MACROECONOMIC MODELLING

CONTRIBUTIONS TO ECONOMIC ANALYSIS

172

Honorary Editor:
J. TINBERGEN

Editors:
D. W. JORGENSON
J. WAELBROECK

NORTH-HOLLAND
AMSTERDAM · NEW YORK · OXFORD · TOKYO

MACROECONOMIC
MODELLING

S. G. HALL

S. G. B. HENRY

Bank of England
London, U.K.

1988

NORTH-HOLLAND
AMSTERDAM · NEW YORK · OXFORD · TOKYO

© ELSEVIER SCIENCE PUBLISHERS B.V., 1988

ISBN: 0 444 70429 9

Publishers:
ELSEVIER SCIENCE PUBLISHERS B.V.
P.O. Box 1991
1000 BZ Amsterdam
The Netherlands

Sole distributors for the U.S.A. and Canada:
ELSEVIER SCIENCE PUBLISHING COMPANY, INC.
52 Vanderbilt Avenue
New York, N.Y. 10017
U.S.A.

LIBRARY OF CONGRESS
Library of Congress Cataloging-in-Publication Data

Hall, S. G.
   Macroeconomic modelling / S.G. Hall, S.G.B. Henry.
      p.   cm. -- (Contributions to economic analysis ; 172)
   Bibliography: p.
   ISBN (invalid) 0-444-70429-9 (U.S.)
   1. Macroeconomics--Mathematical models.   I. Henry, S. G. B.
II. Title.   III. Series.
HB172.5.H355 1988
339'.0724--dc19   88-5379
                                                              CIP

Introduction to the series

This series consists of a number of hitherto unpublished studies, which are introduced by the editors in the belief that they represent fresh contributions to economic science.

The term 'economic analysis' as used in the title of the series has been adopted because it covers both the activities of the theoretical economist and the research worker.

Although the analytical methods used by the various contributors are not the same, they are nevertheless conditioned by the common origin of their studies, namely theoretical problems encountered in practical research. Since for this reason, business cycle research and national accounting, research work on behalf of economic policy, and problems of planning are the main sources of the subjects dealt with, they necessarily determine the manner of approach adopted by the authors. Their methods tend to be 'practical' in the sense of not being too far remote from application to actual economic conditions. In addition they are quantitative.

It is the hope of the editors that the publication of these studies will help to stimulate the exchange of scientific information and to reinforce international cooperation in the field of economics.

The Editors

For Jacqueline and Vivienne

PREFACE

This book arose out of research done by the authors in the period between 1983 and 1987 whilst at the National Institute of Economic and Social Research. A number of things combined to impart the basic thrust of the research; partly the developments in formulating and estimating Rational Expectations Models, and partly actual developments in the UK economy itself. On the latter point, the sharp downturn in output, even more rapid falls in employment, and the large overappreciation of sterling, all posed new demands on empirical model builders. Many existing empirical models simply failed to account for these rapid changes in the aggregate economy since they did not have sufficiently volatile properties. Thus the developments in the Rational Expectations literature seen highly relevant to these phenomena, especially those developments emphasising the real consequences of a combination of inertia in certain markets coupled with fast moving - forward looking - markets elsewhere. In many respects much of the research summarised in this volume recounts the problems in embedding this type of dynamic behaviour in a large scale macro economic model and our, possibly imperfect, resolution of them. We should emphasise that in this endeavour, we have not implanted many of the key behavioural features of, say, the seminal Dornbusch model of exchange rate overshooting. Our research has attempted to build on much of the spirit of this approach, but also attempts to provide robust econometric models of dynamic behaviour, aimed at outperforming alternative backward looking models, as judged by statistical criteria. This leads us to emphasise inertia in the real exchange rate, as well as the likely presence of forward looking expectation formation among foreign exchange operators. We also stress the potential for forward looking behaviour in goods markets, and factor demands. Apart from the econometric issues which this work has entailed (and which we survey in in the first half of the book), there are quite considerable problems in implementing forward looking behaviour in a large scale macroeconomic model, if the model is to be used in a regular way for forecasting and policy simulation. The developments undertaken in this part of our research are summarised in the second half of the book. This shows, we hope, that though the problems are computationally formidable, manageable solutions are distinctly possible, which shed some light on how the British economy has behaved over the last decade.

In our research endeavours over the last few years, our debts to other researchers at the National Institute and elsewhere have been numerous. Among our collegues we would like to single out particularly Andrew Britton, Simon Wren-Lewis, Andreas Drobny, Keith Cuthbertson, and Simon Brooks for their help. For collegues outside the National Institute we would like to thank Andrew Harvey and Andrew Hughes-Hallett for comments on earlier drafts of parts of the manuscript. We also extend thanks to David Currie for general encouragement, and also in his role as supervisor of Stephen Hall's thesis, which was the basis for part of chapter 6.

In preparing the manuscript for the publishers, Patricia Facey made valiant efforts with early drafts. Latterly, Gillian Clisham has dealt with an increasingly difficult schedule of revisions and amendments with great cheerfulness. To both we are extremely grateful.

Lastly, the research reported here was part of a program of econometric research financed by the Macromodelling Consortium of the Economic and Social Research Council. We would like to express our thanks for this support.

CONTENTS

Chapter 4. Macro Models

Chapter 5. Model Solutions, Dynamic Tracking and Mechanical Forecasts

Chapter 6. Stochastic Analysis in Non-Linear Models

Chapter 7. Optimal Control and Dynamic Analysis of Macro Economic

            Models

Chapter 8. The Issue of Time Inconsistency in Macro Policy

Chapter 1

DYNAMIC MODELLING AND RATIONAL EXPECTATIONS

1. Introduction

The link between dynamic modelling and expectation formation has occupied much of the economics profession for well over a decade. The clearest example of the linkage between the two lies in the 'deep structural' approach associated with the Rational Expectations Hypothesis (REH). In this case the behaviour of agents is often described as the optimal outcome of an explicit dynamic program subject to costly adjustment. Then the hypothesis of rationally formed expectations is embedded in this program. In principle, such a model separates lags arising from the economic environment, and lags due to expectation formation, hence avoiding the strictures of the 'Lucas critique'. This approach is in contrast to models where these dynamics are compounded, implying that model reduced form parameters will change as e.g. policy stance and, hence, expectation formation, change. Policy evaluation by simulation techniques could well be invalid in such models.

These propositions are, of course, very familiar. What is surprising perhaps is the limited degree to which empirical models have attempted to implement this distinction, and the purpose of this chapter is to explore some of the consequences of the conjuncture of lags and expectations, and provide illustrations using models of both the labour market and the foreign exchange market. As we suggest in later sections, our reasoning is that these examples are ones where extremely variable behaviour is often manifest. While this property of variability has been associated with exchange rates in the 'overshooting' literature for some time (starting with the seminal article by Dornbusch (1976)), there is also a semblance of similar jumps in employment. We consider some of these points briefly now.

An analysis of employment implying such sharp changes is relatively straightforward (see Henry (1979) and Nickell (1984)). For the continuous case, a simple version of the firm's optimising problem is that it seeks to maximise the discounted functional

$$\int e^{-r(t)} \ [p(t) \ R \ (L, \ t) \ - \ w(t) \ L(t) \ - \ c \ (\dot{L}(t) \ + \ \delta L(t))] \ dt \tag{1}$$

where R(.) is the firm's real revenue function (dependent upon employment (L)), p is output price, w is a given wage rate, and c(.) is an adjustment cost function with the term in $\delta(t)$ representing voluntary quitting. The Euler equation in this case is

$$p(t)R_L = w(t) + (r + \delta) \ c' \ - \ (\ddot{L}(t) + \delta\dot{L}) \ c''(t) \tag{2}$$

The general solution for an equation of this kind, together with its associated transversality condition is given in section 2. It shows that the path of employment depends upon a future weighted stream of expected values of the forcing variables; prices and wages in this case. But if, for illustrative purposes, these forcing variables are held constant, a stationary problem ensues.

The interesting situation is, however, the non-stationary case where forcing variables are not constant. A special case of this is where a single change occurs in the forcing variables. This may be interpreted as a once-for-all change in expected future variables at T let us say. When this happens the new equilibrium for the firm is e.g. L_2^* , produced by a fall in expected future prices, and given by a new equilibrium trajectory. Assuming employment is initially at L_1^*, the subsequent movement of $L(t)$ will be a change in employment which occurs immediately, before the change in forcing variables, moving along that unstable path guaranteed to place $L(t)$ on the new saddlepath at t = T. This is not an immediate jump to the new saddlepath however, as there are costs of adjusting labour.

The dynamic analysis of the foreign exchange market has typically used a related analytical framework to that given already for the case of employment. We may devote a few moments to its salient features here however, because it will be used later in our account of the foreign exchange modelling reported in section 4B, and because this next model has additional features which may also be related to labour market behaviour.

This analysis is usually couched in complete model terms, and takes a general form for the first order matrix case (see Blanchard and Kahn (1980) and Buiter (1982)).

$$\begin{bmatrix} X_{t+1} \\ {}_t P_{t+1} \end{bmatrix} = A \begin{bmatrix} X_t \\ P_t \end{bmatrix} + \gamma Z_t \tag{3}$$

where (X, p) is the state vector, Z the vector of forcing variables. X and p can be vectors (not necessarily of the same order), or in the simplest case, scalars. A and Y are suitably conformable matrices of coefficients. In this representation, X_t is a 'predetermined' variable in Blanchard/Kahn terminology. That is, it is a function only of variables known at time t. p_{t+1} on the other hand, is a 'non-predetermined' variable, and can depend upon variables in the information set at time t+1 (Ω_{t+1}). Compared with our earlier example, the present one differs in a number of respects. The model is linear, although this in turn may be viewed as a linearisation of a non-linear model around a static or growing equilibrium path (see Tinsley (1971). The order of the model is an apparent difference only. High order single equations may be represented as matrix first order cases fairly readily (section 4A below gives an example for the employment case). As we have said, the present example is usually applied to the complete model case. Non-predetermined variables can be interpreted as embodying forward-looking behaviour, usually in financial markets where agents have rational expectations. Predetermined variables, on the other hand, are interpreted as 'backward-looking' variables, and these are often labour market variables.

Much attention has centred on the solution of models such as (3). For the non-predetermined variables, transversality conditions are invoked which, together with the requisite initial conditions for the predetermined variables, provide a unique solution. This solution has the form

$$P_t = - C_{22}^{-1} C_{21} X_t - C_{22}^{-1} \sum_{i=0}^{\infty} J_2^{-i-1} (C_{21} Y_1 + C_{22} Y_2) EZ_{t+i} \qquad (4)$$

$$X_t = X_0, \quad t = 0$$
$$= \beta_{11} J_1 B_{11}^{-1} X_{t-1} + Y_1 Z_t - (\beta_{11} J_1 C_{12} + B_{12} J_2 C_{22}) C_{22}^{-1}$$
$$\sum_{i=0}^{\infty} J_2^{-i-1} (C_{21} Y_1 + C_{22} Y_2) E Z_{t+i}, \qquad t>o$$

where $A = C^{-1} J C$, and J_1 is the matrix of stable eigenvalues, J_2 the matrix of unstable eigenvalues. C is the matrix of associated eigenvectors. In deriving (4) we have decomposed Y conformably into Y_1 and Y_2. [See Buiter (1982) for further details on these solutions.]

Later in this chapter we will describe the estimation of a model of the foreign exchange market, using a first order model such as that in (3) above. Models of employment are also described where the underlying dynamic equation is akin to the solutions for non-predetermined variables given in (4). Before proceeding to the estimation results, we describe some extensions to the dynamic analysis described so far, which will be relevant to the employment models we use. After that, section 3 discusses some of the alternative estimation methods we use in estimating exchange rate and employment models. Finally, section 4 presents econometric results when using these methods.

2. General analysis of dynamic models

The general analysis is provided in Hansen and Sargent (1980) and for convenience, we will relate the analysis to employment decisions in what follows. Clearly a similar analysis could equally be applied to other dynamic models.

Assuming the typical firm minimises

$$\sum_t R^t \{\frac{A}{2} (L_t - L_t^*)^2 - L_t'HL_t - [D(B)L_t]'[D(B)L_t]\} \tag{5}$$

where R is the discount factor, L is taken to be an n x 1 vector of employment - disaggregated by industry, or occupation, H and A are n x n matrices and are positive definite, and $D(B) = \overset{m}{\underset{j}{\Sigma}} D_j B^j$ where B is the lag operator and each matrix is n x n. In this formulation we have costs arising from employment being away from equilibrium, L*, which is defined further below, and other direct costs of employment given by the quadratic term $L_t'HL_t$. Finally, the terms in the matrix polynomial D(B) are general formulations including adjustment costs of, if necessary, more than second order.

In essence the solution proceeds by using certainty equivalence, replacing the unknown L_{t+i}^* (i ≥ 1) [on which the dynamic employment equation will be shown to depend] with $E_t L_{t+i}^*$ where this is the linear least square forecast of L_{t+i}^* based on information available at t. The deterministic Euler equation for the above problem is

$$[(H - A) + D (RB^{-1})' D(B)] L_t = AL^* \tag{6}$$

To solve (6), note first that the roots of

$$det \left[(H - A) + D(RB^{-1})' D(B) \right] = 0$$

come in pairs; thus if z_0 is a root so is Rz_0^{-1}. The matrix polynomial on the LHS of (6) may then be factorised in the form $C(Rz^{-1})' \, C(z)$, where $C(z) = \sum_{j}^{m} C_j z^j$.

Using this factorisation, the Euler equation is

$$C \, (RB^{-1})' \, C(B) \, L_t = AL_t^* \tag{7}$$

which in terms of the familiar backward solution using the stable root, forward solution using the unstable root, is

$$\sum_{j=0}^{m} C_j \, B^j \, L_t = A \sum_{j=0}^{m} \, (C_j \, R^j B^{-j})^{-1} \, L_t^* \tag{8}$$

Hansen and Sargent show that, given the feedback part of this equation, a tractible numerical procedure exists for obtaining the feed-forward part.

One important illustration of an higher order model is the case where the decision rule for employment is second order in both the backward and feed-forward parts. A number of models producing such an equation may be cited. Among the most used are

(i) the assumption of at least second-order adjustment costs;

(ii) the assumption of separate labour markets, each characterised by a first order dynamic model. The aggregate labour market may then be shown to be a second order one (Nickell (1984)). We briefly describe these two cases next.

(1) Higher order adjustment costs

In this case we seek to minimise

$$\sum_{0}^{\infty} R^t \left[\frac{a}{2} (L_t - L^*)^2 + \frac{b}{2} \Delta L_t^2 + \frac{c}{2} (\Delta^2 L_t)^2 \right] \tag{9}$$

The Euler equation for this problem is

$\quad$ $H(B) \, L_t = aL_t^*$, where

$$H(B) = \left[cR^2 B^{-2} - (b + 2c (1 + R)) RB^{-1} + (a + b (1 + R) \right.$$
$$\left. + c (1 + 4R + R^2)) - (b + 2c (1 + R)) B + c B^2 \right] \tag{10}$$

This may be factorised as

$\quad$ $H(B) = (1 - \lambda_1 B - \lambda_2 B^2)(1 - \lambda_1 RB^{-1} - \lambda_2 R^2 B^{-2})$

where the λ_i (1 = 1, 2) terms may be determined by equating coefficients, i.e.

$\quad$ $\lambda_2 = - c$

$\quad$ $R\lambda_1 (\lambda_2 R - 1) = - (b + 2c (1 + R)) R$

$\quad$ $(1 + \lambda_1^2 R + \lambda_2^2 R^2) = [a + b (1 + R) + c (1 + 4R + R^2)]$

The employment equation may then be written

$$(1 - \lambda_1 B - \lambda_2 B^2)L_t = (1 - \lambda_1 RB^{-1} - \lambda_2 R^2 B^{-2})aL^* \tag{11}$$

(2) Disaggregated Labour Markets

The second example may be interpreted as a vector extension to (1) in discrete time, and arises from minimising the discounted cost of adjusting multiple 'quasi-fixed' factors over an infinite time horizon.

The optimal decision rule (again allowing for the operation of suitable transversality conditions) is

$$\underset{\sim}{L}_t = J_1 \underset{\sim}{L}_{t-1} + \sum_{i=0}^{\infty} (R\ J_1)^i\ [1 - R\ J_1]\ [1 - J_1]\ \underset{\sim}{L}^*_{t+i} \tag{12}$$

where $\underset{\sim}{L}^*_t$, is the static equilibrium for the vector of quasi fixed factors $\underset{\sim}{L}_t$, and R is the discount factor. If this is specialised to the case where there are two distinct types of labour, (so $\underset{\sim}{L} = (L_1,\ L_2)$) each with different adjustment costs, we obtain

$$\begin{bmatrix} L_{1t} \\ L_{2t} \end{bmatrix} = J_1 \begin{bmatrix} L_{1t-1} \\ L_{2t-1} \end{bmatrix} + \sum_{i=0}^{\infty} (R\ J_1)^i\ (1 - R\ J_1)\ (1 - J_1) \begin{bmatrix} L^*_{1t+i} \\ L^*_{2t+i} \end{bmatrix}$$

We may aggregate by simply adding the two types of labour, i.e.

$$L_t = \begin{bmatrix} i^T \end{bmatrix} \begin{bmatrix} L_{1t} \\ L_{2t} \end{bmatrix} , \quad \text{where } i^T = (1,\ 1)$$

$$\text{Thus } L_t = \begin{bmatrix} i^T \end{bmatrix} (1 - J_1\ B)^{-1} \sum_{i=0}^{\infty} (R\ J_1)^i\ [1 - R\ J_1]\ [1 - J_1] \begin{bmatrix} L^*_{1t+i} \\ L^*_{2t+i} \end{bmatrix}$$

where B is the lag operator.

Or

$$|1 - J_1\ B| L_t = \begin{bmatrix} i^T \end{bmatrix} \text{adj.}\ [1 - J_1\ B] \sum_{i} (R\ J_1)^i\ [1 - R\ J_1]\ [1 - J_1] \begin{bmatrix} L^*_{1t+i} \\ L^*_{2t+i} \end{bmatrix}$$

As the model is second order, the determinental expression on the LHS is 2 x 2, so that we may write it

$$|1 - J_1 \ B| \ L_t = (1 - (J_{11} + J_{22}) \ B + (J_{11} \ J_{22} - J_{12} \ J_{21}) \ B^2) \ L_t$$

in other words, the LHS is a second order autoregressive equation in aggregate employment (L_t). [See Nickell (1984) for an extended discussion of this case.]

3. Estimation methods

A. Estimating forward-looking models

For the sake of illustration we take the case of employment in the discussion throughout this section. Extensions of similar analysis to other models, such as joint factor demands or dynamic portfolio models may readily be made, though we will not make those extensions here. Applications to other factor demands, wage formation and the demand for money, are presented in Chapter 4. The sort of dynamic equation we have been considering in earlier sections can be written

$$L_t = \lambda_1 \ L_{t-1} + \lambda_2 \ L_{t-2} + a \sum_i^N h(i) \ E_t \ L^*_{t+i} + \epsilon_t \tag{13}$$

In this equation, E_t is the conditional expectations operator using information up to period t, and the $h(i)$ are forward-weighting functions depending upon the roots λ_i (i = 1, 2). Although (13) is a general second order form, obviously including as special cases the first order models such as those deployed for exchange rate models, it is limited to the finite horizon case, which is an important difference to the models previously described. We will invariably use this assumption of a finite planning horizon when estimating dynamic equations in subsequent sections.

The procedures we will be using in estimating equations of this sort are heavily dependent upon the Instrumental Variables (IV) estimators developed in Hansen and Sargent (1982). There are important differences of detail however, in that they use the explicit form for the optimal decision rule for the first-order infinite plan, whereas some of our examples are second-order and are for finite horizons. Moreover they use a version of the substitution method in identifying all model parameters, which, as will be clear below, we do not. In this sense our procedures are closer to the Errors in Variables (EV) techniques extensively discussed by Wickens (1982) and (1986). Below, we provide an outline of the general methods of estimating RE models, and then give details on the distinctive features of the methods used in obtaining our own empirical results. Apart from estimation of the optimal decision rule in the form given by (13), we also outline methods for estimating the stochastic form of the Euler equation, and provide illustrations using EV methods.

(i) Optimal decision rule

To establish the alternative estimation possibilities for the optimal decision rule, we first recall the Hansen and Sargent (1982) method for estimation of a first-order infinite time model. Again using an employment equation example, the relevant equation is

$$L_t = \lambda L_{t-1} - (\lambda/\delta) \sum_{j}^{\infty} (\lambda R)^j \, E_t (Q_{t+j} - a_{t+j}) | \Omega_t \tag{14}$$

where Ω_t is the full information set, δ is a parameter given by adjustment costs, Q is a forcing variable known by the econometrician, and a_t is a technology shock unknown to the econometrician. Estimation by Hansen and Sargents' IV methods, in general, means estimating an equation based on the reduced information set Λ_t. Thus

$$L_t = \lambda L_{t-1} - (\lambda/\delta) \sum_{j}^{\infty} (\lambda R)^j E Q_{t+j} | \Lambda_t + S_t + a_t^*$$

where $S_t = \lambda/\delta \sum_{j}^{\infty} (\lambda R)^j [E Q_{t+j} | \Lambda_t - E Q_{t+j} | \Omega_t]$, and

$$a_t^* = \lambda/\delta \sum_{j}^{\infty} (\lambda R)^j E a_{t+j} | \Omega_t$$

The reduced information set Λ is dependent upon a set of current and lagged variables $\underset{\sim}{X} = (X_t, X_{t-1}, \ldots)$, where $\underset{\sim}{X}$ and a_t are independent. Further, we assume that X_t can be represented as

$$X_{t+1} = \gamma^1(B) X_t + e_{t+1} , \quad E_t(X_t | e_t) = 0 \tag{15}$$

an invertible MA process, and that the conditional expectation of Q_t given Λ_t is the least squares projection on the Xs, i.e.

$$E_t (Q_t | \Lambda_t) = \theta(B) X_t$$
or $\quad Q_t = \theta(B) X_t + u_t$

where u and $\underset{\sim}{X}$ are independent. Using these results, it is possible to write the optimal decision rule as a restricted equation for the dependent variable as a function of current and lagged X's, i.e.

$$L_t = \lambda L_{t-1} + \Pi(B) X_t + S_t + a^*_t$$

where

$$\Pi(B) = \frac{-(\lambda/\delta)}{1-\lambda RB^{-1}} [\theta(B) - \lambda RB^{-1} \theta(\lambda R)\gamma(\lambda R)^{-1} \gamma(B)] \qquad (16)$$

and

$$\gamma(B) = 1 - \gamma^1(B).$$

Equations (15) and (16) now constitute the model, and embody:

(a) the feedback/feedforward restrictions of the optimal rule, and

(b) they incorporate information on the autocovariance function of the

X variables.

Estimation of the model by non-linear methods may be based on the independence (orthogonality) conditions:

$$E((S + a^*)_t , X_{t-j}) = 0 \qquad\qquad j \geq 0$$

and of the independence of X_t with both u_t and e_t.

In the extension to this model which we are interested in, the steady-state equilibrium for the dependent variable is L*, which, for convenience, we are taking as the linear function

$$L^*(t) = \Gamma' Z_t$$

where Z_t is a set of forcing variables and Γ a set of constant parameters. Then implementation of the Hansen-Sargent method could proceed by identifying an information set, say V, where

$$Z_t = J(B) V_t + h_t$$

where h is independent of V. Again the full model would then be the explicit dynamic equation for employment together with the time series representation for the instrument set V_t.

As stressed earlier, the second order case does not readily permit explicit analytical solutions for the optimal decision rule, so that jointly embodying the feedback/forward restrictions and the autocovariance properties of the forcing variables becomes problematic. We therefore adopt simplified procedures in estimating forward versions of the employment equation. The first method we use is described now and this will be described as an Instrumental Variable method. (See 4 ii below). This uses the finite form of the optimal decision rule (13), and applies the feedback/feedforward restrictions by numerical methods. Then the presence of forward expected forcing variables as regressor variables is handled by instrumental variables, treating the equation as an errors-in-variables case by replacing $E_t L^*_{t+I}$ by L^*_{t+i} in the employment equation. Since according to the REH

$$E_t L^*_{t+i} = L^*_{t+i} + n_{t+i}$$

the optimal decision rule is

$$L_t = \lambda_1 L_{t-1} + \lambda_2 L_{t-2} + a\sum_i^N h(i) \Gamma' Z_{t+i} + g_t + \varepsilon_t \qquad (17)$$

where g_t is a weighted sum of led values of n_t. Consequently this equation involves MA(N) error processes. Hayashi and Sims (1983) discuss forward filters which improve the efficiency of estimators of this equation, though these are not applied here. The other feature of

the model is the dependance which exists between its feedback and

feedforward terms.

In our examples this non-linearity of the employment equation is

dealt with by using iterative or non-linear estimation methods, and

examples of each are given in Section 4. The iterative procedure is

described in Hall (1984), and uses the Euler and closed form solution.

If this is applied to the model given by equations (9)-(11) and equation

(13) for example, the steps are:

(a) From initial estimated values of the backward parameters using (if

necessary) arbitrary values for the forward terms, the parameters of the

Euler equation (10) are obtained by factorising.

(b) For given values of the forcing variables Z_t (t = 1 ... T), and

given L_0 and L_T, solve the deterministic from the Euler equation (10)

over t = 1, ..., T, using numerical procedures. The latter is necessary

since t + 1 appears in the Euler equation. Call this solution $L_t^{(1)}$.

(c) Perturb Z_t in the ith period (i = 1 ... k) giving $Z_t^{(2)}$, and

recalculate L_t, giving $L_t^{(2)}$. Since from the closed form equation (13),

assuming $L_t^* = \Gamma' Z_t$,

$$\frac{\partial L_t}{\partial Z_{t+i}} = \Upsilon\lambda_i \cong \frac{L_t^{(1)} - L_t^{(2)}}{Z_t^{(1)} - Z_t^{(2)}}$$

where λ_i is the weight of the ith forward value of Z. Then other

values of the forward weights are constructed in similar fashion, and

the closed form of the employment equation is re-estimated using this

computed forward convolution of the Z variables. The revised values for

the parameters on the lagged dependent values are calculated, and the

next set of weights $\lambda_i^{(2)}$ are recomputed using (b) and (c). The

procedure is continued until convergence. An illustration of a second-

order employment model estimated using this iterative IV method is shown

in Table 1 below (Section 4).

Alternatively a non-linear estimate of the employment equation can

be made using instrumental variables, which for the finite case can be

done using the principle of undetermined coefficients. (See Table 1'

Section 4)

The second method we report for which we give results, uses a

vector autoregression model (VAR) for Z_t, and in many ways is closer to

the procedure used by Hansen and Sargent (see below on the point made

about FIML). The VAR is, say,

$$X_t = \sum_{i}^{4} A_i X_{t-i} + h_t \tag{18}$$

where $X_t = [Z_t, G_t]$. This set includes the forcing variables, but as

the results in Table 2 below indicate, in addition, it also incorporates

proxy measures of fiscal policy (BD) and monetary policy (CC), and

variables affecting the supply of labour, real benefits (RBEN) and a proxy for union power (UM). The estimates we provide are then based on a two-step estimation procedure. Predictions for the forcing variables over the planning period are determined as i^{th} step forecasts conditional upon information available at (t-1) using the VAR model above. These predictions are treated as data, and enter the employment equation, which is then estimated by single equation methods. This alternative method is illustrated in Table 2 in Section 4 below which gives details of the VAR estimates. The results when this is used in estimating a dynamic employment model, are given in Table 3.

Pagan (1984) shows that, contrary to the common assumption, the two-step estimation is asymptotically efficient as compared with the joint estimator of the complete model. However, the Least Squares estimate of the variance of regression coefficients is usually inconsistent except under the null hypothesis that the parameters are zero (the common case in other words). Compared with the IV estimator described earlier, the present one makes similar informational assumptions, albeit on a different instrument set.

We end by noting that for the models we have used, two possible Full Information applications might be made. These are the application of the systems version of Wickens (1982) EV approach, and the full information version of the joint optimal decision rule and the VAR model.

The former requires that $E_t Z_{t+i}$ be replaced by actual Z_{t+i}, but in addition a (structural) equation for each Z_{t+i} (i = 0 ... N) be estimated simultaneously with the optimal decision rule.

Although this does not directly substitute in the restricted reduced form predictions, Wickens argues that the resulting estimated model does embody rationality. This is because FIML replaces endogenous regressors by their restricted reduced form predictions in estimating the model. On convergence, the two procedures coincide.

Note that the auxiliary equations for the (now jointly determined) Zs can include endogenous regressors, but not forward values. Wickens' example uses the reduced form for the equation for Z. Using reduced form equations for the Z variables, where the instrument set is predetermined, makes this method equivalent to our IV method. For this reason we have not pursued this.

Similarly, a system estimator for the optimal decision rule together with the VAR model involves substituting for EX_{t+k} using the (k + 1) period prediction of the VAR model, i.e.

$$EX_{t+k} = A^{k+1} X_{t-1}$$

(assuming the VAR only includes the forcing variables, otherwise a selection vector is required).

The employment equation is then

$$L_t = \lambda_1 L_{t-1} + \lambda_2 L_{t-2} + a\sum_{k}^{N} h(k) A^{k+1} e'X_{t-1} \tag{19}$$

where e' is a selection vector, and this employment equation may be jointly estimated with

$$X_t = \Sigma A_i X_{t-i} + \varepsilon_t \tag{20}$$

Nickell (1984) reports one such FIML estimate, based on a finite horizon. The parameter estimates are almost identical to the two-stage estimates he reports, and so there seems little to be gained from pursuing this system approach in our case.

(ii) Stochastic Euler equation

Instrumental variable procedures are much less demanding in computational terms. Apart from the use of instrumental variables in estimating the decision rule noted earlier, they may also be used to estimate the stochastic Euler equation (see Kennan (1979) and Wickens (1986)). The essence of the procedure can be seen in the case of a single lead, single exogenous variable equation,

$$Q_t = \alpha E_t Q_{t+1} + \beta X_t + e_t \tag{21}$$

Then since by the REH,

$$Q_{t+1} = E_t Q_{t+1} + u_{t+1}$$

where u_{t+1} is the innovation in Q_{t+1}, substituting for $E_t Q_{t+1}$ in (19) gives

$$Q_t = \alpha Q_{t+1} + \beta X_t + e_t - \alpha u_{t+1} \tag{22}$$

which exhibits both a dependence between a regressor and the error term, and moving average error (MA(1)). The former is dealt with by using an IV estimator, and the latter, if ignored, produces inefficient

estimators.   Kennan (1979) describes a two-step estimation procedure
which overcomes this, but this is not confirmed by our results (see
section 4A(ii)).

4. Empirical results

We now move on to the discussion of empirical examples of the models
described in earlier sections.   These are confined to illustrations of
labour   market   (employment)   and   exchange   rate   behaviour,   and   are
described in sections A and B.

A. Employment models

(i) Some simplifying assumptions

The emphasis here will be on employment (numbers employed), so an
explicit treatment of hours worked, or utilisation of labour will not
figure in the present exercise.   [For a joint model of employment and
hours see Hall, Henry, Payne and Wren-Lewis (1985).]   Also, we will
invariably invoke the simplifying assumption that adjustment costs on
labour may be approximated by a quadratic cost function, although there
are well known deficiencies in this assumption.   Moreover, we will
assume this function is defined over changes in employment ΔL, rather
than the more theoretically valid hires and separations, treated as
distinct elements, each affecting employment.   Finally, and perhaps most
importantly, we will effectively be treating the employment decision in
isolation from other factor demands, simply to keep the present analysis
tractable.

There has been increasing attention focussed on the necessity of
treating the labour market as a whole in a theoretically coherent way.

This is largely in reaction to the ad-hoc specifications adopted for wage equations in the Phillips curve literature. Most often, the recommendation amounts to joint models of employment and real wage determination. The approach adopted here is compatible with these views, although here we concentrate only upon labour demand equations. Estimating such single equations, of course, implies potential problems of consistency in estimation, where stochastic regressors - such as the real wage or real demand - appear. These problems are fairly easily dealt with in a single equation model by use of appropriate, consistent, estimation methods.

We specialize the general model to the second-order case which is the case described in detail in section 2 above. Also there is considerable empirical evidence for the usefulness of this case (see, for example, Nickell (1984) and Henry and Wren-Lewis (1984).)

Before proceeding to the discussion of empirical results, we may note that the main contending explanations of employment behaviour depend upon assumptions made about the firm's environment. As we derive the optimal employment rule for a quadratic cost function, these assumptions are implicit, though a largely equivalent derivation can be based on optimising a net revenue function as in Nickell (1984). Essentially there are two issues here: the arguments of the desired level of employment in the long run (L*), and its functional form. On this later question we adopt an extreme simplification and assume linear forms throughout. This is equivalent to assuming that the underlying parameters are not identified, which, as they are identified only for the most basic form of technology in dynamic models of the sort we are interested in, seems justified. Turning to the question of the determinants of L*, we may list the alternatives we pursue as follows.

(a) Price-taking firms:

In this case, with the (K,L,M) production function, the arguments of L* are the real wage, real material prices and the capital stock which we will assume is fixed, so we abstract from decisions about investment. In this model a time trend might enter as a proxy for exogenous technical progress.

(b) Imperfectly competitive firms:

Apart from the real price terms as in case (a), the level of real demand for goods is now an argument in L*. (See Layard and Nickell (1985), (1986).) Many empirical models of employment use the production function to substitute out the capital stock in terms of output in the optimal employment rule. This results in an employment equation dependent upon real prices and real output and, if output is treated as endogenous, and instrumented by variables which affect real demand, then this produces a model empirically indistinguishable from the former.

(c) The demand constrained firm:

In models of this sort, where the firm is constrained by lack of effective demand in the goods market, employment depends upon real output (assuming no stockbuilding, so that sales and output are identical) and relative prices. A synthetic model which nests this alternative has employment depending upon real prices and output. The version depending upon relative prices may then be derived as a restriction on the coefficients of the real price terms.

The next section will discuss how forward-looking versions of the alternative equations obtained under (a) - (c) may be estimated, incorporating backward-forward restrictions.

(ii) Employment models with forward expectations

The objective in this section is to provide estimates of models which are based on the elements of theory described in the previous sections, with explicit forward expectations for forcing variables: real wages (w/p), real material prices (Pm) and real output (Q). Each model is estimated using non-linear methods, and details are provided as we proceed. For purposes of estimation, a finite planning horizon was imposed of five quarters, it being assumed that this was a reasonable horizon in practice and given that the weighting function on forward terms implied by the autoregressive parameter estimates appeared to decay relatively quickly.

Optimal decision rule: single equation estimates

Because it is the most general case we use the general non-competitive model, with exogenous technical progress and/or capital accumulation represented by a time trend.

The equation we estimate may be written

$$L_t = \lambda o + \lambda_1 L_{t-1} + \lambda_2 L_{t-2} + \alpha_3 w^e_t + \alpha_4 P^e_{mt} + \alpha_5 Q^e_t + \alpha_6 t + \varepsilon_t$$

where w^e is the weighted forward convolution of the real wage (over t=0, ..4), and P^e_m and Q^e and defined similarly.

Table 1 shows the results of estimating the model using iterative instrumental variable estimation on a successively simplified version of the model. The version dropping the expected real materials price (column (2)) is preferred among this set. The materials price is not

Table 1. Employment equations with forward expected forcing variables:

iterative estimates using instrumental variables

Sample 1964Q2-1983Q4

	(1)	(2)	(3)
λ_0	0.102 (0.249)	-0.219 (0.597)	-0.196 (0.519)
λ_1	1.327 (11.594)	1.370 (12.219)	1.459 (13.41)
λ_2	-0.417 (3.646)	-0.441 (3.860)	-0.495 (4.302)
α_3	-0.0336 (2.609)	-0.03 (2.381)	
α_4	0.009 (1.695)		
α_5	0.076 (3.037)	0.0877 (3.603)	0.0532 (2.643)
α_6	-0.0003 (2.769)	-0.0003 (2.985)	-0.0003 (2.916)
$se(10^2)$	0.349	0.351	0.362
DW	2.144	2.171	2.21
BP(16)	16.257	15.06	15.697
ARCH	0.353	0.028	0.069
CHOW	4.064	1.074	1.815
$\chi^2(20)$	40.22	10.857	18.726

BP(16) is the Box-Pierce statistic for a random correlogram distributed as χ^2 with 16 degrees of freedom.
LM(4) is Lagrange multiplier statistic for fourth-order residual autocorrelation.
ARCH is Engles's test for autocorrelated squared residuals.
CHOW is the Chow test for parameter stability distributed as F.
χ^2 (20) is one-step forecast test distributed as χ^2 with 20 degrees of freedom.
Figures in parenthesis are t statistics.
All equations estimated by instrumental variables, the instruments being the aggregate replacement ratio, current and lagged; working population, current and lagged; real government expenditure, current and lagged; world raw material priced relative to world manufacturing prices, current and lagged; the average personal, indirect and employers' tax

well determined, and there is considerable improvement in apparent
paramater stability and one step forecast performance in moving from (1)
to (2). Although these statistics do not measure absolute performance,
in this case they are quite revealing. The model in column (1) for
example has substantial forecast errors over the first two years of the
recession, actually seriously underpredicting employment by 100-200
thousand per quarter.   The model in column (2) makes only one
significant error, in the second quarter of 1979.

Re-estimating the employment equation using non-linear instrumental
variables, applying the method of undetermined coefficients produced
very similar results to those listed in table 1. The two non-linear
methods seem therefore to produce similar numerical results to a
reasonably high degree of accuracy. (See Hall, Henry, Payne and Wren-
Lewis (1986) for a review of this latter technique.) For example, the
non-linear instrumental variable estimate of the example shown in column
(2) of table 1 was as follows when estimated over the same sample
period.

Table 1'. Non-Linear Estimate of Column 2 Table 1

λ_1	λ_2	α_3	α_4	α_5	α_6	$se(10^{-2})$	DW
1.359	-0.426	-0.005	-0.287	0.014	$-0.327(10^{-3})$	0.350	2.144
(12.331)	(3.824)	(1.936)	(0.787)	(2.82)	(3.32)		

Optimal decision rule: two-step estimates
The final example we use for the optimal decision rule is a two-step
estimate, using a VAR model for real demand and the real wage. Unlike
the VAR used in the Hansen-Sargent model, which uses lagged values of a
set of forcing variables, our example introduces other variables into

Table 2.   VAR Model for output and the real wage
           (variables in logs) (* signifies t>1, ** signifies t>2)

	Q	BD	WP	CC	BEN	UM
(i)Dependent variable Q						
Lag						
1	0.549**	-1.238*	0.365**	-0.029		
2	-0.054	2.096*	-0.386*	0.337**		
3	-0.081	-1.986*	0.320*	-0.310*		
4	0.154	0.268	-0.096	0.137*		

se(10^{-1}) = 0.14;   DW = 2.13

	Q	BD	WP	CC	BEN	UM
(ii)Dependent variable BD						
Lag						
1	-0.002	1.77**	-0.042*	-0.006		
2	-0.018	-1.449**	-0.08**	0.019		
3	0.039*	0.71**	-0.054*	-0.004		
4	0.019	-0.222*	0.005	-0.002		

se(10^{-1}) = 0.027;   DW = 1.896

	Q	BD	WP	CC	BEN	UM
(iii)Dependent variable WP						
Lag						
1	-0.196*	-0.307	0.66**	-0.389**	-0.057*	0.044*
2	-0.329**	-0.266	-0.284*	0.139	0.154**	-0.023
3	-0.310*	1.799*	0.114	0.06	-0.012	0.051
4	-0.332*	-1.146*	0.052	-0.120*	0.092*	-0.013

se(10^{-1}) = 0.12;   DW = 2.02

	Q	BD	WP	CC	BEN	UM
(iv)Dependent variable CC						
Lag						
1	-0.785**	2.19*	-0.077	1.069**		
2	0.239	-1.156	0.217	-0.579**		
3	0.036	-1.327	0.196	0.745**		
4	0.086	0.439	-0.205*	-0.349**		

se (10^{-1}) = 0.202;   DW = 2.11

the model, with a 'semi-structural' interpretation. Thus, as well as
lagged output and the real wage, we include a measure of external
competitiveness (CC), the cyclically adjusted budget deficit (BD), the
level of unemployment benefit (UBEN) and a measure of union power (UM).
The first two serve as indicators of the stance of monetary and fiscal
policy respectively, and the latter two are exogenous influences upon
the real wage. Each of these variables has figured in the extensive
debate on the causes of UK employment, and for this reason we include
them in our examples here. (For articles concerned in this debate, see
HM Treasury (1985), Henry and Wren-Lewis (1984) and Nickell and Layard
(1985).)

    The VAR model for output, the fiscal deficit, the real wage and
competitiveness is shown in table 2. (RBEN and UM are assumed to be
generated by AR(4) models.) Table 3 then gives the results of
estimating the employment equation with expected values of the forcing
variables given by n step predictions from the VAR model (n = 0, ...,
4). As with previous illustrations, there are well established
dynamics, and evidence of effects from real demand and the real wage
which accord with a-priori views. These latter are not significant at
the 5 per cent level, though again the relative sizes of the two
influences are similar to those found in the previous examples.

Table 3.   Employment Equation: 2-step non-linear estimate using VAR
predictions   Sample 1964Q4-1983Q4

λ_1	λ_2	α_3	α_4	α_5	α_6	$se(10^{-2})$	DW
1.526	-0.581	-0.014	0.096	0.014	$-0.209(10^{-3})$	0.376	2.31
(14.303)	(5.451)	(1.799)	(0.296)	(1.799)	(1.92)		

Stochastic Euler Equation

The final results are estimates of the stochastic Euler equation using
the full set of forcing variables. It is estimated using the two-step
procedure described in Kennan (1979). To estimate the model in this way
we first estimate a version of the closed form of the model,

$$L_t = \lambda_1 L_{t-1} + \lambda_2 L_{t-2} + B'X_t + \mu_t \tag{23}$$

where the forward convolution of future forcing variables is assumed to
be representable by a vector of (current and lagged) exogenous variables
(X_t).   Providing $E(X_t, \mu_t) = 0$, the estimates of λ_i ($i = 1$, 2) are
consistent.   Then, using these estimates, the restricted form of the
Euler equation is estimated in the form

$$\hat{Y}_t = \gamma_0 + \gamma_1 w_t + \gamma_2 P_{mt} + \gamma_3 Q_t + \gamma_4 t + v_t \tag{24}$$

Since the current values of the forcing variables are endogenous, the
model is estimated by IV. $\hat{Y}$ is the restricted sum of lagged and future
employment levels, weighted by the first stage estimates for λ_1 and λ_2.
Results are given in Table 4.

Table 4. Employment: Stochastic Euler Equation

SAMPLE 1964Q4-1983Q4 (2-step estimates)

Equation (26) L_t	λ_1	λ_2	$se(10^{-2})$	DW
	1.52 (18.464)	-0.567 (6.475)	0.274	2.167

(27) $\hat{Y}_t$	Y_0	Y_1	Y_2	Y_3	Y_4	$se(10^{-1})$	DW
	27.42 (9.60)	-0.773 (5.901)	0.256 (4.237)	1.199 (4.438)	$-0.399(10^{-2})$ (3.546)	0.464	0.705

Certain aspects of these results are interesting, though others are less attractive. On the positive side, it is evident that similar lag structures are identified in this version as in our earlier examples. Also the estimates on the forcing variables are of the correct sign and are well determined. On the negative side the equation is subject to powerful serial correlation. The review of this procedure noted the presence of a non-invertible MA process in this model, though in our case inspection of the residual correlogram strongly confirms an autoregressive error process. The problem then appears not only to be one of inefficient estimates, but possible misspecification also. Given these difficulties, these results are presented as initial ones of some interest, though overall our illustrations suggest that more plausible estimates of the rational model are obtained using the optimal decision rule.

Conclusions on Employment equations

In this section we have estimated employment models with an explicit separation of expectations formation and lagged adjustment. Given some simplifying assumptions, alternative methods may be used to estimate this class of model, and these have been illustrated using aggregate data. Two conclusions emerge from this empirical work. Firstly, that plausible models of employment behaviour can be based on explicit forward-looking behaviour and, for the cases we have considered, these appear to perform favourably. Secondly, our results attribute an important statistical role to both real wage and real demand effects in the explanation of employment. This result appears to hold regardless of the procedures we have used in estimating the model.

B. Forward-looking models of the exchange rate

(i) Introduction and motivation

We will not devote much attention to the theoretical underpinnings of exchange rate models. The relevant literature is enormous. Instead, we provide a simple theoretical basis for the class of models we estimate subsequently. As will be evident, there is a fairly close correspondence between this analysis and some of that used for the case of employment in the previous section.

We begin from a simple cost function, which we suppose represents government aspirations (defining E_t to be the log of the exchange rate)

$$C = \sum_{t=0}^{T} \frac{a}{2} (E_t - E_t^*)^2 + \frac{d}{2} (E_t - E_{t-1})^2 \qquad (25)$$

where E* is the exchange rate which the market would set in the absence
of government intervention, or any form of adjustment costs. We further
suppose an (inverse) intervention function

$$E_t = g(I_t)$$

represents government intervention, either through official financing
flows on the foreign exchange market or through direct intervention in
the markets.

If we minimise this expression with respect to I over a finite time
horizon, we get the following first-order conditions

$$a \, g'(g(I_t) - E_t^*) + d \, g'(g(I_t) - g(I_{t-1})) - d \, g'(g(I_{t+1}) - g(I_t)) = 0$$
$$t = 0, \ldots, T - 1 \quad (26)$$

with a special form of this equation for T.

Dividing through by g', equation (26) will yield

$$E_t = \frac{a}{a+2d} E_t^* + \frac{d}{a+2d} (E_{t-1} + E_{t+1}) \qquad (27)$$

To make this model operational, we need to specify the determinants of
E*. We postulate

$$Log(E_t^*) = \alpha(r_{Dt} - r_{Ft}) + B(r_{Dt-1} - r_{Ft-1}) + \phi log(E_{t-1}) \qquad (28)$$

where E_t^* is the exchange rate which the market would set in the absence of any government intervention or any form of adjustment costs. In (28) if $B = 0$, $\alpha > 0$, and $\phi = 1$, then the equation is simply the open arbitrage equation. If $-B = \alpha > 0$ then it is a pure difference term in the real interest rate differential and it suggests an asset stock model in which assets fully adjust to a change in interest rates within the time period. Then substituting (28) into (27) gives

$$E_t = \frac{a}{a+2d} [\alpha(r_{Dt} - r_{Ft}) + B(r_{Dt-1} - r_{Ft-1}) + \phi E_{t+1}]$$

$$+ \frac{d}{a+2d} (E_{t-1} + E_{t+1})$$

So $$E_t = \frac{a}{a+2d} [\alpha(r_{Dt} - r_{Ft}) + B(r_{Dt-1} - r_{Ft-1})]$$

$$+ \frac{\phi(a+d)}{a+2d} E_{t+1} + \frac{d}{a+2d} E_{t-1} \qquad\qquad (29)$$

Equation (29) offers an interesting general equation from which to begin estimation. If $B = 0$, $\phi = 1$, and $d = 0$, the equation reduces to the open arbitrage equation but if any of these restrictions are violated the simple open arbitrage model is rejected in preference for a more complex one. The coefficients on E_{t+1} and E_{t-1} should both be greater than or equal to zero and they should sum to close to unity. (If $\phi = 1$, then they sum to exactly unity.) The next section details how this equation may be estimated, and describes some results of so doing.

(ii) Estimation and results

The estimation will be carried out over the period 197303 to 198406 using monthly data. The exchange rate equation is estimated using the Wickens (1982) Errors in Variable technique described in section 3. To complete this an equation will also be specified for the interest rate differential so as to allow for the possible endogeneity of interest rates. Also equation (29) is specified in real terms, that is as a real exchange rate dependent upon real interest differentials.

The Wickens technique allows us to use actual lead data as a measure of expected future variables. The outturns are then taken to be an estimate of expectations, where the data is subject to a white noise measurement error. The model is estimated by a systems estimation technique (either Three Stage Least Squares (3SLS) or Full Information Maximum likelihood (FIML) where an equation is specified for each of the expectations terms. These equations will generally be an unrestricted reduced form of the model. Specifying these reduced form equations for expectations corrects for the bias produced by the measurement error and the resulting estimates may be shown to be consistent. As the expectations equations do not exploit the structure of the model this technique will not generally be fully efficient.

Before examining the system estimations a useful point of departure is provided by the results of estimating the model by OLS. These results are obviously inconsistent but we introduce them as a useful guide to the effect of the systems estimation.

OLS estimates (sample 197303-198406, monthly data)

$$E_t = -0.016 + 0.52 \ E_{t-1} + 0.48 \ E_{t+1} - 0.003 \ (r_{Dt} - r_{Ft})$$
$$\quad\ \ (0.5) \quad (18.0) \qquad\quad (16.2) \qquad\quad (4.1)$$

$$+ \ 0.003 \ (r_{Dt-1} - r_{Ft-1}) \tag{30}$$
$$(3.6)$$

$\Sigma e^2 = 0.014 \qquad DW = 2.6 \qquad SEE = 0.010 \qquad \bar{R}^2 = 0.994$

This is a well-fitting equation but it violates many of the main conditions of (29). For example, if $\phi = 1$ then as $(a+b) > b$ (for a, b > 0), the coefficient on E_{t+1} must be greater than the coefficient on E_{t-1}. This is not true of equation (30). Also this parameter on the current interest rate term is significant but carries the wrong sign. This is a common finding in exchange rate equations (see Hall (1987)), so the OLS estimates seem to reject the general theory used in deriving this model.

Happily this need not be the end of the story. There are at least two main problems with the OLS results; the first, highlighted by Haache and Townend (1981) and Hall (1983), is that interest rates are endogenous and so are subject to simultaneous equation bias. The second problem is that the expected exchange rate term cannot validly be modelled simply by using the actual future exchange rate. In order to cope with both these problems a three equation model has been estimated using both 3SLS and then FIML where both the forward exchange rate and the interest rate differential are specified as endogenous in addition to the exchange rate. The expected exchange rate equation will not be reported since, within the Wickens estimation framework, this equation has no structural significance.

For our purpose the interest rate equation is not the prime concern so a specific conceptual model is not developed for it. Instead a fairly simple specification will be used which makes interest rates a function of the endogenous exchange rate, two lagged dependent variables and two terms in the annual rate of domestic inflation (ΔP_t). The lagged dependent variables may be thought of as correcting a non-white noise error process induced by missing explanatory variables. On this interpretation, part of the equation is a simple time series model of interest rate movements. If we view the exchange rate term as a government reaction term, i.e. the famous 'leaning into the wind' policy, then we would expect a negative coefficient. The sign of this effect becomes ambiguous, however, if we interpret the term as a market response to the overall expected return of assets.

The results for the unrestricted model are reported in table 5; the picture presented for the exchange rate equation is now radically different. In the 3SLS estimates the term on the future exchange rate is now much larger than the lagged exchange rate, as equation (29) would suggest. The two parameters still sum closely to unity, and the current real interest rate terms are now positive but not significant. The real interest rate equation is fairly well determined with correctly signed parameters. The FIML estimates are perhaps even more satisfactory than the 3SLS estimates. The expected exchange rate term has an even larger parameter, while the interest rates are now both correctly signed and significant.

Table 6 shows the effect of imposing the restriction that the coefficients on the expected future and the lagged exchange rate terms sum to unity.

Table 5. The unrestricted exchange rate and interest rate equation

SAMPLE 197303-198406, monthly

Independent variable	Dependent variable E_t		Independent variable	Dependent variable $(r_D - r_F)_t$	
	3SLS	FIML		3SLS	FIML
Constant	-0.04 (1.2)	-0.05 (1.1)	Constant	0.34 (1.2)	0.48 (1.1)
E_{t-1}	0.35 (5.7)	0.22 (7.2)	$(E_t - E_{t-1})$	-21.8 (1.7)	-1.8 (0.21)
E_{t+1}	0.65 (10.2)	0.79 (26.8)	ΔP_t	-51.2 (5.0)	-56.2 (4.3)
$(r_D - r_F)_t$	0.0005 (0.3)	0.0024 (2.1)	ΔP_{t-1}	48.0 (4.6)	51.6 (3.8)
$(r_D - r_F)_{t-1}$	-0.0009 (0.6)	-0.0031 (2.7)	$(r_D - r_F)_{t-1}$	0.96 (13.2)	0.96 (10.8)
			$(r_D - r_F)_{t-2}$	0.006 (0.08)	-0.03 (0.4)

$\Sigma e^2 = 0.019$ $\Sigma e^2 = 0.0286$ $\Sigma e^2 = 170.1$ $\Sigma e^2 = 85.6$
DW $= 2.3$ DW $= 1.96$ DW $=$ 1.93 DW $= 1.9$

3SLS Minimand = 36.6

Log likelihood function = 515.6

Table 6. Imposing the unit restriction on the model

SAMPLE 197303-198406, monthly

Independent variable	Dependent variable E_t		Independent variable	Dependent variable $(r_D - r_F)_t$	
	3SLS	FIML		3SLS	FIML
Constant	-0.0009 (0.82)	0.0013 (1.3)	Constant	0.34 (1.2)	0.49
α	0.38 (6.5)	0.246 (8.2)	$(E_t - E_{t-1})$	-21.9 (1.7)	-2.5 (0.3)
$(r_D - r_F)_t$	-0.00009 (0.06)	0.0024 (2.3)	ΔP_t	-51.4 (5.0)	-56.2 (4.3)
$(r_D - r_F)_{t-1}$	-0.0003 (0.8)	-0.0029 (1.3)	ΔP_{t-1}	48.2 (4.1)	51.1 (3.8)
			$(r_D - r_F)_{t-1}$	0.96 (13.2)	0.958 (11.0)
			$(r_D - r_F)_{t-2}$	0.007 (0.1)	-0.029 (0.4)

$\Sigma e^2 = 0.017$ $\Sigma e^2 = 0.0267$ $\Sigma e^2 = 170.1$ $\Sigma e^2 = 184.6$
DW $= 2.3$ DW $= 2.0$ DW $= 1.93$ DW $= 1.9$

3SLS Minimand $= 38.66$ Log likelihood
function $= 514.8$

A likelihood ratio test of the imposed restriction in Table 6 gives a
test statistic of 1.6 (the 95 per cent significance level for the Chi Sq
(1) distribution is 3.4), so the restriction is easily accepted by the
data. The Table 6 results differ from those in Table 5 with respect to
the interest rate effects, the FIML estimates now look much more like a
difference term. A further restriction on the model was therefore
imposed to see if the interest rate effect could be re-parameterised as

a difference term.   These results are reported in Table 7.

Table 7.   A restricted interest rate effect

SAMPLE 197303-198406, monthly

Independent variable	Dependent variable E_t	
	3SLS	FIML
Constant	-0.0001 (0.1)	-0.0002 (0.2)
α	0.41 (7.4)	0.242 (8.7)
$(r_D - r_F)_t - (r_D - r_F)_{t-1}$	0.0002 (0.1)	0.0042 (3.9)
	$\Sigma e^2 = 0.017$ DW = 2.4	$\Sigma e^2 = 0.031$ DW = 2.03

Independent variable	Dependent variable $(r_D \ r_F)_t$	
	3SLS	FIML
Constant	0.32 (13.3)	0.56 (1.9)
$(E_t - E_{t-1})$	-23.2 (1.9)	-0.3 (0.04)
ΔP_t	-46.4 (4.6)	-48.0 (3.9)
ΔP_{t-1}	42.9 (4.2)	41.7 (3.3)
$(r_D - r_F)_{t-1}$	0.93 (13.3)	0.91 (11.5)
$(r_D - r_F)_{t-2}$	0.01 (0.17)	-0.02 (0.3)

$\Sigma e^2 = 172.6$ $\Sigma e^2 = 191.9$
DW   =   1.9   DW   =   1.82
3SLS Minimand = 43.08 Log likelihood
function = 512.7

The likelihood ratio test of this restriction against the model in Table 6 is 4.2 which would reject the restriction. The likelihood ratio test of both restrictions jointly (the model in Table 7 as a restricted version of Table 5) is 5.8, which is just within the critical limit of 5.99. It would seem, therefore, that we can comfortably accept the restriction that the parameters on the expected and lagged exchange rate term sum to one. The interest rate terms, however, may not form a simple difference. One problem with both the models outlined in Tables 5 and 6 is that although the current interest rate term is positive, the net effect is negative and so an increase in interest rates will lower the exchange rate. This is not the case for the restricted model in Table 7. To accept the model set out in Table 6 would therefore be to reject the underlying theory. However, one explanation of the results is that stocks adjust to a new equilibrium level but they take more than a month to do it. In order to allow for this possibility a slightly more general restriction was included; this took the form:

$$B(r_D - r_F)_t + \phi(r_D - r_F)_{t-1} - (B + \phi)(r_D - r_F)_{t-2}$$

The assumption in this equation being that adjustment may be spread over two months but the whole term represents an exact difference equation nonetheless. Applying this restriction produced a likelihood ratio test statistic of the restriction (against the model in Table 6) of 1.8, which is easily accepted. The full set of results is presented in Table 8.

It is interesting that throughout this set of regressions the FIML results have been uniformly more acceptable than the 3SLS results. On the basis of the FIML results we can conclusively reject the simple open arbitrage equation on two grounds; first the results indicate that stocks of assets will reach an equilibrium even in the presence of a non-zero interest rate differential. Second, there is a significant effect from the lagged exchange rate so that the exchange rate will not move by discrete jumps but will follow a more gradual path.

Table 8. The preferred, fully restricted model

SAMPLE 197303-198406, monthly

Independent variable	Dependent variable E_t		Independent variable	Dependent variable $(r_D - r_F)_t$	
	3SLS	FIML		3SLS	FIML
Constant	-0.0001 (0.1)	-0.0002 (0.2)	Constant	0.35 (1.2)	0.49 (1.6)
α	0.42 (7.5)	0.265 (9.4)	$(E_t - E_{t-1})$	-20.94 (1.6)	1.0 (0.1)
B	0.00015 (0.1)	0.003659 (3.5)	ΔP_t	-51.82 (1.6)	-52.6 (0.1)
ϕ	-0.00053 (0.3)	-0.003657 (3.0)	ΔP_{t-1}	47.82 (4.6)	47.1 (3.6)
			$(r_D - r_F)_{t-1}$	0.95 (13.0)	0.93 (10.5)
			$(r_D - r_F)_{t-2}$	0.0004 (0.06)	-0.03 (0.3)

$\Sigma e^2 = 0.0166$ $\Sigma e^2 = 0.028$ $\Sigma e^2 = 170.2$ $\Sigma e^2 = 192.1$
DW $= 2.5$ DW $= 2.1$ DW $=$ 1.92 DW $= 1.86$

3SLS Minimand = 40.15   Log likelihood
                        function = 513.9

So far this analysis has been based around equation (29) which assumed that asset markets were sufficiently flexible that they would completely dominate exchange rate movements. This assumption will now be relaxed and possible effects from trade movements will be investigated. A common approach for this purpose would include the current balance in the exchange rate equation, but, largely due to problems in obtaining data for invisibles on a monthly basis, we include a term in the ratio of exports to imports.

By following the same nesting down procedure as outlined earlier, a model similar to that presented in Table 8 can be obtained, the new version now including a term in the ratio of exports to imports (LXM). This model is shown in Table 9.

Table 9. <u>A full restricted version with trade effects</u>

SAMPLE 197303-198406, monthly

Independent variable	Dependent variable E_t		Independent variable	Dependent variable $(r_D - r_F)_t$	
	3SLS	FIML		3SLS	FIML
Constant	0.0017 (1.4)	0.0015 (0.9)	Constant	0.184 (0.7)	0.44 (1.6)
α	0.40 (6.8)	0.19 (6.5)	$(E_t - E_{t-1})$	−43.3 (3.9)	−10.56 (1.3)
β	−0.0008 (0.5)	0.0044 (3.9)	ΔP_t	−44.0 (4.4)	−48.8 (4.1)
ϕ	0.0006 (0.4)	−0.0041 (3.2)	ΔP_{t-1}	43.0 (4.4)	43.9 (3.6)
LXM	0.016 (2.2)	0.016 (1.95)	$(r_D - r_F)_{t-1}$	0.98 (14.0)	0.93 (11.1)
			$(r_D - r_F)_{t-2}$	0.03 (0.5)	−0.01 (0.2)

$\Sigma e^2 = 0.015$ $\Sigma e^2 = 0.032$ $\Sigma e^2 = 189.9$ $\Sigma e^2 = 176.89$
DW = 2.3   DW = 1.89   DW = 1.92   DW = 1.88
              3SLS Minimand = 45.7   Log likelihood
                                     function = 523.242

The addition of LXM has produced a dramatic increase in the log likelihood function, the parameter on LXM in the exchange rate equation is correctly signed with a t-value of close to 2 for both the 3SLS and FIML results. The coefficient on the change in the exchange rate in the interest rate equation has now taken its expected negative sign in the FIML results. It is interesting that despite the obvious improvement in the likelihood function the 3SLS minimand has risen. This is caused by the addition of LXM to the instrument set in the 3SLS estimation process.

So a number of conclusions emerge from these monthly estimates of an exchange rate equation estimated using the Wickens IV technique. The model rejects the open arbitrage condition in three important ways. It finds a significant role for the lagged exchange rate, suggesting that the exchange rate cannot jump sufficiently freely to meet the open arbitrage condition. Secondly, it finds that asset stocks seem to reach an equilibrium before the interest rate differential is removed, so that a non-zero differential does not lead to a constantly changing exchange rate. Finally, it finds a significant role for the trade balance in exchange rate determination, thereby rejecting the assumption that in the short run asset markets completely dominate exchange rate determination. Next, we consider the problems of estimating the model using quarterly data, with the view that a quarterly exchange rate model may be derived suitable for use in a quarterly macroeconometric model. [A fuller illustration of this is provided in Chapter 4].

A quarterly model

The larger sample which is afforded by monthly data is very important
when systems estimation, such as FIML, is being used. So it is of
interest to establish what effects re-estimating the model using
quarterly data has.

The set of quarterly results presented below are for an identical
model to that presented in table 8 except that the two period lag on the
interest rates was found to be unnecessary in the case of quarterly
data. This is not surprising; if monthly data suggests that asset
stocks achieve equilibrium in two months, we would expect quarterly data
to suggest equilibrium in one quarter. The likelihood ratio test of the
zero parameter restriction on the second lagged interest rate term for
quarterly data is 0.8. Table 10 presents a set of quarterly results for
the model; only FIML results are reported.

These results are very similar to those of table 8. The effect of
interest rates on the exchange rate is correctly signed and significant.
As we might expect, with quarterly data the effect of the lagged
exchange rate has fallen in magnitude and it is marginally
insignificant. However, the earlier conclusions seem to be born out by
this quarterly model.

The final set of results in table 11 present a quarterly version of
table 9 which includes the ratio of exports to imports.

Table 10. The quarterly model (FIML estimates)

SAMPLE 19701-1984Q2

Independent variable	Dependent variable E_t	Independent variable	Dependent variable $(r_D - r_F)_t$
Constant	0.0004 (0.06)	Constant	0.8 (1.0)
α	0.1 (1.3)	$(E_t - E_{t-1})$	7.5 (0.69)
B	0.009 (2.5)	ΔP_t	-13.5 (2.8)
		ΔP_{t-1}	0 (0)
		$(r_D - r_F)_{t-1}$	0.85 (7.7)
		$(r_D - r_F)_{t-2}$	-0.23 (2.1)

$$\Sigma e^2 = 0.08 \qquad\qquad\qquad\qquad \Sigma e^2 = 270.4$$
$$\Delta W = 2.1 \qquad\qquad\qquad\qquad\qquad DW = 1.7$$
$$\text{Log likelihood function} = 78.2$$

Table 11. A quarterly model with trade effects (FIML)

SAMPLE 197201 - 198402

Independent variable	Dependent variable E_t	Independent variable	Dependent variable $(r_D - r_F)_t$
Constant	0.0016 (0.26)	Constant	0.65 (0.6)
α	0.215 (3.2)	$(E_t - E_{t-1})$	41.9 (4.4)
β	0.010 (4.3)	ΔP_t	-14.6 (2.5)
LXM	0.101 (3.3)	ΔP_{t-1}	0.0 (-)
		$(r_D - r_F)_{t-1}$	0.82 (6.6)
		$(r_D - r_F)_{t-2}$	0.32 (-2.45)

$$\Sigma e^2 = 0.06 \qquad\qquad\qquad\qquad \Sigma e^2 = 4.21$$
$$DW = 2.4 \qquad\qquad\qquad\qquad\qquad DW = 1.8$$
$$\text{Log likelihood function} = 83.84$$

The addition of trade effects to the exchange rate equation has again had a marked effect on the value of the log likelihood function. It has also produced a general rise in the t-values associated with the exchange rate equation.

The results for the quarterly model therefore confirm the picture presented by the earlier monthly model. The open arbitrage equation is again rejected on three counts: the presence of a significant effect from trade, the lagged exchange rate and the lagged interest differential.

Conclusions on Exchange Rate equations

So to conclude this section we note that the simple open arbitrage equation which lies at the heart of many current exchange rate models is significantly rejected by both monthly and quarterly data on a number of counts in favour of a richer and more complex model. In Chapter 4 we will consider other applications of some of these ideas to exchange rate modelling.

DYNAMIC MODELLING AND COINTEGRATION

1. Introduction

Prior to the development of cointegration theory and the recent work on
estimation using non-stationary variables, the main thrust of
econometric and statistical theory had developed within a stationary
framework. The vast majority of variables which are of interest to the
applied economist are obviously non-stationary. Econometricians have
taken a variety of approaches to dealing with this conflict; at the
simplest level many early practitioners simply ignored the stationarity
requirement. This practice led to a substantial literature dealing with
the 'spurious regression' problem which culminated in the Box-Jenkins
approach to modelling which used only stationary variables. In turn the
reaction to this approach was the view that important information could
be lost by pre-filtering data to render it stationary and that the long-
run properties of the data, in particular, was being completely ignored.
This reaction developed into the dynamic modelling approach which is
often encapsulated in the error correction model. This approach uses a
mixture of stationary and non-stationary variables in the same equation
and has proved a powerful tool although its foundations in statistical
theory have always been weak.

The concept of cointegration provides a firmer theoretical
foundation for dynamic modelling, in addition to giving a number of new
insights into the long-run properties of data. This makes this new body
of theory important to both applied econometricians and theoretical
statisticians.

2. Stationarity

A key concept underlying this chapter is the idea of stationarity, so it seems appropriate to give a basic account of this before proceeding. A detailed mathematical exposition of the underlying theory may be found in Jazwinski (1970). Let $(x_t, t \epsilon T)$ be a stochastic process, then we define strict stationarity (or stationarity in the strict sense) to hold when the process has the same probability law as the process $(x_{t+i}, t \epsilon T)$ for any $i \epsilon T$. So if $P(.)$ defines the joint density function, strict stationarity implies that

$$P(x_{t_1} \ldots, x_{t_N}) = P(x_{t_1+i} \ldots, x_{t_N+i}) \tag{1}$$

In fact for most applications this definition is unnecessarily restrictive and all that is required is weak stationarity (wide sense or co-variance stationarity). A series is said to be weakly stationary if it has finite second moments and the mean value of the series and its correlation function are time invariant. So $E(x_t^2) < \infty$ for all $t \epsilon T$; this in turn implies that the mean value, correlation and co-variance functions exist.

The properties of a weakly stationary [we will henceforth say simply 'stationary'] series and a non-stationary series are quite different. A stationary series will have a well-determined mean which will not vary greatly with the sampling period; moreover it will tend to constantly return to its mean value and fluctuations around this mean will have a broadly constant amptitude. A non-stationary series on the other hand will exhibit a time varying mean and we can not in general properly use the term mean without referring to some particular time period.

The simplest example of a non-stationary process is the random walk.

$$x_t = x_{t-1} + \varepsilon_t \text{ where } \varepsilon_t \sim IN(0, \sigma^2) \tag{2}$$

So that if $x_0 = 0$

$$x_t = \sum_{i=1}^{t} \varepsilon_i \tag{3}$$

The variance of x_t is $t\sigma^2$ and this becomes indefinitely large as $t \to \infty$. It is also clear that the concept of a mean value for x_t has no meaning. In fact if at some point $x_t = C$ then the expected time until x_t again returns to C is infinite.

3. The background to cointegration theory

A detailed account of the development of the ideas leading up to the introduction of the concept of cointegration may be found in Hendry and Morgan (1986) and Hendry (1986). The pitfalls of using non-stationary data have been known for a considerable period of time: Jevons (1884) and Hooker (1901) both show that they are aware of the spurious correlation which can occur when trended data is being used. The first formal analysis of the problem, that we are aware of, is Yule (1926) who constructed a number of experiments to show that standard theory worked well in the case of stationary variables but could give highly misleading results when variables were non-stationary.

Despite this clear analysis of the problems implied by non-stationary data econometricians proceeded to carry out research based on conventional techniques which assumed stationarity but applied this to trended economic variables. A good example is the development of the literature on consumption functions including Kuznets (1942), Haavelmo (1947), Davis (1952), Brown (1952), Evans (1969) and Hendry (1973). This work centred around regressions of the level of consumption on the level of income, two obviously non-stationary variables.

Partly as a reaction to this widespread disregard for conventional theory, Box and Jenkins (1970) proposed a system of modelling which involved pre-filtering all data to render it stationary before proceeding to estimate or identify a suitable model structure. Granger and Newbold (1974) re-emphasised the warnings of Yule concerning the use of non-stationary data; they coined the term 'spurious' regression for the results obtained by using two trended variables in a regression when the variables were actually unrelated. An interesting point raised by this paper, in the light of the recent cointegration literature, is that they noticed that the 'spurious' regressions were typically characterised by a very low Durbin-Watson statistic.

An alternative strand of research to the approach of Box and Jenkins was founded on the work of Sargan (1964) and Phillips (1957). This approach to dynamic modelling using the Error Correction formulation, is distinguished by a mixture of both stationary and non-stationary terms in the regression equation. The non-stationary (levels) terms are interpreted as determining the long-run equilibrium relationship exhibited by the data. The dependant variable is, however, typically a stationary first difference term and sufficient other difference terms are included in the equation to produce a white noise stationary error process. Subsequent developments in this area have been made by Davidson et al (1978), Hendry and von Ungern-Sternberg (1980), Hendry and Mizon (1978) and Currie (1981).

A further major contribution in setting the scene for the introduction of the cointegration literature came from researchers working on serial correlation and the properties of test statistics, when data is a random walk. Important contributions in this area include Fuller (1976), Dickey and Fuller (1979) and (1981), Evans and Savin (1981), Nelson and Kang (1981), Nelson and Plosser (1982), and Sargan and Bhargava (1983). This literature has produced a more detailed understanding of the properties of regression with non-stationary variables and the distribution of various test statistics under the assumption that the data is generated by random walk processes. It has also proposed a number of tests of the random walk hypothesis which have proved useful.

4.   Integrated variables and cointegration

The concept of integrated series was introduced into econometrics in Granger (1980) and (1981); the basic idea had been in use in the electrical and hydraulic engineering literature for some time. This basic idea is that the order of integration of a series is given by the number of times the series must be differenced in order to produce a stationary series. So if we consider the simple random walk model (2), differencing this series once will produce a stationary variable, x_t^1 = ε_t. This implies that the series generated by (2) is integrated of order one. A more formal definition may be stated thus. A series, x_t, is said to be integrated of order d (denoted $x_t \sim I(d)$) if it is a series which has a stationary, invertible, non-deterministic ARMA representation after differencing d times.

The importance of this definition lies in the Granger (1981) proof that in general if we take a linear combination of two series, each integrated at a different level, then the resulting series will be integrated at the highest of the two orders of integration. So suppose

$$Z_t = b\ x_t + c\ Y_t \tag{4}$$

where $x_t \sim I(dx)$, $Y \sim I(dy)$ then in general $Z_t = I(\max(dx, dy))$. This is demonstrated by noting that the spectrum of Z_t is

$$f_z(w) = b^2 f_x(w) + c^2 f_y(w) + 2bc(r(w) + r(w)) \tag{5}$$

where $r(w)$ is the cross spectrum between x and y which has the property that $|r(w)|^2 \leq f_x(w).f_y(w)$. Now when w is small we are considering the low frequencies of the spectrum and for small w

$$f_x(w) = A_1 w^{-2dx}\ ,\qquad f_y(w) = A_2 w^{-2dy} \tag{6}$$

and so the term with the largest d_i will dominate. This need not always be the case of course, and it is the exceptions to this general rule which allow the case of cointegration. However, when this rule does hold it illustrates the problem of estimation using variables which are not I(0). In this case the error term itself will generally be integrated at the highest order of any of the variables in the regression. So the error term will be non-stationary, it will have no properly defined mean or variance, and the basic assumption of OLS is violated.

The important exception to this rule is where the low frequency (or trend) components of the spectrums of two or more variables exactly offset each other to give a stationary Z series. This is the case of a set of cointegrating variables. The basic idea is that if, in the long run, two or more series move closely together, even though the series themselves are trended, the difference between them is constant. We may regard these series as defining a long-run equilibrium relationship and, as the difference between them is stationary, the error term in a regression will have well defined first and second moments. So traditional OLS regression becomes feasible in this case. The term equilibrium has many meanings in economics and its use in the cointegration literature is rather different from most definitions of equilibrium. Within the cointegration literature all that is meant by equilibrium is that it is an observed relationship which has, on average, been maintained by a set of variables for a long period. It implies none of the usual theoretical implications of market clearing or full employment and neither does it imply that the system is at rest.

Cointegration may be formally defined as follows: the components of the vector X_t are said to be cointegrated of order d, b (denoted X_t ~ (I(d,b))) if:

    i) all components of X_t are I(d)

and

    ii) there exists a vector $\alpha(\neq 0)$ so that

$$Z_t = \alpha' X_t \sim I(d - b), \ b > 0;$$

the vector α is then called the cointegrating vector.

An important implication of this definition is that if we have two variables which are integrated at different orders of integration then these two series cannot possibly be cointegrated. This is an intuitively clear result; it would be very strange to propose a relationship between an I(0) series and an I(1) series. The I(0) series would have a constant mean while the mean of the I(1) would go to infinity and so the error between them would be expected to become infinitely large. It is however possible to have a mixture of different order series when there are three or more series under consideration.

In this case a subset of the higher order series must cointegrate to the order of the low order series. For example suppose Y ~ I(1), X ~ I(2) and W ~ I(2), then if

$$V_t = a\,X_t + c\,W_t \sim I(2 - 1) \tag{7}$$

and $\quad Z_t = e\,V_t + f\,Y_t \sim I(1 - 1) \tag{8}$

then X and W $\sim$ (I (2, 1)) and V and Y $\sim$ (I(1, 1)) and $Z_t \sim I(0)$.

Clearly many such combinations are possible and an example of one will be given later in the chapter.

Perhaps the most important result using this definition of cointegration is the Granger Representation theorem (Granger (1983)). This theorem states that if a set of variables are cointegrated (d = 1, b = 1) then there exists a valid error-correction representation of the data. So if X_t is an N x 1 vector such that $X_t \sim$ (1, 1) and α is the cointegrating vector then the following general ECM model may be derived where $Z_t = \alpha'X_t$

$$A(L)\,(1 - L)\,X_t = -\,\Upsilon'Z_{t-1} + d(L)\epsilon_t \tag{9}$$

where A(L) is a finite order polynomial with $A(0) = I_N$ and d(L) is a finite order lag polynomial.

Equation (9) is a regression model containing only stationary variables and so the usual stationery regression theory applies. This provides a complete theoretical basis for the ECM model when the levels terms cointegrate. The Granger Representation theorem also demonstrates that if the data generation process is an equation such as (9) then X_t

must be a cointegrated set of variables. The practical implications of this for dynamic modelling are profound: in order for an error-correction model to be immune from the spurious regression problem it must contain a set of levels terms which cointegrate to give a stationary error term. The danger with dynamic estimation is that the very richness of the dynamic structure may make the residual process appear to be white noise in a small sample when in fact the levels terms do not cointegrate and so the true residual process must be non-stationary.

There are a number of other, more minor, implications which follow from a set of variables being cointegrated; first if X_t and Y_t are cointegrated then because Y_t and Y_{t-i} will be cointegrated for any i, X_t and $\alpha Y_{t-i} + W_t$ (where $W_t \sim I(0)$) will be cointegrated. Second, if X_t and Y_t are cointegrated and $I(1)$ then either X_t must Granger cause Y_t or Y_t must Granger cause X_t or both of these statements is true. This follows essentially from the existence of the ECM model which suggests that, at the very least, the lagged value of the variables must enter one determining equation. Finally it is interesting to note that if X_t and Y_t are a pair of prices from two efficient speculative markets without adjustment costs then they cannot be cointegrated. This follows from the fact that if they were cointegrated then one would Granger cause the other and so it could be used to forecast the other price.

5. Estimating the cointegrating vector

One approach to estimating the cointegrating vector would be to work with (9), the ECM representation of the data. This however is not an easy procedure to implement properly as it must be remembered that (9)

is a complete system of equations determining all the elements of X_t.

Further, there is the cross-equation restriction that the same

parameters should occur in the levels parts of all the equations. So it

would need to be estimated as a full system subject to this non-linear

constraint. In fact consistent estimates may be achieved much more

easily following a suggestion made by Granger and Engle (1985) which

relies on two theorems given in Stock (1985). These theorems use the

concept of the order of a sequence which may be defined as follows:

Definition: The sequence (bn) is at most of order n^λ denoted $O(n^\lambda)$ if

and only if for some real number Δ, $0 < \Delta < \infty$, there exists a finite

integer N such that for all $n \geq N$, $| n^{-\lambda} b_n | < \Delta$.

The suggestion is simply that the static model may be estimated by OLS

to give consistent estimates of the cointegrating vector. Stock (1984)

in his theorem 2 demonstrates that under very weak assumptions

$$T^{1-\delta} (\hat{\alpha} - \alpha) \xrightarrow{p} 0 \qquad \delta > 0 \qquad\qquad (10)$$

which demonstrates that $\hat{\alpha}$, the OLS estimates of the cointegrating

vector, are consistent estimates of α. A more surprising result is

that in theorem 4 Stock demonstrates that the order of convergence of

the OLS estimates is $O(T^1)$; this contrasts with standard estimation in

the stationary case where the order of convergence is $O(T^{1/2})$. This means

that the OLS estimates in the non-stationary case converge on

their true parameter values much faster than in the stationary case.
This property is sometimes referred to as 'super consistency'. However,
offsetting this rapid convergence to the true parameter values is a
result based on Stocks' theorem 1 which shows that there is a small
sample bias present in the OLS estimator and that the limiting
distribution is non-normal with a non-zero mean. Banerjee et al (1986)
suggest that this small sample bias may be important in some cases and
they show that for certain simple models the bias is related to $1 - R^2$
of the regression, so that a very high R^2 is associated with very little
bias.

It is important to note that the proof of the consistency of the
OLS estimator does not require the assumption that the RHS variables are
uncorrelated with the error term. In fact any of the variables may be
used as the dependent variable in the regression and the estimates
remain consistent. This means that problems do not arise when we have
endogenous RHS variables or when these variables are measured with
error. The reason for this may be seen quite easily at an intuitive
level, the error process in the regression is I(0) while the variables
are I(1) (or higher) so the means of the variables are time-dependent
and will go to infinity. In effect what happens is that the growth in
the means of the variables swamp the error process. This may be seen
graphically in the following simple diagram.

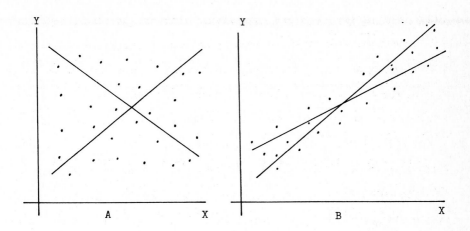

In A we present a scatter of data points and two regression lines, $Y = \alpha X + c_1$ and $X = \beta Y + c_2$. The regression lines are different because of the well-known property of OLS that $\alpha \neq \frac{1}{\beta}$. Now if the data is stationary and we increase the number of observations nothing significant will change in diagram A: the scatter of points will become more dense, that is all. However, if the data is non-stationary then increasing the number of observations will have the effect of spreading the diagram over a larger area, and because the error term is stationary the variance of the errors will be constant. This is illustrated in B; it is obvious that the two regression lines will be forced closer together and as the number of observations becomes infinite the two regression lines become identical so that $\alpha = \frac{1}{\beta}$. This also explains the importance of a high R^2 in ensuring that the small sample bias is unimportant. When the $R^2 = 1$, i.e. the equation is a perfect fit, $\alpha = \frac{1}{\beta}$ even in the stationary case. In the non-stationary case the goodness of fit determines how effective the trended nature of the data is at swamping the constant variance error term.

Granger and Engle (1985) demonstrate that once OLS has been used to estimate the cointegrating vector then the other parameters of the Error Correction Model may be consistently estimated by imposing the first-stage estimates of the cointegrating vector on a second-stage ECM. This is done simply by including the residuals from the first-stage regression in a general ECM. This procedure is sometimes referred to as the two-step Granger and Engle estimation procedure. They also demonstrate that the OLS standard errors obtained at the second stage are consistent estimates of the true standard errors.

The advantages of the two-step procedure are that it allows us to make use of the super convergence properties of the first-stage estimates and that at the first stage it is possible to test that the vector of variables properly cointegrates. Thus we are sure that the full ECM model is not a spurious regression.

6. Testing for cointegration

Much of the early applications of cointegration (e.g. Granger and Weiss (1983) or Hall and Brooks (1985)) was hampered by the difficulty of testing for cointegration between a set of variables. The early practice was to rely on an informal inspection of the correlogram of the error process. If the correlogram quickly approaches zero and then remains close to zero the error process would be judged stationary. The problem here is obviously how to define quickly and that no form of statistical rigour could be brought to bear on the question. Granger and Engle (1985) proposed a range of seven possible tests which may be used for cointegration testing; these tests are related to, or stem from, the unit root literature mentioned above but their use in this case is more complex. The situation is that we have an OLS estimate of the cointegrating vector $\hat{\alpha}$ and we may define the OLS residuals from the cointegrating regression as

$$Z_t = \hat{\alpha} X_t' \qquad (11)$$

Now suppose Z_t follows an AR(1) process so that

$$Z_t = \rho Z_{t-1} \qquad (12)$$

then cointegration would imply that $\rho < 1$ which suggests the null hypothesis that $\rho = 1$ and the test that the error process is a random walk. The Dickey-Fuller test and the use of the Durbin-Watson statistic proposed by Sargan and Bhargava (1983) can both be used to test this hypothesis. There is however a further complication: if α were known then we could simply use the standard tables from Dickey and Fuller (1981) for example to test the relevant hypothesis. When $\hat{\alpha}$ is not known, the problem is much more complex, under the null hypothesis that $\rho = 1$ we cannot estimate α in an unbiased way. Because OLS will seek to produce minimum squared residuals this will mean that the Dickey-Fuller tables will tend to reject the null too often. So we have to construct tables of critical values for each data generation process individually under the null hypothesis. Granger and Engle present some sample calculations of critical values for some simple models. We will discuss the three of their proposed test procedures which have been most commonly used. These are defined below.

The Dickey-Fuller (DF) test:

Perform the regression $\Delta Z_t = \emptyset_1 \, Z_{t-1} + \varepsilon_t$ then under the null that $\rho = 1$, $\emptyset_1 = 0$, if $\rho < 1$, $\emptyset_1 < 0$ so we perform a t-test to test whether $\emptyset_1$ is significantly less than zero. The t-statistic on $\emptyset_1$ is the DF statistic.

The Augmented Dickey-Fuller (ADF) test:

Perform the regression $\Delta Z_t = \emptyset_1 \, Z_{t-1} + \sum_{i=1}^{p} \Upsilon_i \Delta Z_{t-i} + \varepsilon_t$ again under the null that $\rho = 1$, $\emptyset_1 = 0$ and if $\rho < 1$, $\emptyset_1 < 0$ so we again use the t-test to test that $\emptyset_1$ is significantly less than zero. The t-statistic on $\emptyset_1$ is the ADF statistic.

The Cointegrating Regression Durbin-Watson (CRDW) test:

The Durbin-Watson from the cointegrating regression may be used to test the null that $\rho = 1$. Under this hypothesis the CRDW = 0 and so we seek a value of the CRDW which is high enough to reject the proposal that it actually is zero.

The following table gives the critical values which have been derived for the 2- and 3-variable case by Monte Carlo approximation:

Table 1. Critical values for tests of cointegration

	1%	5%	10%
2 variable case			
CRDW	.511	.386	.322
DF	-4.07	-3.37	-3.03
ADF	-3.77	-3.17	-2.84
3 variable case			
CRDW	.488	.367	.308
ADR	-3.89	-3.13	-2.82

Source: 2-variable case: Granger and Engle (1985).
3-variable case: thanks are due to Professor Granger
for permission to report these results.

It is clear that the critical values do not change enormously as we move
from a 2-variable model to a 3-variable model. Nonetheless in the
application given below we will be working outside of the strict limits
of these tables and so we must exert caution in the interpretation of
these critical values.

Maximum likelihood estimation of the cointegrating vector
There are a number of drawbacks to the procedure outlined above; testing
the model for cointegration is difficult given that the distribution of
the test statistics varies with each model. Practical experience
suggests that the tests often have fairly low power. A more fundamental
problem however is that the above procedure makes the assumption that
the cointegrating vector is unique. In general if we have a set of N
I(1) variables then there may exist r cointegrating vectors between the

variables where $r \equiv N-1$. If we restate equation (9), the general ECM
model as

$$A(L)(1 - L) \ X_t = - \ \Upsilon' \ B \ X_{t-1} + d(L)\varepsilon_t \qquad (13)$$

where B is now an N x N matrix of cointegrating vectors. Then r, the
number of distinct cointegrating vectors will be given by the rank of B.
Given that at most $r = N-1$ we see immediately that B is singular. Where
the cointegrating vector is unique, $r = 1$, all the rows of B are linear
combinations of each other.

We therefore need a procedure to estimate all the cointegrating
vectors which exist between a set of variables and to test for the
number of distinct cointegrating vectors which exist. Johansen (1987)
has proposed a method which gives maximum likelihood estimates of B, the
full cointegrating matrix and also produces a likelihood ratio test
statistic for the maximum number of distinct cointegrating vectors in
the matrix.

Johansen sets his analysis within a slightly different framework to
that used above, so we begin by defining the general polynomial
distributed lag (PDL) form of the model as

$$X_t = \Pi_1 \ X_{t-1} + \ldots + \Pi_k \ X_{t-k} + \varepsilon_t \qquad (14)$$

where X is a vector of N variables of interest; and ε_t is an IID N
dimensional vector with zero mean and variance matrix Ω. Within this

framework the long run, or cointegrating matrix is given by

$$I - \Pi_1 - \Pi_2 \ldots \Pi_k = \Pi \qquad\qquad (15)$$

and so the rank of Π, r, defines the number of distinct cointegrating vectors. Now we define two matrices α, β both of which are N x r such that

$$\Pi = \alpha \; \beta '$$

and so the rows of β form the r distinct cointegrating vectors.

Johansen then demonstrates the following Theorem.

Theorem : The maximum likelihood estimates of the space spanned by β is the space spanned by the r canonical variates corresponding to the r largest squared canonical correlations between the residuals of X_{t-k} and ΔX_t corrected for the effect of the lagged differences of the X process. The likelihood ratio test statistic for the hypothesis that there are at most r cointegrating vectors is

$$- \; 2 \; \ln Q = - \; T \sum_{i=r+1}^{N} \ln(1 - \hat{\lambda}_i) \qquad\qquad (16)$$

where $\hat{\lambda}_{r+1} \ldots \hat{\lambda}_N$ are the N - r smallest squared canonical correlations. Johansen then goes on to demonstrate the consistency of the maximum likelihood estimates and, more importantly, he shows that the likelihood ratio test has an exact distribution which is a function of a N - r Brownian motion. This means that a set of exact critical values can be tabulated which will be correct for all models.

In order to implement this Theorem we begin by reparameterising (14) into the following ECM model.

$$\Delta X_t = \Gamma_1 \Delta X_{t-1} + \quad + \Gamma_{k-1} \Delta X_{t-k+1} + \Gamma_k X_{t-k} + \epsilon_t \tag{17}$$

where

$$\Gamma_i = I + \Pi_1 + \ldots \Pi_i \ ; \ i = 1 \ldots K$$

The equilibrium matrix Π is now clearly identified as Γ_k.

Johansen's suggested procedure begins by regressing ΔX_t on the lagged differences of ΔX_t and defining a set of residuals R_{ot}. Then regressing X_{t-k} on the lagged residuals and defining a further set of residuals, R_{kt}. The likelihood function, in terms of $\alpha\beta$ and Ω, is then proportional to

$$L(\alpha \ \beta \ \Omega) = |\Omega|^{-T/2} \ \text{EXP} \ [-\frac{1}{2}\sum_{t=1}^{T} (R_{ot} + \alpha \ \beta' R_{kt})'$$
$$\Omega^{-1} \ (R_{ot} + \alpha \ \beta' \ R_{kt})] \tag{18}$$

If β were fixed we can maximise over α and Ω by a regression of R_{ot} on $-\beta' R_{kt}$ which gives

$$\hat{\alpha}(\beta) = - S_{ok} \ \beta(\beta' S_{kk} \ \beta)^{-1} \tag{19}$$

and

$$\hat{\Omega}(\beta) = S_{oo} - S_{ok} \beta (\beta' S_{kk} \beta)^{-1} \beta' S_{ko} \tag{20}$$

where $S_{ij} = T^{-1} \sum_{t=1}^{T} R_{it} R'_{jt} \qquad i,j = 0,K$

and so the likelihood function may be reduced to minimising

$$\left| S_{oo} - S_{ok} \beta (\beta' S_{kk} \beta)^{-1} \beta' S_{ko} \right| \tag{21}$$

and it may be shown that (21) will be minimised when

$$\left| \beta' S_{kk} \beta - \beta' S_{ko} S_{oo}^{-1} S_{ok} \beta \right| / \left| \beta' S_{kk} \beta \right| \tag{22}$$

attains a minimum.

We now define a diagonal matrix D which consists of the ordered eigenvalues $\lambda_1 > \ldots > \lambda_p$ of $S_{ko} S_{oo}^{-1} S_{ok}$ with respect to S_{kk}. That is λ_i satisfies

$$\left| \lambda S_{kk} - S_{ko} S_{oo}^{-1} S_{ok} \right| = 0$$

and define E to be the corresponding matrix of eigenvectors so that

$$S_{kk} E D = S_{ko} S_{oo}^{-1} S_{ok} E$$

where we normalise E such that $E' S_{kk} E = I$.

The maximum likelihood estimator of $\hat{\beta}$ is now given by the first r rows of E, that is, the first r eigenvectors of $S_{ko}S_{oo}^{-1}S_{ok}$ with respect to S_{kk}. These are the canonical variates and the corresponding eigenvalues are the squared canonical correlation of R_k with respect to R_o. These eigenvalues may then be used in the test proposed in (16) to test either for the existence of a cointegrating vector $r = 1$, or for the number of cointegrating vectors $N > r > 1$.

An application to the UK wage data

Using this concept of cointegration to construct an aggregate model of wage determination is particularly apt as the earliest examples of the application of ECM models in econometrics were applied to this sector (see Sargan (1964)). The early models involved only level terms in real wages and a trend representing target real wages. More recent models have also included elements from the Phillips curve literature with the level of unemployment also entering the formulation (see Hall, Henry and Trinder (1983), and Chapter 4).

Before proceeding to test the sets of variables for cointegration it is sensible to establish the properties of the individual series. Much of the theory of cointegration has been developed for the case where all the series are I(1). Higher orders are of course possible and are allowed for under the general definition of cointegration given above. Complications arise, however, when the series are integrated of different orders (e.g. one series might be I(1) and another I(2)); the two series cannot then be co-integrated. In this section we will be concerned with five series; these are: LW: the log of wages; LP: the log of the consumer price index; LPROD: the log of aggregate productivity, UPC: the percentage unemployment rate; and LAVH: the log of average weekly hours worked.

In order to test the level of integration of these variables the Dickey-Fuller (DF) and an Augmented Dickey-Fuller (ADF) test will be used. These are both t tests and rely on rejecting the hypothesis that the series is a random walk in favour of stationarity; this requires a negative and significant test statistic. Table 2 reports the DF and ADF statistics for the five series and their first differences.

Table 2. The time series properties of the variables

	TEST	
Variable	DF	ADF
LW	10.9	2.6
LP	14.5	1.9
LPROD	3.8	3.3
LAVH	-0.3	-0.5
UPC	5.2	1.8
ΔLW	-3.5	-1.4
ΔLP	-1.4	-0.9
ΔLPROD	-8.0	-2.4
ΔLAVH	-11.3	-4.6
ΔUPC	-2.4	-2.5
LW-LP	2.6	2.2
Δ(LW-LP)	-8.5	-3.6

First if we consider the levels of the five variables it is quite obvious that none of them are stationary processes. Four of the variables actually have positive test statistics and the one negative one (LAVH) is highly insignificant. The next five rows in the table are the first difference of the variables, of these ΔLPROD, ΔLAVH and ΔUPC are negative and significant on both tests. So we may conclude that as differencing once produces stationarity these series are I(1). The two remaining series ΔLW and ΔLP are not significant on both tests so it is not possible to reject the hypothesis that they are a random walk in first difference. This indicates that both LW and LP are probably I(2). In the case of three or more variables it is possible to have a subset of the variables which are integrated at a higher order than the remaining variables and still have a valid cointegrating vector if the sub-set of variables together is integrated at the same order as the remaining variables. In this case the remaining two rows of table 2 show that the real wage (LW-LP) is I(1) even though both LW and LP separately are I(2). It is therefore possible that all the variables could form a cointegrating set.

The original Sargan wage bargaining model suggested that real wages would grow steadily along a simple trend, which was interpreted as the desired or target real wage growth of the union sector. There are two problems with this simple original formulation from the point of view of this paper. The first is simply that as the final wage equation is explaining nominal wages then in order to set up a full cointegrating vector of variables we should relax the unit coefficient on prices. The second problem arises from the definition of cointegration, given above, that the variables must be non-deterministic. A time trend is clearly deterministic and must strictly fall outside the definition of cointegration. It is however worth noting that this is also true of the constant, which is invariably included in the cointegrating regression. There are other reasons also for abandoning the use of a simple trend in this equation, in particular the existence of the long-term rise in real wages is widely associated with the long-term growth in productivity. So it may be preferable to use aggregate productivity rather than a simple time trend for this reason also.

The basic Sargan model using smoothed productivity (LPRODS) instead of a time trend may be tested as a cointegrating vector in the following regression

$$LW = -5.49 + 0.99 \ LP + 1.1 \ LPRODS \qquad\qquad (23)$$

CRDW = 0.24   DF = -1.7   ADF = -2.6 R^2 = 0.9972

RCO: 0.86   0.72   0.52   0.35   0.18   0.04   0.08

            -0.20   -0.27   -0.29   -0.32   -0.34

Sample 1963Q4-1984Q4.

RCO is the residual correlogram.

On the basis of the CRDW, the DF, and the ADF test statistics we are unable to reject the assumption that equation (23), the simple Sargan model, represents a non cointegrating vector of level terms.

If we go on to add the percentage level of unemployment to the vector of variables we can test whether incorporating this element of Phillips curve effect produces a set of cointegrating variables.   The relevant cointegrating equation is then

$$LW = - 5.6 + 1.03 \ LP + 1.07 \ LPRODS - 0.72 \ UPC \qquad\qquad (24)$$

CRDW = 0.28   DF = -2.12   ADF = -3.0 R^2 = 0.9974

RCO: 0.85   0.70   0.49   0.29   0.10   -0.06   -0.18

            -0.31   -0.37   -0.39   -0.41   -0.43

All the parameter values of this regression have reasonable values and are correctly signed. However, the CRDW and the DF statistic are well below their critical value, although they have risen considerably from equation (23). Again, we cannot reject the hypothesis that these variables are not a cointegrated vector.

There is, however, another term which often appears in the specification of aggregate wage equations in the UK. This term is the log of average hours worked. The reason for its inclusion is due to the way the aggregate wage data is generated. The way this is often done is to take total wages and salaries for the UK as a whole from the National Accounts and divide this number by the product of employment and hours to give the average hourly wage. This means that a change in hours worked will have a direct effect on the measured wage if total wages and salaries do not move enough to offset it. As many workers are salaried rather than paid hourly this may well be the case. Another effect is that if overtime hours are paid at a different rate than basic hours, then marginal changes in hours incur overtime payments so the weighting pattern of basic and overtime wage rates will vary with hours worked. Some researchers have tried to remove this effect by making an ad hoc adjustment to wages for hours worked. A more successful practice is simply to include hours as one of the explanatory variables. Equation (25) presents a cointegrating regression which includes such a term in hours.

$$LW = 2.88 + 1.02\ LP + 0.93\ LPRODS - 0.61\ UPC - 1.79\ LAVH \qquad (25)$$

CRDW = 0.74   DF = -4.07   ADF = -2.88 R^2 = 0.9993

RCO: 0.63   0.39   0.09   -0.1   -0.03   -0.06   -0.05

$\qquad\qquad$ -0.04   -0.06   -0.05   -0.06   -0.02

where LAVH is the log of average hours.

The CRDW test now rejects the hypothesis of non cointegration decisively, as does the DF test; the ADF test statistic has actually fallen slightly compared with (24): it is still fairly high although it is not able to reject non cointegration. The residual correlogram also would strongly suggest a stationary error process. It would seem reasonable to conclude that the five variables in (25) constitute a co-integrating vector. By comparing (25) with (24) we know that the inclusion of LAVH is necessary, but any of the others might be excluded at this stage and cointegration still retained. In order to test this, each of the three variables (LP, LPRODS and UPC) were dropped, one at a time, and cointegration tests were performed. These are reported in table 3. In all cases the test statistics are considerably lower than

Table 3. Testing for the exclusion of three of the variables

		Excluded variable	
	LP	LPRODS	UPC
CRDW	0.05	0.339	0 64
DF	-0.68	-2.648	-3.66
ADF	-1.43	-1.378	-2.14
R^2	0.9502	0.9968	0.9990
RCO 1	0.96	0.82	0.68
2	0.92	0.73	0.47
3	0.86	0.64	0.22
4	0.78	0.55	0.06
5	0.72	0.57	0.14
6	0.65	0.52	0.13
7	0.58	0.46	0.14
8	0.50	0.40	0.16
9	0.41	0.31	0.13
10	0.32	0.25	0.11
11	0.23	0.23	0.20
12	0.13	0.17	0.16

in equation (25) and the residual correlograms do not strongly suggest
stationarity.   However, the exclusion of both LPRODS and UPC are both
suggested   by the CRDW test (at the 5 per cent level).   Given the
uncertainty surrounding the Granger and Engle critical values for this
model there may be a strong argument for relying more heavily on the
informal evidence of the correlogram.   So in order to estimate a valid
ECM model of UK wage determination, we include the full cointegrating
vector in the levels part of the model.   That is to say, we must include
the level of wages, prices, unemployment, productivity and average hours
to achieve a stationary error process.

Before going on to look at the second stage equation there is a
further complication which needs to be considered.   Equation (25) is a
valid cointegrating regression involving five variables.   In general,
however, we would not expect it to be unique.   It would have been quite
in order to have used any of the four independent variables in (25) as
the dependent variable in a regression.   However, given the properties
of OLS, the resulting equilibrium relationship implied by the regression
would not normally be identical to (25).   It is important therefore to
know just how different the implied equilibrium relationship given by
the different inversions of (25) would be.   This question is
investigated in table 4 below, which shows the various inversions of
equation (25);   the table actually shows the various regressions
rearranged so that LW is on the LHS for ease of comparison. R^2 is the
standard statistic associated with the regression.

Estimating the equation in its different inversions produces different estimates of the equilibrium parameters, as we would expect. The interpretation of this divergence is not entirely satisfactory at present; in the light of Stock (1985) theorem 3, which establishes that the estimates of the cointegrating regression are consistent but subject to a small sample bias, we would assume that the various estimates in table 4 are all estimating the same cointegrating vector and that the divergences are simply due to small sample bias. The properties of the OLS estimator are not well understood when the cointegrating vector is not unique, in this case it is possible to get estimates of differing cointegrating vectors in different inversions. It is possible to investigate this by using the Johansen estimator and test procedure. We would conjecture that even when the cointegrating vector is not unique, estimation by OLS is only likely to detect the cointegrating vector with minimum variance. It is not likely therefore to detect distinct cointegrating vectors. In the light of these problems, we will continue the estimation on the basis of the equation normalised on LW as this gave the highest R^2.

Table 4. The effects on the equilibrium relationship of changing the dependent variable

Coefficients

Dependent variable	Constant	LP	LPRODS	UPC	LAVH	R^2
LW	2.88	1.02	0.93	-0.61	-1.79	0.9993
LP	2.79	1.03	0.88	-0.73	-1.78	0.9988
UPC	1.74	1.20	0.85	-3.52	-1.65	0.8508
LAVH	6.89	1.01	0.86	-0.57	-2.64	0.8096
LPRODS	2.28	0.966	1.21	-0.56	-1.66	0.9746

Now having achieved a suitable specification of the cointegrating equation we can proceed to the second stage of the Granger and Engle procedure. If we define Z to be the derived residual from equation (25) we may then include these residuals in a standard ECM model. In our case a fairly simple search procedure produced the following equation

$$\Delta LW = -0.007 + 1.04 \ EDP - 1.18 \ \Delta^2 UPC_{-1} - 0.98 \ \Delta LAVH \qquad (26)$$
$$(1.4) \quad (6.0) \qquad (1.4) \qquad (8.6)$$

$$+ \ 0.22 \ \Delta LW_{-2} - 0.26 \ Z_{-1}$$
$$(2.9) \qquad (3.3)$$

IV estimates

DW = 1.99   BP(16) = 23.7   SEE = 0.01285

CHISQ(12) = 2.3   CHOW(64,12) = 0.22

Data period: 1965Q3-1984Q3.

Instrumental variable estimation has been used, following the suggestion of McCallum (1976), to allow for the simultaneity in expected future inflation (EDP). Some noteworthy features of this equation are the near unit coefficient on prices and the good out of sample forecasting performance described by the CHOW and CHISQ statistics (derived from this model when estimated without the last 12 observations). BP(16) is the Box-Pierce test for a random correlogram.

In order to get some idea of how influential the two-step estimation procedure has been it seems sensible to relax the restriction implied by the cointegration regression and estimate a free ECM equation. Exactly the same dynamic specification as equation (26) has been used, to give

$$\Delta LW = 1.02 + 1.1 \ EDP - 1.3 \ \Delta^2 UPC_{-1} - 1.01 \ \Delta LAVH \qquad (27)$$
$$(1.5) \quad (2.2) \qquad (1.5) \qquad\qquad (7.3)$$

$$+ 0.23 \ \Delta LW_{-2} - 0.28 \ LW_{-1}$$
$$(2.6) \qquad\quad (2.1)$$

$$+ 0.29 \ LP_{-1} - 0.14 \ UPC_{-1} - 0.55 \ LAVH_{-1}$$
$$(2.2) \qquad (0.6) \qquad\quad (2.0)$$

$$+ 0.21 \ LPRODS_{-1}$$
$$(2.6)$$

IV estimates

DW = 2.03   BP(16) = 24.9   SEE = 0.01298

CHISQ(12) = 65.5   CHOW(60,12) = 6.5

Data period: 1965Q3-1984Q3.

The implications of this regression are somewhat different to (25) and (26). This equation would suggest dropping the level of unemployment altogether, even though table 2 showed that this had a major effect on the properties of the cointegrating regression. It is also interesting to note that the out of sample stability tests indicate considerable parameter instability for this equation. The coefficient on expected price inflation is also considerably larger than unity, suggesting that this equation does not exhibit derivative homogeneity in prices. If the object of this exercise were simply to carry out a normal estimation process, an obvious move at this stage would be to combine the levels terms in wages and prices into a real wage term. This restriction was easily accepted by the data and produced a large improvement in the parameter stability tests (CHISQ(12) = 7.9, CHOW(60,12) = 0.75). However, the coefficient on expected price inflation fell to 0.82 and the level of unemployment remained insignificant. Finally, let us consider the static long-run solution to the model (27)

$$LW = 3.64 + 1.03 \text{ LP} + 0.75 \text{ LPRODS} - 0.50 \text{ UPC} - 1.96 \text{ LAVH} \qquad (28)$$

If we interpret the parameters in table 4 as limiting bounds on the
equilibrium sub-space then the coefficients on LP, LPRODS and LAVH all
lie within this space, but the coefficient on unemployment is just
outside the range suggested by table 4.

In conclusion, while the concept of cointegration is clearly an
important theoretical underpinning to the error correction model there
are still a number of problems surrounding its practical application;
the critical values and small sample performance of many of the tests
are unknown for a wide range of models, and informed inspection of the
correlogram may still be an important tool. The interpretation of the
equilibrium relationship when it is not unique also presents some
problems. Nevertheless in the example presented here the two-stage
procedure seems to perform well and to offer a number of insights into
the data in terms of the time series properties of the variables both in
isolation and in combination.

Cointegration and Dynamic Homogeneity

In an important paper Currie (1981) considered some of the long-run
properties of dynamic models which arise from the general polynomial
distributed lag form of dynamic modelling. He pointed out that if the
long-run properties of a model were to be invariant to the rate of
growth of the steady state equilibrium, then a particular non-linear
restriction on the parameters was implied. This restriction could be
tested and, in the case of a single equation error correction model, it

involved only a simple linear constraint on the parameters.

Hall and Drobny (1986) point out the implication of this analysis for the two step cointegration procedure which has been outlined above. They demonstrate that a possible conflict may arise between the long run solution of the first and second stage if a complex non-linear constraint is not imposed on the equation. In order to illustrate these propositions, we use a general formulation of a dynamic model, and relate this to the error correction model. An example based on the wage model used above concludes the section.

Long-run properties

Consider the long-run relationship between a set of variables which are all integrated of order I(1); that is, the variables are stationary only after first differencing. If, on the other hand, stationarity is achieved by taking a linear combination of the variables expressed in levels form, then the variables are said to cointegrate. A crucial property of cointegrated variables is that they can be represented by an ECM. The Engle and Granger two-step estimation procedure builds on this notion. The first stage of the procedure is to estimate the following levels regression:

$$Y_t = \alpha_o + \sum_{i=1}^{K} \alpha_i X_{it} + U_t \tag{29}$$

where Y_t and all the X_{it}'s are I(1) variables, and U_t is an unobservable stochastic term. If equation (29) passes the usual tests for cointegration, then the α_i (i=o$_,$ ..., K) coefficients are treated as long-run parameters defining the equilibrium or long-run relationship between Y and the X_i's. Further, successful cointegration of (29) implies that U_t must be a stationary variable ($I(0)$). The residuals from (29) are therefore also $I(0)$, and represent (stationary) deviations from the equilibrium relationship. The second stage of the procedure takes these residuals lagged one period (V_{t-1}) and enters them into a typical dynamic equation such as:

$$\Delta Y_t = B_0 + \sum_{J=1}^{N} (B_J \Delta Y_{t-J} + \sum_{i=1}^{K} B_{Ji} \Delta X_{it-J}) + \emptyset V_{t-1} + \varepsilon_t \qquad (30)$$

where ε_t is a white noise residual error. Notice that all variables in (30) are by construction $I(0)$. The close similarity between (30) and traditional ECM equations should be clear. The two types of equations are identical except that the residuals from (29) included in equation (30) replace the levels or error-correction part of the usual model.

The long-run solution to equation (30) is (following Currie)

$$Y = \alpha_0 + \sum_{i=1}^{K} \alpha_i X_i + \emptyset^{-1} [(1 - \sum_{J=1}^{N} B_J) \Delta Y - \sum_{i=1}^{K} \Delta X_i \sum_{J=1}^{N} B_{Ji} - B_0] \qquad (31)$$

where $\Delta Y_t = \Delta Y$ and $\Delta X_{it-j} = \Delta X_i$ in steady state.

The analysis below is motivated by considering the difference in the long-run solutions implied by equations (31) and (29). Engle and Granger's elaboration of the two step procedure is based on considering $I(1)$ variables with zero mean drift. The assumption of zero mean drift implies that the expected values of the first differences of the variables in steady states are zero. Under this assumption the expected value of the last term of equation (3) becomes B_o in steady state, which may also be set equal to zero to give complete consistency between equations (29) and (31).

However restricting the analysis to processes with zero mean drift does tend to reduce the applicability of the two step procedure. It is quite obvious that many economic series exhibit persistent trend like behaviour. "Over the last century, most economic variables have changed radically in mean and often in variance so that their first two moments are far from constant" (Hendry, 1986 page 201). It is precisely such variables which would be ruled out by the zero mean drift assumption. If however we relax this assumption then the last term in equation (31) will not generally be zero and so an obvious conflict may result in the implied steady state behaviour between (29) and (31). If the final term in equation (31) equals zero, the equation is said to exhibit derivative homogenity. This may occur either because the first differences of the data have zero means or because the equation obeys a set of non-linear parameter restrictions which exactly set this last term to zero. The simple condition that this term is zero is a necessary condition for consistency between (29) and (31) but it is not sufficient. This is because there are many combinations of parameters and rates of growth of the variables which will set this term equal to zero while violating the levels equation. Equation (29), however, constrains the rates of growth of the variables to be in a fixed relationship. By taking the first difference of (29) we get:

$$\Delta Y = \sum_{i=1}^{K} \alpha_i \, \Delta X_i \tag{32}$$

To obtain consistency between (29) and (30) the rates of growth in steady state in (30) must obey the restriction implied by (32). The appropriate restriction can then be derived in the following way. From (32), we may rewrite the last term in (31) as

$$(1 - \sum_{J=1}^{N} B_J) \sum_{i=1}^{K} \alpha_i \, \Delta X_i - \sum_{i=1}^{K} \Delta X_i \sum_{J=1}^{N} B_{Ji} = B_0 \qquad (33)$$

If we define:

$$(1 - \sum_{J=1}^{N} B_J) = \Gamma_0 \qquad \text{and} \qquad \sum_{J=1}^{N} B_{Ji} = \Gamma_i$$

we may write (33) as

$$\sum_{i=1}^{K} (\Gamma_0 \alpha_i - \Gamma_i) \, \Delta X_i = B_0 \qquad (34)$$

Equation (34) is then the general restriction which must hold for (29) and (30) to be consistent.

Equation (34) is a highly non-linear restriction involving the steady state values, ΔX_i, which are unknown. There are however special cases of (34) which may be expressed as a linear restriction and which may be easily tested. The most natural case is to consider

$$(\Gamma_0 \alpha_i - \Gamma_i) = 0 \qquad (i=1, \ldots, K) \qquad (35)$$

and $B_0 = 0.$

This may be tested by defining $\Delta Z_i = \alpha_i \Delta X_i$ and estimating the following equation:

$$\Delta Y_t = \sum_{J=1}^{N} (B_J \Delta Y_{t-j} + \sum_{i=1}^{K} \Omega_{iJ} \Delta Z_{it-J}) + \emptyset V_{t-1} + \varepsilon_t \qquad (36)$$

The constraint that $(\Gamma_0 - \sum_{J=1}^{N} \Omega_{iJ}) = 0$ for all i is then equivalent to

(35). This is the restriction suggested by Hall and Drobny (1987) to obtain consistency between (29) and (30) above. Below is an example using and testing the restriction in (36).

A more restricted, but still relevant special case is where the rates of growth of all the variables are equal in equilibrium. This might be the case for a nominal price system for example. In this case $\Delta X_i = \Pi$ for all i and so when $B_0 = 0$, (34) becomes

$$\sum_{i=1}^{K} (\Gamma_0 \alpha_i - \Gamma_i) = 0 \text{ , or} \qquad (37)$$

$$\Gamma_0 \sum_{i=1}^{K} \alpha_i = \sum_{i=1}^{K} \Gamma_i \qquad (38)$$

If we now define $\Delta Z_i = \Pi \sum_{i=1}^{K} \alpha_i$, and again estimate an equation such as

(36), then the constraint that $\Gamma_0 = \sum_{i=1}^{K} \sum_{J=1}^{N} \Omega_{iJ}$ is equivalent to (38).

An Example

In this section we provide a short example illustrating the imposition of derivative homogeneity on a wage equation estimated using the two-step procedure. The example extends the a wage model presented earlier. We did not address the question above of whether the series in fact exhibit zero mean drift. This question is investigated in the following table which reports the value of the constant from a fourth order autoregression of the first differences of the five variables entering the model. The constant should be insignificantly different from zero if the variable exhibits zero mean drift. In addition to the value of the constant we also present the Lagrange Multiplier test for serial correlation in the residuals of first, second and fourth orders (LM(1), LM(2), LM(4) respectively).

Table 5. Testing the zero mean drift assumption

Dependent Variable	Constant (t statistics in parentheses)		LM(1)	LM(2)	LM(4)
ΔLW	0.013	(3.2)	4.0	4.3	4.6
ΔLP	0.004	(2.0)	0.02	0.06	1.4
ΔLPRODS	0.001	(2.8)	0.8	0.9	4.0
ΔUPC	0.0004	(1.7)	0.3	0.5	2.4
ΔLAVH	-0.0002	(0.1)	0.1	0.1	0.2

Among the five variables considered in this table only LAVH is arguably not a zero mean series. LW, LP and LPRODS are almost certainly not zero mean series; this is of course hardly a surprising result as all three series show well defined long term trend like behaviour.

The first stage, cointegrating regression is the same as that used in Hall (1986) although the sample period is different. The results are as follows:

$$LW = 8.7 + 1.04 \ LP + 0.96 \ LPRODS - 0.75 \ UPC - 1.80 \ LAVH \qquad (39)$$

Data period: 1967Q1-1986Q2

CRDW = 0.77   DF = 4.33   ADF = 2.63 R^2 = 0.9992

RCO: 0.62   0.40   0.12   -0.05   0.04   0.02

     -0.02   -0.05   -0.07   -0.06   0.06   0.01

We now proceed to transform the RHS variables of (39) by multiplying each of them by their coefficient. So let, for example,

$$LP^T = LP \ x \ 1.04$$

This transformation has the effect of making all the coefficients in a cointegrating regression, when carried out with the transformed variables, equal unity.

The following, unrestricted dynamic regression was then estimated with the transformed first difference terms:

$$\Delta LW = 0.02 + 0.14 \Delta LW_{t-2} + 0.47 \Delta LP^T_t + 2.3 \Delta UPC^T_{t-1}$$
$$(3.3) \quad (1.8) \qquad\qquad (3.3) \qquad (2.8)$$

$$-1.38 \Delta LPRODS^T_t + 0.51 \Delta LAVH^T_t - 0.29 RES_{t-1} \qquad\qquad (40)$$
$$(2.0) \qquad\qquad (7.9) \qquad (4.0)$$

DW = 1.9   LM(8) = 10.9   LM(1) = 0.18

BP(16) = 2.70   SEE = 0.012 R^2 = 0.71

where RES is the residual from equation (39).

The constraint that $(\Gamma_0 - \sum_{J=1}^{N} \Omega_{iJ}) = 0$ for all i would imply that

the coefficients on each of the first difference terms should be set
equal to the sum of the coefficients on the ΔLW terms and that the
constant should equal zero. Clearly the t-statistics for each term in
(40) taken in isolation suggest rejection of the hypothesis. However
the appropriate test is a joint test to see if all the constraints can
be imposed at once as shown by equation (36) of section 2. This is
accomplished by creating a new variable defined as

$$S = \Delta LW - \Delta LP^T - \Delta UPC^T - \Delta LPRODS^T - \Delta LAVH^T$$

and then estimating a general regression of the form

$$S = \alpha_0(L)S_{t-1} + \alpha_1(L)\Delta\Delta LW_t + \alpha_2(L)\Delta\Delta LP^T_t + \alpha_3(L)\Delta\Delta UPC^T_t +$$
$$\alpha_4(L)\Delta\Delta LPRODS^T_t + \alpha_5(L)\Delta\Delta LAVH^T_t + B\ RES_{t-1}$$

where $\alpha_i(L)$ is a lag polynomial. This equation now imposes the value of $(1 - \sum \alpha_0)$ on all the long-run first difference terms.

These sets of restrictions were applied to the variables included in (40), yielding the following restricted version of the dynamic equation (arrived at after a conventional testing down procedure)[1]:

$$S = \underset{(4.3)}{0.51}\ S_{t-1} \quad - \underset{(4.2)}{0.28}\ \Delta\Delta LW_{t-1} \quad - \underset{(3.2)}{0.54}\ \Delta\Delta LP^T_{\ t} \quad - \underset{(6.3)}{0.37}\ \Delta\Delta LAVH^T_{\ t}$$

$$\underset{(2.8)}{-0.44}\ \Delta\Delta LPRODS^T_{\ t} \quad - \underset{(3.9)}{0.31}\ RES_{t-1} \tag{41}$$

DW = 2.0   LM(8) = 13.9   LM(1) = 0.23

BP (16) = 22.6   SEE = 0.013 R^2 = 0.520

Equation (41) imposed five restrictions on (40): that the constant is zero and that the sum of the coefficients on each of the four independent variables equals the sum of the coefficients on the dependent variables. The F-test of the restricted equation (41) against equation (40) is $F(5,72) = 2.16$, which does not reject the restriction

---

(1)   The general equation included 4 lags on all the variables (including $\Delta\Delta UPC^T$ where the coefficients on all the lags were insignificant).

at the 5% level. Equation (41) is therefore completely consistent with
the cointegrating regression (39), and thus the long run solution to
(41) is (39).   The long run dynamic implications of (41) are also
consistent with it.   This is not true of equation (40).   The long run
solution to (40) will vary with the steady-state rate of growth of wages
and prices, which directly contradicts the equilibrium equation (39).

DISEQUILIBRIUM MODELS

1. Introduction

This chapter considers material which is rather different from that in
the other chapters and will explore the estimation and application of
disequilibrium modelling techniques. The example of the labour market
used in Section 4, however, will extend material used in Chapter 1 to
the disequilibrium case.

The concept of equilibrium is obviously an important one in
economics but it is not entirely unambiguous. Equilibrium is sometimes
taken to mean that demand is equal to supply (in all markets if more
than one market is being considered); an alternative definition is that
the economic system is 'at rest' and so there are no forces tending to
bring about change. These two definitions are not identical, we can for
example consider the equilibrium position for a monopolist who fixes a
market price subject to a known demand curve. The system has no
tendency to move and is in equilibrium in the second sense but clearly
demand does not equal supply and the first definition of equilibrium is
inappropriate. This concept of an equilibrium which is defined by an
absence of change is fundamental to much of the theoretical literature
on disequilibrium or temporary equilibrium which has grown out of the
work of Clower (1965) and Leijonhufvud (1968).

In its most fundamental form we can model a market with the

following two equations

$$D_t = \alpha_1 P_t + B_1 Z_t + U_{1t} \tag{1}$$

$$S_t = \alpha_2 P_t + B_2 Z_t + U_{2t} \tag{2}$$

Equation (1) is a demand curve, which relates demand for any good to its real price (P_t), a set of other factors Z_t, which may be a vector, and U_{1t} a stochastic error term. Equation (2) similarly relates supply to the price of the good, a set of other factors and an error term U_{2t}. The coefficient vectors B_1 and B_2 are such that the model is identified. These two equations are common to all forms of market analyses, the various approaches differing in their assumptions about what is observed and how the real price is determined. A full equilibrium approach, for example, would assume that $D_t = S_t = Q_t$ (where Q_t is observed), and that the real price is determined simply where $D_t = S_t$. An assumption of imperfect competition often amounts to assuming that the market is dominated by a monopolist (monopsonist) and that therefore we only observe points on the Demand (Supply) Curve, i.e. in the monopoly case $D_t = Q_t$ and the supply curve is unobservable. The distinguishing feature of the discrete disequilibrium approach is the assumption that the observed quantity actually being traded will always be on the short side of the market, that is

$$Q_t = Min(D_t, S_t) \tag{3}$$

The justification for this approach is based on the notion of voluntary exchange, a demand or supply curve may be thought of as defining the maximum amount of a good which will be exchanged voluntarily at a given price. If someone is offered a smaller quantity than he demands at a given price, he will generally accept this trade as profitable, but an individual will not generally purchase a larger quantity than indicated by his demand curve.

In order to close the disequilibrium model it is necessary to make some assumption about the determination of prices. The usual assumption which is made is that

$$P_t = P_{t-1} - \gamma(D_t - S_t) + U_{3t}, \quad \gamma > 0 \tag{4}$$

so that if demand is greater than supply the real price will rise and if it is less than supply the price will fall. Equations (1)-(4) then constitute a full statement of the single market disequilibrium model. Over time the real price will tend to adjust to the market clearing price and the speed at which it does this is governed by γ. If γ becomes very large the disequilibrium model will move very quickly towards equilibrium. If γ is small then disequilibrium will persist for a considerable time. One of the advantages of using an empirical model based on (1)-(4) therefore is that the estimate of γ will give us an indication of how closely the model approximates a market clearing model.

In this chapter we will be concerned with describing and estimating explicit disequilibrium models. For the single market, these, in essence, will convey two things. Firstly, they estimate the underlying demand and supply functions together with a price adjustment equation for that market.   Secondly, they allow for discrete switches to take place in the regime - be it a demand or supply constraint in that market.   The advantages of such an explicit recognition of disequilibrium to more informal notions of disequilibrium are obvious. One is that it is possible to place rival views about equilibrating/non-equilibrating models within a general disequilibrium model and test for the presence of discrete regime changes and the speed of adjustment. Furthermore, incorporating discrete switches in regime is an advance over the sort of modelling which simply introduces an activity variable into a behavioural equation, attributing to this the characteristics of a non-Walrasian function with spillover.   The limitations of this latter, very widespread, practice is that it leaves unspecified the analytics of spillover effects between markets, and hence cannot be used as a test of them.   It also assumes, by implication, that a particular regime is in force throughout the sample period, and again, does not test this key assumption.   Thus the use of measured output as an additional variable in a Walrasian labour-demand equation entails that a goods market constraint is in force throughout the sample.   A two-market disequilibrium model in contrast could adjudicate on the realism of this assumption.   (An account of the multi-market case with explicit rationing is given in section 2B).

In the remainder of this chapter we describe some of the analytics of the disequilibrium approach (section 2) and outline some estimation procedures (section 3).   Then in section 4 we describe the application of some of these concepts and techniques to the labour market using the UK as our example.

2. Disequilibrium models

A. The single market

To start with we look at the simplest case, that of disequilibrium in a single market.   The extension of the multiple markets is described later.

While the theoretical literature on disequilibrium models has grown very quickly over the last 15 years, examples with empirical applications of the approach have been sporadic.   The reason for this lies in the difficulty of actually estimating a model of the form (1)-(4) where we do not know 'a priori' whether an observation Q_t should be assigned to the demand curve or the supply curve.   The paper which founded the work on empirical applications is Fair and Jaffee (1972); this paper considered a model like (1)-(4) except that (4), the price equation, was assumed to hold exactly.   This meant that the direction of price movements could be used as an exact guide as to whether the observation was on the demand or supply curve.   To see what this entails we can rewrite (4), if $U_{3t} \equiv 0$, as

$$D_t - S_t = \frac{1}{\gamma} \Delta P_t .$$

Now when $D_t < S_t$, $Q_t = S_t + (D_t - S_t) = S_t + \frac{1}{\gamma} \Delta P_t$,
So that when $D_t < S_t$ we can write (1) and (2) as

$$Q_t = \alpha_1 P_t + B_1 Z_t + U_{1t}$$

$$Q_t = \alpha_2 P_t + B_2 Z_t + \frac{1}{\gamma} \Delta P_t + U_{2t}$$

Similarly when $S_t < D_t$, $Q_t = D_t + D_t - S_t$

$$Q_t = D + \frac{1}{\gamma} \Delta P_t,$$

Thus the model is

$$Q_t = \alpha_1 P_t + B_1 Z_t + \frac{1}{\gamma} \Delta P_t + U_{1t}$$

$$Q_t = \alpha_2 P_t + B_2 Z_t + U_{2t}$$

These two sets of equations can be re-expressed as one by defining two new variables

$$\Delta P_t^1 = \begin{cases} \Delta P_t \text{ if } \Delta P_t > 0 \\ \\ 0 \text{ otherwise} \end{cases}$$

$$\Delta P_t^2 = \begin{cases} \Delta P_t \text{ if } \Delta P_t < 0 \\ \\ 0 \text{ otherwise} \end{cases}$$

Using these conventions the whole model can be estimated by instrumental variables (to allow for the endogeneity of P_t, ΔP_t^1 and ΔP_t^2), i.e. by estimating,

$$Q_t = \alpha_1 P_t + B_1 Z_t + \frac{1}{\gamma} \Delta P_t^1 + U_{1t}$$

$$Q_t = \alpha_2 P_t + B_2 Z_t + \frac{1}{\gamma} \Delta P_t^2 + U_{2t}.$$

This solution to the switching problem is undoubtedly very elegant but it rests on two crucial assumptions; the first is that $U_{3t} = 0$ and the second that nothing other than $(D_t - S_t)$ affects the real price. Both of these assumptions are unlikely to be realistic and it is for this reason that the Fair-Jaffee approach has been used to only a limited extent. An alternative approach to the Fair-Jaffee technique was proposed by Maddala and Nelson (1974) who were able to derive the appropriate density function for a model such as (1)-(4). This made it possible to carry out maximum likelihood estimation of such models, and it is this approach which has formed the basis of most empirical applications and is one which we will use here. A survey of much of this literature may be found in Quandt (1982); we will provide a detailed account of the derivation of the likelihood function in section 3 below.

Given the extreme complexity of the full switching likelihood function, it is perhaps not surprising that alternative methods have been suggested for estimating disequilibrium models. The main alternative is discussed and applied to the labour market by Andrews and Nickell (1986). Its genesis can be seen partly as a response to the difficulty of full maximum likelihood estimation, and partly in response to the assumption of the discrete switching model that the whole market could be treated as a homogeneous unit. This alternative approach views the aggregate market as being composed of many sub-markets, each of which may be in disequilibrium. The aggregate market then contains elements, some of which are demand constrained and some of which are supply constrained. In constrast the single aggregate switching model assumes that all parts of the market are either demand constrained or supply constrained at one time, while the disaggregated approach allows sub-sections of the market to be in different regimes.

It is perhaps worth noting that the assumption in the aggregate switching model that there is a homogenous market is common to many widely used modelling approaches, of both the competitive and non-competitive types. It might also be argued that if aggregation has such important consequences then perhaps the answer is to model the disaggregated sub-markets in isolation.

To compare the disaggregated disequilibrium model with the aggregate model, let us briefly consider the labour market case. In the disaggregated labour market assume there are N separate markets, but also that there is a uniform wage. The ith market demand and supply of labour is then

$$n_i^d = X'\alpha + U + U_i \qquad (i = 1, \ldots, N)$$
$$n_i^s = Z'\beta + V + V_i$$

where X and Z are sets of regressor variables including the real wage, U and V are white noise error terms, and U_i, V_i are independently distributed between i. Aggregate employment is given by summing across markets in excess supply (i ϵ U) and those in excess demand (i ϵ C), i.e.

$$n_t = \sum_{i \varepsilon U} (X'\alpha + U + U_i) + \sum_{i \varepsilon C} (Z'\beta + V + V_i)$$

$$= \lambda\ N(X'\alpha + U + f_2) + (1 - \lambda)\ N(Z'\beta + V + f_3)$$

λ is the proportion of markets in excess supply, $f_2 = \sum_{i \varepsilon U} U_i\ (\lambda N)^{-1}$ and $f_3 = \sum_{i \varepsilon C} V_i\ ((1 - \lambda)N)^{-1}$, where N is the number of markets and is 'large'. Assuming the errors are bivariate normal, with zero mean and parameters $(\sigma_1,\ \sigma_2,\ \rho)$, then the model of employment can be written

$$n_t = (X'\alpha + U) - g(Y\gamma + \eta;\ \sigma_3) \tag{5}$$

where g is a function of $Y\gamma + \eta$ which, in turn, is

$$Y\gamma + \eta = X'\alpha - Z'\beta + U - V$$

and where $\sigma_3 = N(\sigma_1{}^2 + \sigma_2{}^2 - 2\sigma_1\sigma_2\rho)^{\frac{1}{2}}$

(see Andrews and Nickell, 1986 for full details). Then equation (5) may be reinterpretated as the aggregate demand for labour (which is the first term on the RHS) and a function g(.). One of the appealing features of this model is that if g(.) is zero, the model reduces to the equilibrium model. On the other hand if σ_3 - which concerns the variability of disequilibrium across markets - is zero, then (5) is similar to the disequilibrium model reviewed earlier, in that it implies a demand side determination of employment during times of excess supply and contra. However, although this model appears to incorporate the discrete switching model as a special case, such a conclusion is unwarranted for several reasons. Firstly, the disaggregated model just described implicitly assumes a fixed allocation of disequilibria across markets which is constant throughout the sample. The parameter λ is fixed in other words. This assumption can be relaxed somewhat if a time series of λ is known, but this adds little to the model. Thus regime changes which are such an important characteristic of the discrete switching model, do not occur in the present case. Secondly, the specification of the price adjustment model does not arise naturally in this model, unlike the case of the discrete switching model, and ad hoc formulations are used. Finally, although it is often the case that estimating the discrete switching model poses considerable difficulty, the present model if anything appears more difficult. Particular difficulty arises with the estimation of the crucial σ_3 parameter, which is a pity, given its potential role in selecting between alternative disequilibrium formations. (See Andrews and Nickell, op. cit. for an example illustrating the problems in identifying this term.)

B. Multi-market disequilibrium

The theoretical literature on disequilibrium has stressed the interactions between markets; this is sometimes referred to as 'spillover' effects from one market to another. So, for example, if individuals are constrained in their supply of labour in the labour market then this will be reflected in the goods market by an effect from their income limiting the demand for goods. The empirical literature has concentrated to a large extent on single market models, where the implicit assumption is that other markets in the system are not allowed to switch regime. This is clearly a very serious limitation and in this section we will discuss the extension of the single market switching model to the two market case. Within this limited framework, the

Clower/Leijonhufved, dual decision hypothesis for the single time period
is fully confronted (see for example Gourieroux et al, 1980). For the
two agents involved in the model, households and firms, we distinguish
Walrasian and fixed-price equilibria. These latter arise when one or
both agents face a non-Walrasian constraint in at least one market:
goods or labour. Thus the Walrasian program for the consumer is the
solution to

Max U (M/p, C, L) where   C   = consumption

                                         L   = labour supply

                                         M/p = real money balances
subject to the constraint
pC + M = wL + Π + Mo   w   = wages

                                         Π   = distributed profits

                                         Mo = initial money

                                               balances.

The alternative program results from introducing a further constraint

$$pC + M = w\bar{L} + Π + Mo, \text{ where } \bar{L} \leq L$$

Here $\bar{L}$ is an additional constraint, produced, for example, by excess
supply in the labour market. In the Walrasian case, consumption is

$$C^W (p, w)$$

and in the constrained case, we have instead

$$C^C (p, w, \bar{L})$$

In general terms then we can invoke a dependence of decisions in one
market upon transactions in the other; these are spillover effects.

Hence, we may define the constrained decisions (see Gourieroux et al, op. cit.), where the goods market is market 1, and labour is market 2, as

$$D_1^{\,c} = \alpha_1\, Q_2 + \delta_1\, (p,\, w)$$

$$S_1^{\,c} = \beta_1\, Q_2 + \lambda_1\, (p,\, w)$$

$$D_2^{\,c} = \alpha_2\, Q_1 + \delta_2\, (p,\, w)$$

$$S_2^{\,c} = \beta_2\, Q_1 + \lambda_2\, (p,\, w)$$

These equations express the general idea of constrained demand and supplies. Thus the first equation, for example, defines a case where the demand for goods is constrained on the labour market by Q_2. The coefficient α_1 then indicates the spillover effect from one market to the other. Four regimes of fixed price equilibria are then possible

(1) Repressed inflation

$$S_1 = Q_1 = \beta_1\, S_2 + \lambda_1$$

$$S_2 = Q_2 = \beta_2\, S_1 + \lambda_2$$

$$D_1 = \frac{1}{(1-\alpha_1\beta_2)}\, (\alpha_2\lambda_2 - S_1)$$

$$D_2 = \frac{1}{(1-\alpha_2\beta_1)}\, (\delta_2 + \alpha_2\, \lambda_1)$$

(2) Classical unemployment

$$D_1 = \alpha_1 D_2 + \delta_1$$

$$S_2 = \beta_2 S_1 + \lambda_2$$

and $S_1 = Q_1 = \dfrac{1}{(1-\alpha_1\beta_i)} (\lambda_1 + \beta_1 S_2)$

$$D_2 = Q_2 = \dfrac{1}{(1-\alpha_2\beta_1)} (\delta_2 + \alpha_2 \lambda_1)$$

(3) Keynesian unemployment

$$D_1 = Q_1 = \alpha_1 D_2 + \delta_1$$

$$D_2 = Q_2 = \alpha_2 D_1 + \delta_2$$

$$S_1 = \dfrac{1}{(1-\beta_1\alpha_2)} (\lambda_1 + \beta_1 S_2)$$

$$S_2 = \dfrac{1}{(1-\alpha_1\beta_2)} (\lambda_2 + \beta_2 S_1)$$

(4) Underconsumption

$$S_1 = \beta_1 S_2 + \lambda_1$$

$$D_2 = \alpha_2 D_1 + \delta_2$$

$$D_1 = \dfrac{1}{(1-\alpha_1\beta_2)} (\alpha_1\lambda_2 + S_1)$$

$$S_2 = \dfrac{1}{(1-\alpha_1\beta_2)} (\lambda_2 + \beta_2 S_1)$$

The important thing to emphasise about these formulations is that they are representations of fixed price equilibria for the unit period. In this, essentially static, framework a meaningful reduced form to the model occurs if the model is 'coherent' (Gourieroux et al, op. cit.). This means that the model, which is globally non-linear, but piecewise linear, may yield determinable comparative static results for changes in exogenous variables (contained in the λ (.), δ (.) functions in the equations above). Gourieroux et. al. show that in the two-market case these coherency conditions are equivalent to local stability conditions for quantity adjustment.

The trouble with these models lies in their static formulation. The solutions considered so far are described as 'temporary equilibrium with quantity rationing' (Muellbauer and Portes, 1978), and the system is thought of as being at rest (i.e. in equilibrium in that sense) although markets do not clear. There are two ways in which this feature may be amended. First, as for the single market case, a set of price adjustment equations is appended to the model, i.e.

$$\Delta \underset{\sim}{P} = \Upsilon \left[(\underset{\sim}{D} - \underset{\sim}{S}), Z : U_3 \right] \tag{6}$$

$\underset{\sim}{P}$ is a vector of prices, Υ a matrix of adjustment coefficients, $(\underset{\sim}{D} - \underset{\sim}{S})$ a vector of excess demand terms, Z is a set of variables independently affecting P, and U_3 is a vector of error terms. It might be noted in passing that this is invariably the form in which the single market model is estimated. It is an ad hoc formulation however, though it might be observed that pretty well all dynamic models (explicitly disequilibrium or otherwise) use something like this. The voluminous

Phillips Curve literature is but one case in point. At a more fundamental level dynamic issues are concerned in the micro foundations of inter-temporal household and firms decisions when faced by these additional constraints. Muellbauer and Portes (op. cit.) for example introduce inventories into firms' behaviour, attributing to these a buffer stock role. The given constraint Q_1 in the goods market is then a perceived sales constraint. If this is in error, unexpected sales can be met from stocks. It is also not hard to see that the role of the buffer stock is to enable the firm to learn (converge onto) the correct sales constraint. The rigorous development of such a joint model with inter-temporal optimising in the light of quantity constraints is extremely difficult, and has not yet been achieved.

3. Estimation methods

We next outline maximum likelihood methods of estimating the disequilibrium model, and these are the techniques used in the empirical examples later. For this, we revert to the single market case, since our empirical examples will be exclusively single market ones. Let the model be

$$
\begin{aligned}
D_t &= a_1 P_t^1 + b_{1t} + U_{1t} \\
S_t &= a_2 P_t + b_{2t} + U_{2t} \\
P_t &= a_3 (D_t - S_t) + P_{t-1} + b_{3t} + U_{3t} \\
Q_t &= \mathrm{Min}(D_t, S_t) \\
P_t^1 &= \alpha(t) P_t + \beta(t)
\end{aligned}
\tag{7}
$$

In this model b_{1t}, b_{2t}, b_{3t} are linear _functions_ of exogenous variables with coefficients to be estimated, and we have adopted this convention to simplify the subsequent notation.

$$\text{Assume } (U_{1t}, U_{2t}, U_{3t}) \sim N \left[0, \begin{bmatrix} \sigma_3^2 & 0 & 0 \\ 0 & \sigma_2^2 & 0 \\ 0 & 0 & \sigma_3^2 \end{bmatrix} \right]$$

Assuming the observations are independent, the log likelihood function is

$$\Sigma_t \ln h(Q_t, P_t) \text{ where}$$

$$h(Q_t, P_t) = \int_{Q_t}^{\infty} g(D_t, Q_t, P_t)dD_t + \int_{Q_t}^{\infty} g(Q_t, S_t, P_t)dS_t \tag{8}$$

and $g(D_t, Q_t, P_t)$ is given by

$$\frac{(1 + a_3(a_2 - a_1\alpha(t))) \exp \left[-\frac{1}{2}(U_{1t}, U_{2t}, U_{3t})\right] \begin{bmatrix} \sigma_1^{\frac{1}{2}} & 0 & 0 \\ 0 & \sigma_2^{\frac{1}{2}} & 0 \\ 0 & 0 & \sigma_3^{\frac{1}{2}} \end{bmatrix} \begin{bmatrix} U_{1t} \\ U_{2t} \\ U_{3t} \end{bmatrix}}{(2\pi)^{3/2}\sigma_1\sigma_2\sigma_3} \tag{9}$$

$$= J(t) \exp \left(-\frac{1}{2} E_t\right) \text{ say.}$$

$$\text{Now } E(t) = \frac{1}{\sigma_1^2}(D_t - a_1P_t^1 - b_{1t})^2 + \frac{1}{\sigma_2^2}(S_t - a_2P_t - b_{2t})^2 +$$

$$+ \frac{1}{\sigma_3^2}(P_t - a_3D_t + a_3S_t - P_{t-1} - b_{3t})^2$$

For the first integral, replace S_t by Q_t, then $E(t)$ becomes

$$\frac{1}{\sigma_1^2} (D_t - a_1 P_t^1 - b_{1t})^2 + \frac{1}{\sigma_2^2} (Q_t - a_2 P_t - b_{2t})^2 +$$

$$\frac{1}{\sigma_3^2} (P_t - a_3 D_t + a_3 Q_t - P_{t-1} - b_{3t})^2$$

$$= A_1 D_t^2 + 2A_{2t} D_t + A_{3t}$$

where $A_1 = \dfrac{1}{\sigma_1^2} + \dfrac{a_3^2}{\sigma_1^2}$

$$A_2 t = \frac{1}{\sigma_1^2} (a_1 P_t^1 + b_{1t}) - \frac{a_3}{\sigma_3^2} (P_t + a_3 Q_t - P_{t-1} - b_{3t})$$

$$A_{3t} = \frac{1}{\sigma_1^2} (a_1 P_t^1 + b_{1t}) + \frac{1}{\sigma_2^2} (Q_t + a_2 P_t - b_{2t})^2$$

$$\frac{1}{\sigma_3^2} (P_t + a_3 Q_t - P_{t-1} - b_{3t})^2$$

$$A_1 D_t^2 + 2A_{2t} D_t + A_{3t} = A_1 (D_t + \frac{A_{2t}}{A_1})^2 + B_{1t}$$

where $B_{1t} = A_{3t} - \dfrac{A_{2t}^2}{A_1} = \dfrac{A_1 A_{3t} - A_{2t}^2}{A_1}$

So the first integral of (8) is

$$J(t) \int_{Q_t}^{\infty} \exp \; [- \frac{A_1}{2} (D_t + \frac{A_{2t}}{A_1})^2 - \frac{B_{1t}}{2}] \; dD_t$$

$$= J(t) \exp \; (- \frac{1}{2} B_{1t}) \int_{Q_t}^{\infty} \exp \; [- \frac{A_1}{2} (D_t + \frac{A_{2t}}{A_1})^2] \; dD_t$$

Putting $x = A_1^{1/2} (D_t + \frac{A_{2t}}{A_1})$, this integral may be written as

$$J(t) \exp(-\frac{1}{2}B_{1t}) \int_{A_1^{1/2}(Q_t + \frac{A_{2t}}{A_1})}^{\infty} \exp(-\frac{1}{2}x^2) \frac{1}{A_1^{1/2}} dx$$

$$= J(t) \exp(-\frac{1}{2}B_{1t}) A_1^{1/2} [1 - \Phi(1_{1t})] (2\Pi)^{1/2}$$

where $1_{1t} = A_1^{1/2} (Q_t + \frac{A_{2t}}{A_1})$.

For the second integral of (8), replace D_t by Q_t. Then E(t) becomes

$$\frac{1}{\sigma_1^2} (Q_t - a_1 P_t^1 - b_{1t})^2 + \frac{1}{\sigma_2^2} (S_t - a_2 P_t - b_{2t})^2 +$$

$$\frac{1}{\sigma_3^2} (P_t - a_3 Q_t + a_3 S_t - P_{t-1} - b_{3t})^2$$

$$= A_4 S_t^2 + 2A_{5t} S_t + A_{6t}$$

where $A_4 = \frac{1}{\sigma_1^2} + \frac{a_3^2}{\sigma_3^2}$

$$A_5 t = \frac{1}{\sigma_1^2} (a_2 P_t^2 + b_{2t}) - \frac{a_3}{\sigma_3^2} (P_t - a_3 Q_t - P_{t-1} - b_{3t})$$

$$A_{6t} = \frac{1}{\sigma_1^2} (Q_t - a_1 P_t^1 - b_{1t})^2 + \frac{1}{\sigma_2^2} (a_2 P_t + b_{2t})^2 +$$

$$\frac{1}{\sigma_3^2} (P_t + a_3 Q_t - P_{t-1} - b_{3t})^2$$

$$A_4 S_t^2 + 2A_{5t} S_t + A_{6t} = A_4 (S_t + \frac{A_{5t}}{A_4})^2 + B_{2t}$$

where $B_{2t} = A_{6t} - \frac{A_{5t}^2}{A_4} = \frac{A_4 A_{6t} - A_{5t}^2}{A_4}$

So this integral is given by

$$J(t) \int_{Q_t}^{\infty} \exp \quad [- \frac{A_4}{2} (S_t + \frac{A_{5t}}{A_4})^2 - \frac{B_{2t}}{2}] \ dS_t$$

$$= J(t) \exp (- \frac{1}{2}B_{2t}) \int_{Q_t}^{\infty} \exp \quad [- \frac{A_4}{2} (S_t + \frac{A_{5t}}{A_4})^2] \ dS_t$$

Putting $x = A_4^{\frac{1}{2}} (S_t + \frac{A_{5t}}{A_4})$, the integral is

$$= J(t) \exp (- \frac{1}{2} B_{2t}) \ A_4^{\frac{1}{2}} [1 - \Phi(1_{2t})] \ (2\Pi)^{\frac{1}{2}}$$

where $1_{2t} = A_4^{\frac{1}{2}} (Q_t + \frac{A_{5t}}{A_4})$.

Thus $h(Q_t, P_t) =$

$$J(t)(2\Pi)^{\frac{1}{2}} [\frac{e^{-\frac{1}{2}B_{1t}}}{A_1^{\frac{1}{2}}} \ (1-\Phi(1_{1t})) + \frac{e^{-\frac{1}{2}B_{2t}}}{A_4^{\frac{1}{2}}} \ (1-\Phi(1_{1t}))] \qquad (10)$$

Assuming the observations are independent, the likelihood function is

$$L = \sum_{t}^{T} \ln h(Q_t, P_t), \text{ where T is the sample size.}$$

Two extensions to this basic model may be mentioned. These are, firstly, the multi-market case and secondly, the presence of lagged endogenous variables. The first is discussed in Gourieroux et al (1980) and in Quandt (1983), though also refer to a somewhat simpler approach by Maddala and Chandra (1983). The second is discussed by Laffont and Monfort (1979).

(i) Multimarket disequilibria

A typical model may be written (see Quandt, 1983)

$$Y_1 = \alpha_1 Z + U_1 \quad : \quad Z_1 = \alpha_3 Y + U_3$$
$$Y_2 = \alpha_2 Z + U_2 \quad : \quad Z_2 = \alpha_4 Y + U_4$$
$$Y = Min(Y_1, Y_2) \quad : \quad Z = Min(Z_1, Z_2)$$

The Min condition determines the observed value of the dependent variable in the ith market which goes into the functions in the jth market, and contra. The four possible regimes for this model are given by the convex cones,

$$C_1 = (Y_1 \leqq Y_2, Z_1 \leqq Z_2)$$
$$C_2 = (Y_1 \leqq Y_2, Z_1 > Z_2)$$
$$C_3 = (Y_1 > Y_2, Z_1 \leqq Z_2) \quad \text{and}$$
$$C_4 = (Y_1 > Y_2, Z_1 > Z_2)$$

Each regime implies a linear mapping of U (the error vector) onto the vector of dependent variables $V = (Y_1, Y_2, Z_1, Z_2)$. Thus, for example

$$\begin{bmatrix} 1 & 0 & -\alpha_1 & 0 \\ 0 & 1 & -\alpha_2 & 0 \\ -\alpha_3 & 0 & 1 & 0 \\ -\alpha_4 & 0 & 0 & 1 \end{bmatrix} \begin{bmatrix} Y_1 \\ Y_2 \\ Z_1 \\ Z_2 \end{bmatrix} = \begin{bmatrix} U_1 \\ U_2 \\ U_3 \\ U_4 \end{bmatrix} \tag{11}$$

or $A_1 V = U,$

is the regime given by C_1 above. The general mapping of U onto V is

$$f = \sum_{i}^{4} A_i \, I_i \tag{12}$$

where $I = 1$ if $V \in C_i$,

$\quad\quad\quad = 0$ otherwise.

As noted earlier, Gourieroux et al (1980) derive conditions under which this function is <u>coherent</u>, i.e. essentially the conditions under which the function f is one to one, so that, given a pdf for U, the pdf of V is defined.

The derivation of the required density function for the multi-market model above then proceeds by extension to the single market case already discussed. Thus under C_i the pdf of V is

$$| \det (A_i) | \quad g \ (A_i \ V)$$

where the pdf of U is defined as g (U).   Hence the joint density function for the unobserved variables (Y, Z) is

$$
\begin{aligned}
h \ (Y, \ Z) \ = \ &\int \ldots \int \ | \ \det (A_1) \ \ g \ (A_1, \ V_1) \ | \ dY_2 \, dZ_2 \ + \ldots + \\
&\quad Y_2 > Y \\
&\quad Z_2 > Z \\
&+ \int \ldots \int \ \det (A_4) \ \ g \ (A_4, \ V_4) \ dY_1 \, dZ_1 \\
&\quad Y_1 > Y \\
&\quad Z_1 > Z
\end{aligned}
$$

i.e. the integral evaluated under $C_1, \ldots, C_4$.   (See Quandt, 1983)

In this expression $V_1' = (Y, Y_2, Z, Z_2)$; $V_2' = (Y, Y_2, Z_1, Z)$,

$V_3' = (Y_1, Y, Z, Z_2)$ and $V_4' = (Y_1, Y, Z_1, Z)$.

Note that the extension of the model can allow for price adjustment, in a way that we have described earlier for the single market case. However, as the existing formulation makes clear, the multimarket case is highly complex, and likely to be very expensive to compute. For example, T observations require the calculation of 4T double integrals per evaluation, and given that numerical approximations must be used for these models, this puts severe limits on the size of the model which might be estimated. Goldfeld and Quandt (1980) suggest a two-market or possibly a three-market model is the maximum feasible size. (See Artus and Muet (1983) for an empirical illustration of a model with several regimes.)

(ii) Lagged endogenous variables

Problems arise in the disequilibrium model if the demand and supply incorporate lagged dependent variables, such as

$$E_t^D = \alpha_0 X + \alpha_1 P + \alpha_2 E_{t-1}^D + \alpha_3 E_{t-1}^S + U_1$$

$$E_t^S = \beta_0 X + \beta_1 P + \beta_2 E_{t-1}^D + \beta_3 E_{t-1}^S + U_2$$

(13)

Since with the operation of the Min condition $Q_t = Min (D, S)$ only the exchanged quantity Q_t is observed, implying that the lagged endogenous variables are non-observable. Lafont and Monfort (1979) discuss conditions under which such a model might be estimated. It should be emphasised that this situation does not arise in the next section however where we use dynamic equations for the labour market in an empirical application. There the employment decision is subject to lags due to adjustment costs on actual employment (net employment in fact, though that does not affect this point). In consequence, actual lagged employment appears as a regressor variable, and this is observable.

4. The specification and estimation of a disequilibrium model of the labour market

The rest of this chapter brings together some of the points already discussed in an application of the disequilibrium model for the single market to the case of the UK labour market. This section first discusses the detailed specification of the demand and supply of labour, and later sections provide results. The model of labour demand in chapter 1 which uses forward-looking expectation formation, is again used here, to provide comparison of the rival estimation methods for this equation.

(i) The model

It is fair to say that most, if not all, estimated disequilibrium models of the labour market are based on a simple static neoclassical model of both demand and supply. Apart from the Min condition, the only difference from the standard model is the inclusion of the level of output in the demand function. A typical example would be

$$E^D = \alpha_0 + \alpha_1 (W/P)' + \alpha_2 Q + \alpha_3 t + U_D$$

(14)

$$E^S = \beta_0 + \beta_1 (W/P) + \beta_2 B + \beta_3 P + U_S$$

In this model, $(W/P)'$ is the real product wage, Q the level of the output, (W/P) the real consumption wage, B the replacement ratio, P the population of working age and t is a time trend. (For a recent example of such a model used in a disequilibrium study, see Smyth, 1983.)

(a) The determinants of the demand for labour

The role of Q in the demand function is evidently to incorporate an element of dual-decision behaviour, since in this model it represents the quantity constraint in the goods market. It is of course possible to introduce output into a profit maximising employment rule without assuming quantity constraints. For example, Rosen and Quandt (1978) use the production function to substitute out the capital stock in the marginal productivity of labour equation. This is not a very satisfactory procedure, to fully implement the dual decision hypothesis two markets, with quantity rationing being possible in each, are required. We will not follow this procedure due to the difficulty in providing aggregate demand and supply models of the goods market. So what we use is in the nature of second best procedures. We simply note; firstly, if the goods market is in excess demand so that the supply of goods is not constrained, this implies that profit maximising leads to the first order condition for labour

$$E^D = f_1 \; ((W/P)', \; Pm/P, \; \ldots)$$

where $(W/P)'$ is the real wage, Pm/P the real price of raw material imports, and we are assuming a two factor production function dependent on labour and raw materials (capital services could be separable for instance).

Alternatively, if the goods market is in excess supply, a <u>sales constraint</u> operates on the firm, and its factor demand for labour parallels those produced by the familiar cost minimising subject to a sales constraint, so

$$E^D = f_2 \; (W/Pm, \; Q)$$

in this case, where Q is perceived sales (since we ignore inventories, we equate this with output).

As a statistical procedure we will use a composite function of the form

$$E^D = f_3 \; (W/P, \; Pm/P, \; Q)$$

which nests the unconstrained case $(Q = 0, \; W/P = Pm/P \neq 0)$ and the constrained case $(Q \neq 0, \; W/P = - Pm/P)$. But in this formulation, regime switching in the goods market within the sample period is ruled out, so that for example the finding of a significant effect on Q implies a sales constraint (possibly of a varying form) holding throughout the sample. The demand function we take is

$$E_t = \alpha_0 + \alpha_1 \, (W/P)_t' + \alpha_2 \, Q_t^e + \alpha_3 \, t + \alpha_4 \, E_{t-1} + \alpha_5 \, E_{t-2}$$
$$+ \alpha_6 \, (Pm/p)_t \tag{15}$$

where

(1)   Labour input is measured by numbers employed, so the hours dimension is ignored. (See Hall, Henry, Payne and Wren-Lewis, 1985 for this extension however.)

(2)   Implicitly, the model assumes a production function dependent upon the capital stock, labour input (employment) and raw material inputs (including energy). In all subsequent discussion we will assume that the labour/materials decision is made independently of the optimal decision by the firm regarding its capital input. Capital is thus taken to be predetermined, and is represented in the empirical applications reported below by a time-trend.

(3)   Lags appear in the equation because we assume there are <u>quadratic</u> costs of changing employment. As we described in Chapter 1, such an assumption implies that forward expected values of price terms (assuming inter-temporal profit maximising subject to a technology constraint) occur in the optimal decision rule, i.e. (ignoring error terms, and taking the first order case for simplicity).

$$E_t = (\gamma_0 \, \lambda)^{-1} \, E_{t-1} + \gamma_1 \, \overset{\infty}{\Sigma} \, (\lambda)^{-i-1} \, (\gamma_{t+1} \, g \, (.)) \tag{16}$$

where λ is the unstable root, γ is a vector of parameters depending upon underlying cost structures, and g (.) are the relevant forcing terms including real price and output terms.

If the g (.) are exogenous to the firm's employment decision, and representable by a time-series model, say by vector AR (n) process, then the forward terms in g (.) may be substituted out in terms of lagged g's and the resulting equation may be efficiently estimated if the implied restrictions in the reduced form equation are applied. In our application with lagged output, we will assume that substitution has been effected, though we will not attempt to apply restrictions in estimation. (The resulting equations may at best be only consistent.)

(4) The role of expected output Q^e needs further clarification. The interpretation placed on it here is that it represents an output (or more properly a sales) constraint operating in the goods market. A separate model for output is then required.

Applying the substitution method using a complete dynamic macromodel, assuming forward expectations, is computationally formidable, a problem we have discussed extensively in chapter 1. So here again we use the method described in that chapter which essentially replace the unknown future expectations by generated or predicted values derived in turn by a first stage estimation procedure.

As before, in the present application we assume that agents use a subset of variables from which to produce expected values of output, and we again assume that the employment decision depends on expected variables over a four quarter planning horizon. To repeat, for convenience, what we described in chapter 1, we assume equations for the expected regressor variables Q, of the form

$$Q_t = \frac{\phi(B)}{\theta(B)} Z_t + n_t \qquad (17)$$

where Z_t is taken to be a set of variables considered by the typical agent to be important in influencing aggregate activity. These are assumed to be the real adjusted fiscal deficit (BD) and competitiveness (C). Since lagged values of Z occur in (17), we need equations for Z to produce sufficient future leads of Q. These in turn are taken to be

$$Q_t = a_{11} Q_{t-1} + \cdots a_{1K} BD_{t-1} + \cdots a_{1J} C_{t-1} + \cdots$$

$$BD_t = c_{11} BD_{t-1} + \cdots c_{1N} Q_{t-1} + \cdots c_{1L} C_{t-1} + \cdots \qquad (18)$$

$$C_t = d_{11} C_{t-1} + \cdots d_{1M} Q_{t-1} + \cdots d_{1P} BD_{t-1} + \cdots$$

The model to be estimated is then the employment equation (15) and the VAR model (18) for the expected regressor variables.

When estimating the employment equation the backward/forward restriction as implied by the optimising theory are applied. In these examples we again use the numerical procedure which is outlined in chapter 1.

(b) <u>Inter-temporal theory of the household, and the determinants of the supply of labour</u>

Labour supply is taken to be

$$E_t^S = \beta_0 + \beta_1 (W/P)_t + \beta_2 BN_t + \beta_3 POP_t + \beta_4 UP_t + \beta_5 RRI_t \qquad (19)$$

Apart from the real consumption wage and the working population (W/P and POP respectively), other variables used in the supply function are

(1)   BN. This is the real value of unemployment benefits. It enters here separately, though sometimes the replacement ratio (benefits relative to net income in work) is used. In our specification this would hold if $\beta_1 = -\beta_2$. (See Andrews, 1983.)

(2)   UP. Union power is often incorporated in a supply function to proxy possible effects of unions on restricting entry (e.g. closed shop arrangements). In real wage equations with a bargaining interpretation the role of the union is to exact a monopoly price (real wage). Again this would have negative effects on the supply of workers in the union sector. More generally it produces an upward shift in supply implying higher real wages in aggregate at given employment (if the increase in the union wage exceeds the decrease in the non-unionised wage, suitably weighted by employment proportions in the two sectors).

(3)   RRI. The real interest rate enters via the inter-temporal supply of labour analysis suggested by Lucas and Barro. Here an increase in the real interest rate increases current work effort and decreases future effort. That is to say, the discounted value of future output foregone (by increased future effort) is reduced as the real interest rate rises. This enhances future leisure relative to current.

There may be lags in supply of labour due to, for example, loss of seniority rights, imperfect capital markets, and so on. We allow for up to two lags to provide a fairly rich dynamic specification.

(ii) Disequilibrium estimate of the model

In full, the labour market model we estimate is

$$E_t^D = A_0 + A_1 (W/P)' + A_2 Q^e + A_3 T + A_4 E_{t-1} + A_5 E_{t-2} + A_6 Pm/p_t$$

$$E_t^S = B_0 + B_1 (W/P)_t + B_2 BN_t + B_3 POP_t + B_4 UP_t + B_5 RRI + B_6 E_{t-1}$$
$$+ B_7 E_{t-2}$$

$$E_t = Min (E^D, E^S)_t \tag{20}$$

$$(W/P)_t' = \alpha (W/P)_t$$

$$\Delta_4 (W/P)_t = C_0 + C_1 (E^D - E^S)_t + C_2 UP_t + C_3 NTAX_t + C_4 IP_t$$

In these equations $(W/P)'$ is the demand price of labour, given by gross earnings per employee plus employer taxes deflated by producer prices. The variable Q^e is expected output (= expected sales), described earlier. Real raw materials and energy prices in real terms are given by Pm/p. Finally, the remaining variable in the demand equation is time (T). The supply function includes the supply price of labour (the net level of earnings per worker deflated by the price of consumer goods), the real level of unemployment benefit (BN), the working population (POP), a measure of union strength (UP) and the real interest rate (RRI). In the last equation, NTAX is employers' tax as a proportion of employees' income, and IP is an incomes policy variable reported by Whitley. (This is described in Whitley, 1983.)

Table 1 presents the results for various forms of the model given in equation (20). In the results for the demand function, expected

Table 1. Estimates of the Disequilibrium Model
          Sample 1965Q4 - 1982Q4

Parameter	Spcfn.(1)	(2)	(3)	(4)	(5)
A_0	0.14	0.14	0.164	0.095	0.300
	(0.8)	(0.91)	(1.13)	0.74)	(2.008)
A_1	-0.0012	0.012	0.002	-0.02	-0.002
	(0.07)	(1.02)	(0.194)	(1.90)	(0.245)
A_2	0.06	0.037	0.063	0.047	0.047
	(4.85)	(4.77)	(5.33)	(6.00)	(4.17)
A_3	-0.003	-0.00004	-0.0003	+0.000	-0.0003
	(3.0)	(0.5)	(4.54)	(0.79)	(4.18)
A_4	1.63	1.56	1.603	1.578	1.514
	(128.5)	(53.34)	(69.73)	(36.42)	(175.72)
A_5	-0.72	-0.61	-0.0069	-0.009	-
	(21.1)	(15.1)	(17.32)	(43.29)	(18.34)
A_6	-	-	0.0069	-0.009	-
			(1:447)	(1.76)	
B_0	-0.06	-0.31	-0.058	-0.286	-1.334
	(0.4)	(1.5)	(0.71)	(1.24)	(14.6)
B_1	0.08	0.08	0.081	0.085	0.049
	(4.7)	(3.7)	(4.81)	(4.32)	(2.32)
B_2	-0.04	-0.04	-0.043	-0.041	-0.041
	(4.6)	(1.87)	(4.24)	(2.08)	(4.03)
B_3	1.12	1.18	1.125	1.179	1.318
	(27.3)	(21.56)	(59.302)	(15.749)	(14.51)
B_4	-0.18	-0.19	-0.18	-0.191	-0.363
	(16.1)	(5.7)	(12.78)	(6.26)	(10.21)
B_5	-	-	-	-	-0.137
	-	-	-	-	-
B_6					
B_7	-	-	-	-	-
C_0	0.029	0.03	0.0278	0.03	0.030
	(6.3)	(6.3)	(6.33)	(6.46)	(6.46)
C_1*	0.22	0.24	0.217	0.253	0.219
	(1.43)	(1.93)	(1.738)	(2.01)	(1.929)
C_2	-0.07	-0.104	-0.08	-0.119	-0.044
	(0.2)	(0.32)	(0.24)	(0.369)	(0.149)
C_3	-0.65	0.647	-0.65	-0.64	-0.653
	(3.58)	(3.5)	(3.57)	(3.557)	(3.69)
C_4	0.0068	0.007	0.007	0.007	0.007
	(5.17)	(5.2)	(5.15)	(5.21)	(5.05)
Log L.F.	626.35	625.71	627.34	626.84	626.43

Odd numbered columns use lagged output as a regressor. The remainder
use the VAR model.

Table 1 (cont)

Parameter	Spcfn.(6)	(7)	(8)	(9)	(10)
A_0	0.141	0.177	0.173	0.308	0.179
	(1.02)	(1.14)	(1.08)	(2.2)	(1.3)
A_1	-0.006	0.0017	-0.014	-0.001	-0.006
	(0.056)	(0.014)	(1.0)	(0.1)	(0.6)
A_2	0.028	0.051	0.037	0.05	0.028
	(4.60)	(4.2)	(4.5)	(4.0)	(4.4)
A_3	-0.0001	-0.0003	-0.0001	-0.0003	-0.0001
	(1.57)	(3.9)	(0.6)	(4.0)	(1.7)
A_4	1.52	1.637	1.58	1.48	1.49
	(75.48)	(117.2)	(182.7)	(149.0)	(85.0)
A_5	-0.579	-0.724	-0.64	-0.60	-0.55
	(31.1)	(21.1)	(20.25)	(18.7)	(23.5)
A_6	-	-	-	-	-
B_0	-1.24	1.137	-0.94	-3.4	-3.78
	(19.96)	(4.2)	(3.1)	(20.5)	(63.7)
B_1	0.045	0.085	0.07	-0.06	-0.059
	(2.17)	(4.8)	(3.1)	(2.9)	(3.0)
B_2	-0.043	-0.035	-0.035	-0.045	-0.04
	(3.95)	(3.16)	(2.8)	(4.3)	(4.0)
B_3	1.303	0.957	0.989	1.84	1.91
	(59.44)	(66.21)	(36.2)	(71.8)	(68.7)
B_4	-0.36	-0.299	-0.305	-0.008	-0.01
	(9.89)	(13.15)	(11.8)	(0.5)	(0.8)
B_5	-0.15	-	-	-	-
	(2.74)				
B_6	-	-0.095	0.067	-	-
		(0.5)	(0.3)		
B_7		0.367	0.141		
		(2.3)	(5.9)		
C_0	0.028	0.029	0.028	0.03	0.03
	(6.4)	(6.5)	(5.9)	(6.7)	(6.7)
C_1*	0.226	0.28	0.25	0.107	0.11
	(1.9)	(2.0)	(1.5)	(1.7)	(1.8)
C_2	-0.045	-0.09	-0.06	-0.03	-0.03
	(0.15)	(0.29)	(0.2)	(0.7)	(0.7)
C_3	-0.648	-0.66	-0.62	-0.66	-0.67
	(3.6)	(3.6)	(3.4)	(3.7)	(3.7)
C_4	0.007	0.0067	0.0068	0.007	0.0067
	(5.42)	(5.17)	(5.2)	(5.6)	(5.7)
Log L.F	626.86	632.25	630.45	625.3	625.63

* The t statistic for the variable is constructed on the null hypothesis that $\frac{1}{C_1} = 0$, i.e. $C_1 = \infty$, which implies a full clearing model.

output is proxied either by lagged output [in equations (1), (3), (5), (7) and (9)] or by the expected convolution of predicted output derived from the VAR model.   In all versions of the model certain general features pertain: the estimated effect of demand is similar, the parameters in the supply functions are quite close to each other, and are correctly signed and generally significant. The differences between the alternative models mainly involve the demand equation.   In column (1) which uses lagged output, the real wage is completely insignificant, while in column (2) it has a t-statistic of only 1.02 and column (4) 1.9. So this is not a particularly good result for this model; the lagged output version of the model might well be entertained as the preferred version - it generally has the largest likelihood - and it estimates that the real wage effect in the demand function is not significantly different from zero.

The estimated wage adjustment equation shows a great deal of uniformity between all the alternative specifications in table 1.   Two things stand out: first there is no evidence from these results that union density has any effect on the speed of real wage adjustment. Second, the incomes policy variable is uniformly correctly signed and significant, suggesting that incomes policy does have effects on wage changes.   The t-statistic on C_1 is constructed to test the null hypothesis $\frac{1}{C_1} = 0$, which implies $C_1 = \infty$.   Under this null hypothesis the disequilibrium model tends towards becoming a market clearing model. The C_1 parameter is always correctly signed but it is not sufficiently well determined to reject, convincingly, the market clearing hypothesis. Finally, the regular appearance of a well-determined constant in this equation reflects the growth in real wages over the period.

The remaining columns show further refinements on the first two. Columns (3) and (4) enter a real raw material and energy price term in the demand function (A_6 in equations (1,5)) and columns (5) and (6) enter the real interest rate effect in the supply function.

Of these results, columns (3) and (4) display the disconcerting property that materials and labour inputs are substitutes in column (3) but complements in (4)! Other researchers find similar problems: Beenstock and Warburton (1984) have a substitution relation here, but in Layard and Nickell (1985) materials and energy were complementary factors in production. Overall, the model in column (4) is probably preferable, since among other things, the real wage effect on demand is quite well determined and correctly signed. In both equations (5) and (6) the real interest rate gets the wrong sign, implying increases in the real interest rate decrease current work effort. Moreover, the real wage effect in the demand function is again incorrectly signed in both equations.

In columns (7) and (8), the wrongly signed real interest rate is dropped, and two lags on employment are used in the supply functions. The second of these is correctly signed and significant. The results here are relatively unaffected by the use of lagged output or the VAR output series to proxy expected output. Finally, columns (9) and (10) revert to the static form of the supply function, and illustrate the use of an alternate measure of union pushfulness. This is the measure of the union mark-up as reported in Layard and Nickell (1985) in place of the union density variable used in our earlier regressions. It will be seen that this variable also does not appear to have a significant influence upon labour supply in the results in column (9) (which uses lagged output in the demand function) and in column (10) (using the VAR expected output series).

Overall, however, there is a considerable measure of uniformity between these alternative specifications, and many of the important parameters are well determined and correctly signed, indicating that the disequilibrium approach can produce meaningful estimates, a conclusion at odds with recent results such as Stenius and Viren (1984). Their rather sceptical note on the disequilibrium approach was based on the lack of robustness of the Rosen and Quandt (1978) study. What we have endeavoured to show is that, suitably elaborated, results that compare with other market studies may be obtained using the disequilibrium approach. The results we report do suggest an important role for a labour demand constraint over the latter part of the 1970s and early 1980s. This is true of most of the models we report in table 1. To pursue this point further, we report (in table 2) our preferred version of the model.

The choice of equations from table 1 to be used as the preferred model is not straightforward. Overall, the highest log likelihood function is given by column (7). However this model has an incorrectly signed wage effect in the demand curve and one of the lags in the supply function is insignificant. We considered the most suitable model for

Table 2. The preferred model and a test of its stablity

SAMPLE	1964(4)-1982(4)	1964(4)-1980(4)
Parameter	1	2
A_0	0.072 (0.5)	-0.44 (1.1)
A_1	-0.014 (2.9)	-0.018 (3.2)
A_2	0.042 (5.8)	0.068 (3.7)
A_4	1.588 (119.0)	1.637 (308.0)
A_5	-0.630 (21.0)	-0.510 (7.4)
A_6	-0.007 (1.6)	-0.013 (2.3)
B_0	-2.87 (1.9)	-0.187 (0.8)
B_1	0.083 (4.0)	0.092 (4.9)
B_2	-0.041 (4.8)	-0.048 (8.8)
B_3	1.179 (26.0)	1.153 (28.8)
B_4	-0.188 (14.5)	-0.187 (17.9)
C_0	0.029 (6.9)	0.028 (5.8)
C_1	0.223 (2.21)	1.124 (3.5)
C_3	-0.651 (3.6)	-0.556 (2.7)
C_4	0.007 (5.7)	0.005 (4.2)
log likelihood function	626.68	559.459

simplification to be that represented by column (4), which has the most well determined wage effect on demand as well as a fairly well determined effect of real material prices. We removed the effect of unionisation from this model (C_2) and the insignificant time trend (A_3) to give our preferred model, presented in column (1) of table 2.

This model is clearly very similar to the others presented in table 1. The long-run elasticity of demand with respect to expected output is almost exactly unity while with respect to the real wage it is -0.33. All the coefficients in the supply function and real wage adjustment equation are correctly signed and significant.

The question of the stability of our results to the chosen sample period is, of course, crucial. Conventional forecasting tests are not defined for a system estimation technique such as used here, so as a simple second-best procedure we have reestimated our preferred model without the last eight observations. This is presented in column (2) of table 2. It should be emphasised that this test is in fact a very demanding one as these eight observations are the main period of demand side dominance. They are also a period in which the time series behaviour of employment altered markedly. Given this, the parameters seem quite satisfactorily stable.

Figure 1 shows the ex post forecasts of the preferred model with its implied allocation between demand and supply constraints. It is clear from this that for much of the period (1964-82), the model

Figure 1. <u>Comparison of Labour Demand and Supply</u>

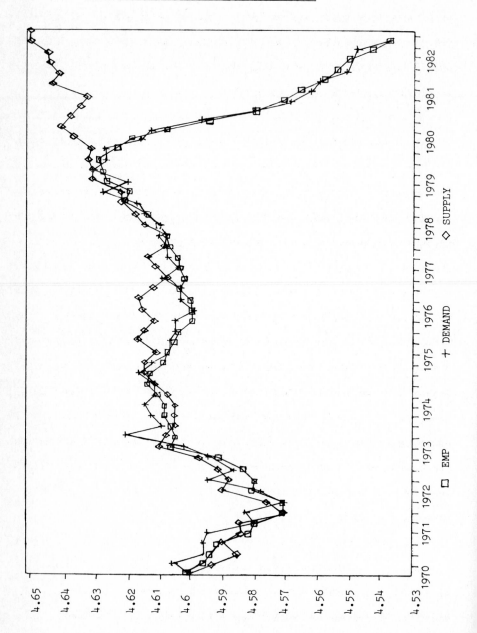

suggests that demand and supply of labour were fairly close. This is consistent with the labour market being approximately in equilibrium. The period 1980-82 however is characterised by a very large fall in actual employment, which, according to our estimates, is largely explained by a fall in the demand for labour, so that this period is characterised as one of large scale excess supply.

To test whether the labour market is in equilibrium or not it is necessary to nest the equilibrium within the disequilibrium model and use an appropriate test statistic, such as a likelihood ratio test, to adjudicate between them. As Monfort (1983) points out, in the case where the price adjustment equation is stochastic, which is the case we deal with, two problems in hypothesis testing (including the hypothesis of equilibrium versus disequilibrium) arise. These are that the parameters C_2 ... C_N in our adjustment equation, other than that on the excess demand term, and the variance of the error on the price adjustment term are not identified under the equilibrium hypothesis (C_1 = + ∞). If the identification question is dealt with by the reparameterisation C_1 = $1/C_1$, C_2 = $1/C_2$ etc., then the likelihood function is not differentiable in the region of H_0, as it is not defined here for σ_3 < 0 (see Monfort p. 76).

In spite of these general problems in testing equilibrium versus disequilibrium models, we present an estimate of an equilibrium model below for comparison with our earlier results. This takes the specification of the demand and supply functions used in column (1) of

table 1, using lagged output as the expected sales proxy in the demand
function.   The supply function is postulated to depend on the real
consumption wage, real benefits, the working population and union
density.   The conventional method of estimating this model would be to
solve the demand and supply equations for a pair of reduced form
equations for employment and the real wage.   The disadvantage of this
approach is that if, as in this case, the model is over-identified, the
structural parameters are not recoverable.   So the apparently good
reduced form estimates could hide the failure of one of the structural
equations.   We will therefore estimate the model in structural form,
making an allowance for the endogeneity of real wages.   The model then
comprises demand and supply functions, and the reduced form real wage
equation

$$(W/P)_t = D_0 + D_1 Y^e_{-1} + D_2 t + D_3 E_{t-1} + D_4 E_{t-2} + D_5 BN_t + D_6 POP_t$$

$$+ D_7 UP_t \qquad\qquad\qquad (21)$$

This is a somewhat unfamiliar representation of the model under the
full equilibrium assumption.   It may be recognised as equivalent to the
estimation of two structural equations, for demand and supply, where the
real wage (a regressor variable in the structural equations) is also
stochastic.   The orthodox treatment of this case is to use instrumental
variable (IV) estimation to recover consistent parameter estimates.   In
this context, the real wage equation above may be seen as an
instrumenting equation.   Estimating the three equations, demand, supply
and the real wage, by a system method (3SLS or FIML) is then similar to
an IV estimate of the demand and supply function using

the predetermined variables on the RHS of the real wage equation as instruments.[1]   The results for this model (the demand and supply functions from (1) in Table 1, and equation (21)) are shown in table 3.

Table 3. Equilibrium model

SAMPLE 1964Q4-1982Q4

Demand	A_0	A_1	A_2	A_4	A_5	A_6	SEE	DW
	0.61	-0.03	0.03	1.17	-0.30	0.005	0.0043	1.84
	(3.0)	(3.3)	(2.9)	(10.9)	(2.5)	(0.9)		

Supply	B_0	B_1	B_2	B_3	B_4		SEE	DW
	5.8	-0.0083	-0.65	-0.22	0.012		0.019	0.09
	(5.3)	(0.8)	1.2	(0.8)	(0.16)			

Real wage	D_0	D_1	D_2	D_3	D_4	D_5	D_6	D_7		
	17.6	-0.4	0.009	4.2	-2.8	-0.08	3.5	0.4	0.027	1.12
	(4.7)	(3.1)	(5.4)	(4.7)	(3.8)	(0.8)	(3.8)	(2.6)		

As the results show, the demand equation fares reasonably well, with most parameters quite well determined, though not as well as in the disequilibrium case. The supply function performs badly however. This evidence makes it clear

(1) If the model were exactly identified then the structural coefficients could be obtained directly from reduced form estimates of employment and the real wage.

why for this specification the disequilibrium model is superior.   The latter part of the period has a sharp decrease in actual employment produced by demand constraints, and an equilibrium formulation means the supply (or at least this supply) function cannot cope.   Its performance over the earlier part of the period is also much worse.

To conclude this chapter we should stress again some themes which have recurred throughout our account of the disequilibrium approach. One which we have emphasised is the considerable difficulty in applying the disequilibrium hypothesis in a way which adequately captures the dual decisions hypothesis.   Moreover, we have also noted the poor quality of many previous empirical applications of disequilibrium models even when applied to single markets, with implied spillover effects. Nonetheless we consider that the results provided in the last section of this chapter give an insight into the role of demand and supply effects in the UK labour market.   Beginning from a new classical equilibrium approach based on optimal inter-temporal behaviour by firms and households, extended to allow for non-market clearing, there is considerable evidence that meaningful estimates of the disequilibrium model may be obtained.   Our results also indicate that the sharp falls in employment after 1979 were due to a rapid fall in labour demand. Thus, in the world hypothesised in our model with many new classical attributes, the high levels of unemployment since 1979 are attributed to deficient demand.

MACRO MODELS

1. Introduction

In this book we are generally concerned with the estimation and use of
structural macro-econometric models.   The term structural is important
here as it explicitly excludes the, non theoretical, time series models
of the vector auto regressive (VAR) type.   A structural model, in our
use of the term, is a formalization of some theoretical view of how the
economy functions.   The individual equations can then be given causal
interpretation and the model represents a testable version of the
underlying theory.   Given this definition of a model it is possible to
classify most structural models according to the theory which they
represent.

All structural models may be thought of as representing a set of
markets which together describe the macro economy.   In the very broadest
sense we can describe almost all models within the following set of
equations.

$$X_i^D = f\ (P,\ X^D,\ X^S,\ X,\ Z)$$
$$X_i^S = g\ (P,\ X^D,\ X^S,\ X,\ Z)$$
$$X_i = h\ (P,\ X^D,\ X^S,\ X,\ Z)$$
$$P_i = j\ (P,\ X^D,\ X^S,\ X,\ Z)$$
$$i = 1\ \dots\ N$$

That is, the economy is made up of N markets with endogenous
variables X_i, $i = 1\ \dots\ N$, and each market has a demand X^D, and a supply

X^S.   The actual quantity traded, X, is a function of prices P, the endogenous variables Z, and the demand, supply and quantity traded in all markets.   Different classes of models are then produced by imposing broad restriction on this very general structure.

By far the most important class of model, at least in terms of its popularity, is the income-expenditure model.   It is often thought of as the implementation of conventional Keynesian theoretical views.   In this model the assumption is generally made that the demand side of the model is dominant, so that $X = X^D$.   The supply side of many of the markets are then virtually ignored, and prices are set on a fairly 'ad hoc' cost mark up basis.   To be more specific, total output in such a model is generally determined by total demand which, in turn, is determined by summing the components of aggregate expenditures, consumption, investment, stockbuilding, etc.   The central, expenditure, part of the model then determines the real components of the economy, and it is around this central structure that additional sectors determining prices and monetary aggregates may be added.   Most of the large forecasting models follow this general structure and although the largest may involve several thousand variables the conceptual approach is common.

Other classes of models include equilibrium models, supply-side models, disequilibrium models and bargaining models.   All of these may, at least in part, be seen as attempts to relax the restrictive assumption of demand side dominance of the income expenditure model, and to cope with the question of how prices are actually determined within the system.

An equilibrium model, for example, makes the general assumption that markets continuously clear so $X = X^D = X^S$, and prices are set so that market clearing occurs. In order to deal with the regular fluctuations which actually occur in real variables, such models often distinguish between the actual value of a variable and its equilibrium value, and simply postulate that the two come together quickly. While the assumption of continuous market clearing may be viewed as an extreme one, a major advantage of this approach is that it does offer a sound theoretical foundation for the determination of prices within the model.

It is worth distinguishing the idea of a 'supply side' model from the model just discussed given the increasing attention now paid to supply side factors. The concept of a supply side model, however, has no clearly defined meaning, we might use the natural analogue to a demand side definition which would be that all markets are assumed to be determined on the supply side. But models which are given the name 'supply side' do not generally make such an extreme assumption. Instead the term is generally taken to mean that the supply side of the market has some important influence in the determination of the quantities actually traded. In practice this often means that an unusually large role is played by relative price effects in expenditure equations, without the model being explicitly formed in terms of demand or supply functions with full market clearing.

In a bargaining model the demand and supply functions become boundaries or constraints on the region of possible trade, and prices and traded quantities are set within this region by some, largely unspecified, bargaining system. This approach produces fairly rich equation specifications for both quantity and price determination as demand and supply factors may enter the model equations.

Prices are also seen as being determined by the bargaining process and so, at least conceptually, pricing behaviour has a better foundation in this model than in the income-expenditure model. The general form of the model does however mean that the final equation can sometimes be observationally equivalent to both the supply side models and to the competitive models.

Disequilibrium models were discussed at length in Chapter 3 and, in terms of our present discussion, the class of complete disequilibrium macro models would be a multi-market analogue of the single market disequilibrium case. Both demand and supply are defined in this model, and trading takes place at the minimum of the two, with prices adjusting possibly extremely slowly to clear the market. There are, however, very few examples applying the disequilibrium approach to complete macro models.

In the context of this brief review of the alternative approaches which may be taken in estimating a macro econometric model, the model described in the rest of this chapter is firmly within the income-expenditure class. We have generally adopted the practice of completing a major re-estimation of the macro model each year. Model 8

(first used in November 1985) introduced widespread forward looking
behaviour into the model. Model 9 (first used in November 1986) made
substantial changes to pricing behaviour, the exchange rate and
consumption. This chapter then presents the key behavioural parts of
the macro model, and in the main will concentrate on Model 8 since this
is most widely represented in the subsequent chapters.   Important
changes which lead to Model 9 will be noted in the text as we proceed.
Also, it is unecessary to detail all equations from each of the two
models, so only the important equations are discussed here.   A full
listing is given in National Institute (1985) for Model 8 and National
Institute (1986) for Model 9.

    In the rest of this chapter we will outline the basis of the
consumption equations, company sector expenditures on employment,
stocks, and investment, the trade equations, wages, prices and the
exchange rate, and finally provide some notes on the monetary sector.
In some equations, forward looking behaviour is an important
characteristic, and these examples are based on the ideas and apply the
techniques discussed in Chapter 1.   Other examples embody two stage
estimation procedures for error correction models, and the general
properties of these estimation methods were extensively described in
Chapter 2.

2. The key equations in the macro model

We will now give a detailed account of the income-expenditure model
which forms the main vehicle for the illustration given in this book,

the National Institute's aggregate quarterly model of the UK economy.

A.   The model in outline

The model can be thought of as explaining the components of the standard national income, expenditure and output identities in constant and current prices. GDP is built up from the expenditure side of the accounts with all variables expressed in real (i.e. constant price) terms.

Thus GDP at factor cost can be expressed as

$$QGDP = QTFS + QDS - QM - QAFC$$

where

$$QTFS = QCE + QDK + QEX + \overline{QPAC}$$

QTFS is total final sales

QDS is stockbuilding

QM is imports of goods and services

QAFC is adjustment to factor cost

QCE is consumers' expenditure

QDK is gross fixed investment

QEX is exports of goods and services

and QPAC is general government expenditure on goods and services.

All variables are measured quarterly at 1980 prices and data is seasonally adjusted. A superior rule denotes an exogenous variable.

There are therefore five categories of expenditure to be determined

endogenously: QDS, QM, QCE, QDK and QEX.   Of these, consumers'
expenditure is the largest and is disaggregated into expenditure on
durables and on non-durables.   The model of consumer expenditure is
described later in Section B.

Total investment is divided into nine categories of which four are
endogenous and determined by behavioural equations in the model.   The
first of these is investment in private dwellings, determined by a
demand function for housing.   The equation for net investment in
manufacturing (inclusive of leasing) will be discussed in section C.   It
assumes that the investment decision   depends upon the lagged capital
stock, retirements and expected future output.   The capital stock and
retirements series differ from the CSO annual data, being adjusted to
imply similar movements in the capital output ratio as the CBI series on
capacity utilisation.   The distribution, financial and business services
sector adopts a similar approach in determining investment, but without
the adjustment to the capital stock and retirements made in the
manufacturing sector.   The final endogenous category, investment in the
rest of industry, is a distributed lag equation dependent on output and
a time trend.

The third of the five endogenous components of the expenditure GDP
identity to be described subsequently is stockbuilding.   In the model
this is divided into three sub-components: manufacturing, distributive
trades and the rest.   Each of these categories is expressed as a
function of expected future output, with lagged adjustment.

Leaving aside the adjustment to factor cost since we will not be
providing details on this in the present chapter, the expenditure
identities above are completed by the explanation of the trade balance.
Some categories are treated as exogenous. We will concentrate on
describing the equations which are explained by demand functions with
activity and relative price variables as the main arguments.

The explanation of expenditures in the economy has required the
introduction of five groups of further endogenous variables. They are:

(i)   incomes

(ii)   output and capacity utilisation

(iii) monetary aggregates and interest rates

(iv)   prices

(v)   the rate of exchange.

Incomes from employment are derived by multiplication of average
hours and employment by the wage rate. The wage rate plays a crucial
role in the model as it is also a major determinant of prices. The wage
equation described in detail below (see section D) emphasises the role
of real earnings targets and unemployment as determinants of wage
inflation.

The remaining categories of income are also endogenous in the
model, but are not discussed further in subsequent sections. Rents are
related to the change in GDP at market prices; income from self-
employment (after stock appreciation) is related to average earnings of

employees and gross trading profits of companies after tax and stock appreciation; property incomes are related to interest rates and each sector's holdings of financial assets; and net profits are determined as the difference between income GDP and the sum of income from employment and income from rent and self-employment. Gross profits include, in addition, stock appreciation. The direct tax model determines income after tax; adding current grants gives personal sector disposable income.

Having built up GDP from expenditures it is then divided amongst the output sectors of the economy, with implications for productivity, capacity utilisation, employment and unemployment. Sectoral output is determined by a form of input-output matrix although we will not be emphasising this in our later discussions, as it is a fairly conventional translation of expenditure into output.

As described in chapter 1, employment is a part of the model where expected future variables play an important role. In this case expected future output is identified as a determinant of all categories of employment, and the expected future real wage is a determinant of manufacturing employment. Changes in unemployment then depend upon changes in employment, with important differences depending upon the division between employment changes in manufacturing or non-manufacturing, and demographic changes to the work force.

Turning to the monetary sector, this is a set of demand equations

for financial assets and an equation which determines the term structure
of interest rates.   The net acquisition of financial assets by each
sector is determined in the 'income-expenditure' section of the model.
The public sector deficit must be financed by borrowing from the other
sectors: by sales of debt to the non-bank private sector, by issuing
currency, by borrowing from the domestic banking systems, and by
borrowing from the overseas sector.   The model equations are demand
equations which determine the stock of government debt and currency held
by the non-bank private sector.   (Bank lending to the public sector is a
residual item).   Equations for bank lending to various sub-categories of
the private sector enable £M3 to be determined from the assets side of
the banking system.   The demand for narrow money (M1) depends on
expected prices, income and interest rates, using a buffer stock model.

The final items of note in the model are then prices and the
exchange rate.   The price equations are of a mark up variety, where cost
items are labour and material costs.   Export and import prices depend
both upon domestic and overseas prices.   The model is completed by the
exchange rate equation the form of which was discussed in Chapter 1.
This is a model of the real exchange rate, dependent in part upon the
forward expected exchange rate assumed to be formed rationally.

We next turn to an account of the more important behavioural parts
of the model, beginning with the consumption sector.

In presenting the econometric results, the following summary statistics will be used:

> SEE is the standard error of the regression
>
> R^2 is the familiar R squared
>
> LM(r)is the Lagrange Multiplier test for r^{th} order residual
>   auto correlation
>
> DW   is the Durbin Watson test of auto correlated residuals
>
> BP(n)is the Box Pierce residual correlogram statistic distributed
>   at $\chi^2(n)$ with n degrees of freedom

Figures in parentheses are 't' statistics

B. Consumer expenditure

Total consumer expenditure (QCE) is disaggregated into non durable
(QCND) and durable consumption expenditure (QDURABLE).

In Model 8 non-durable consumption is determined as a distributed
lag on real personal disposable income (QRDY). In addition it is
hypothesised that consumption decisions are affected by households plan
both to hold a share of their wealth as financial assets, and to try to
maintain a constant ratio of such financial wealth to real income.
Inflation effects will then tend to decrease non-durable consumption.

Model 9 has a consumption function for non durables which is rather
different. This is the one quoted below. In this model the level of
non-durable expenditure is assumed to be dependent upon the form of

income, real financial wealth, and the distribution of income. The
argument for the first term, the form of income, is that the propensity
to consume is likely to be higher out of transfer payments than out of
disposable income. Hence income is distinguished as real disposable
income (QRDY) and current grants (CG). To allow for an income
distribution effect we introduce a proxy variable, the ratio of tax
payments at the standard rate to those at higher rates. This ratio is
defined by the variable URT.

The equation is estimated by instrumental variables (IV) using a
two step procedure as described in Chapter 2. The econometric results
for the equation are shown as (1) below.

$$\Delta \ln QCND_t = 0.003 - 0.149 \, \Delta\ln QCND_{t-1} - 0.347 \, \Delta \ln QRDY_t \tag{1}$$
$$(2.8) \quad (1.4) \qquad\qquad (5.3)$$

$$+0.144 \, \Delta \ln QRDY_{t-1} - 0.345 \, \hat{v}_{t-1}$$
$$(2.8) \qquad\qquad (3.1)$$

where $\hat{v} = \ln QCND - [1.609 + 0.777 \ln QRDY + 0.045 \, (FAPER/CPI)$

$$+86.21. \, CG/CPI/QRDY + 0.096 \, URT]$$

SEE = 0.007, LM(4) = 3.94, DW = 1.96.

Instruments: lagged prices, other personal incomes and further lags on
variables in (1).

In this equation FAPER is financial acquisitions by the personal
sector, and CPI is the consumer price index.

Generally speaking the equation is quite successful, with well determined effects which accord with a-priori conventions, including the long-run or equilibrium effect given by the $\hat{v}$ term which in turn is obtained from a first stage equation.

The durable consumption equation is rather more straightforward, and so can be dealt with briefly. It is a demand equation dependent upon disposable income and various changes in hire-purchase regulations. We also find an anticipations effect due to pre announced tax changes in the budgets of 1968, 1973 and 1979. The equation for Model 9 is shown by (2). (Model 8 had a very similar form and is not discussed separately).

$$\ln \text{QDURABLE} = -3.25 + 0.533 \ln \text{QDURABLE}_{t-1} + 0.857 \, \Delta \ln \text{QRDY}_t$$
$$\phantom{\ln \text{QDURABLE} = } (2.9) \quad (5.5) \phantom{\ln \text{QDURABLE}_{t-1}} (3.4)$$

$$+0.519 \, \Delta \ln \text{QRDY}_{t-1} \; +0.674 \ln \text{QRDY}_{t-1} \qquad\qquad (2)$$
$$(2.1) \phantom{\Delta \ln \text{QRDY}_{t-1}} (3.9)$$

$$-0.003 \, \text{DHP} + \sum a_i \, D_i$$
$$(4.9)$$

$$\text{SEE} = 0.0392 , \quad \text{LM}(4) = 2.3. , \quad R^2 = 0.98$$

In this equation DHP is a Hire Purchase dummy, and D_i are the dummy variables to allow for the effects of anticipated tax changes.

C. Company sector expenditures

This section deals with the modelling of expenditure in employment, stockbuilding and investment by the typical firm. It introduces forward looking behaviour into the sector as a whole, again based on the concepts discussed earlier in Chapter 1.

(i) Employment

The model we use is a labour demand model based on intertemporal profit-maximising with a production function dependent on labour, raw materials and fuel inputs. Implicitly we assume an adjustment cost function depending on changes in employment. These costs include the location and hiring of new workers as well as their costs in on-the-job training (measured in terms of possible output foregone). Disengagements involve redundancy payments and other legal costs. One limitation with this cost function is that it assumes costs are incurred for net changes in employment only. Clearly this is a simplification, since the firm incurs adjustment costs from both hiring and firing, so that adjustment costs are non-zero when new hires equal disengagements.

For the present, however, we will simply state the typical dynamic equation concerned, which is of the form

$$N_t = \lambda_1 N_{t-1} + \lambda_2 N_{t-2} + \sum_i \mu_{1i}(Q^e_{t+i})$$

$$\sum_i \mu_{2i}((w/p)^e_{t+1}) + \sum_i \mu_{3i}((pm/p)^e_{t+i}) \tag{3}$$

In this equation, Q^e is expected output, $(w/p)^e$ is the expected real product wage, and $(pm/p)^e$ is the expected real price of materials and fuel. The second order autoregressive dynamics may be justified by assuming the equation aggregates over different labour types, or over straight-time and overtime working.   Equations of this form are estimated for three sectors of the economy: manufacturing, mainly public and other private, and the preferred results are reported in table 1.

(ii) Stockbuilding

An approach similar to that described for employment is used in obtaining a decision rule for the firm's optimal stockholding assuming that stocks are held as a buffer (see Hall, Henry and Wren-Lewis, 1985).

For brevity we simply note that the optimal decision rule for inventories is of the form

$$S_t = \lambda_1 S_{t-1} + \lambda_2 S_{t-2} + \sum_{i=0}^{\infty} \mu_i (S^*_{t+i})$$

where the μ_i are functions of the parameters λ_1 and λ_2, and S^* is

$$S^*_t = \tau_1 (r-\Pi)_t + \tau_2 Y_t$$

where R-Π is the real interest rate and Y is sales.   Finally, we need to allow for the possibility that stock plans may not be precisely fulfilled.   In particular, if sales differ from their expected level, involuntary changes in finished goods stocks may occur.   This suggests a final equation of the form

$$S_t = \lambda_1 S_{t-1} + \lambda_2 S_{t-2} + \sum_{i=0}^{\infty} \mu_1 (\tau_1 (r-\Pi)_{t+j}^e + \tau_2 Y_{t+j}^e) \qquad (4)$$

$$+ \beta((Y_t)^e - Y_t)$$

Again results for sectoral stocks equations are shown in table 2.

(iii) Investment

A similar approach, based on the presence of adjustment costs, was adopted for the investment equations. Again the typical firm is postulated to undertake an optimal decision over time with respect to its investment plans. Allowing for adjustment costs related to changes in the capital stock implies that equal changes in gross investment (I) and retirements (R) incur no adjustment cost as net investment is zero. Rather than assume this, an objective function is taken which penalises movements from the desired capital stock (ΔK), and changes in gross investment (ΔI). Thus we assume the firm minimises

$$\Sigma d^t [\alpha_1 (K-K^*)^2 + \alpha_2 (\Delta K)^2 + \alpha_3 (\Delta I)^2]$$

where d is a discount factor, and K^* is a function of expected output (Q^e). To proceed with implementing this approach we assume that retirements are exogenous and that the investment decision is separable from other expenditure decisions. Both assumptions are made in the interests of deriving relatively simple dynamic equations. Optimising produces a fairly complex relationship between the capital stock and retirements, and again to ease econometric estimation, a simpler version was taken of the form

$$I_t - R_t = (\lambda_1 - 1)K_{t-1} + \lambda_2 K_{t-2} - \theta(L)\Delta R_t$$
$$+ (\alpha + \beta t)(1 - \lambda_1 L^{-1} - \lambda_2 L^{-2})^{-1} Q_t^e \qquad (5)$$

where $\theta(.)$ is a polynomial in the lag operator (L), to be determined by the data. The $\lambda_1 (i=1, 2)$ are parameters derived from the assumed quadratic costs of adjustment. Furthermore, forward terms in expected output occur in the equation as the desired capital stock is assumed to depend on this. The parameter β allows the desired capital/output ratio to vary through time reflecting technical progress.

Cost of capital terms of a simple variety were included in the original specification, but these were found to be insignificant. The complete results are shown in table 3.

Table 1. <u>Sectoral employment equations (N_t)</u>

Sample 1964 II-1983 IV, quarterly

Sector	Constant	N_{t-1}	N_{t-2}	Q^e	$(w/p)^e$	Time	BP(16)	DW	SEE
Manufac-turing	0.188 (5.8)	-2.67 (6.1)	0.122	0.103			21.46	2.31	0.003
Mainly public	-0.131 (2.337)	1.36 (12.40)	-0.382 (3.542)	0.029 (2.34)		–	18.40	2.09	0.004
Other private	-0.449 (0.831)	0.974 (26.825)		0.015 (2.344)		-0.0004 (1.709)	9.358	1.59	0.008

Table 2.   Sectoral stocks equations (S_t)

SAMPLE 1964 I-1983 I, quarterly

Sector	Constant	S_{t-1}	S_{t-2}	Q^e	SRLD	R^2	BP(16)	DW	SEE
Manufac- turing	31.6 (0.6)	1.40 (14.8)	-0.52 (5.8)	37.3 (4.9)	276.7 (2.5)	0.99	8.73	2.0	288.8
Rest	-1362.5 (2.7)	0.786 (15.7)	-	51.6 (4.0)	-163.6 (2.3)	0.99	22.3	2.0	181.9
Distri- bution	-2559.0 (2.6)	1.34 (11.6)	-0.44 (4.1)	39.9 (3.3)	225.0 (2.7)	0.99	19.4	2.0	174.9

SRLD is a stock relief dummy variable, equal to unity between 1974 and 1981 and zero elsewhere.

Table 3.   Sectoral investment equations $(I-R)_t$

SAMPLE 1966 I-1983 IV, quarterly - manufacturing

SAMPLE 1970 I-1983 IV, quarterly - distribution

K_{t-1}	K_{t-2}	$Q^{e(a)}$		K_{t-3}	ΔR	ΔR_{t-1}	ΔR_{t-2}	ΔR_{t-3}	SEE	BP(16)	DW
Distribution											
0.844 (11.5)	-0.850 (11.7)	9.76 (1.9)	0.094 (1.8)	-0.92 (2.1)	-0.66 (1.5)				73.0	12.46	2.3
Manufacturing											
0.605 (5.0)	-0.236 (1.0)	11.2 (3.2)	0.032 (2.4)	-0.376 (3.1)	-0.98 (20.2)	-0.39 (2.9)	-0.06 (1.6)	-0.07 (1.7)	64.5	12.81	1.9

(a) This term is estimated in the form of $\sum_0^4 \mu_1 Q_{t+1}^e (\alpha + \beta t)$ where Q^e is expected output and t is an time trend. The parameters in the table are estimated value of α and β.

D. Wages, Prices and the Exchange Rate

(i) Wages

There is a single aggregate wage equation in the model, and it is clearly a crucial relationship in determining the overall properties of the model. We briefly comment next on both the form of the equation used in the model and on the estimation methods applied to it.

The wage equation used in both Model 8 and 9 has a similar basis since in each real wage resistance plays an important role in wage behaviour, this being modified by variations in labour market conditions however. In Model 8, the level of real wages is influenced in an important way by a time trend representing workers real wage aspirations.   In Model 9 this trend is replaced by a smoothed productivity variable. Since the version in Model 9 is a generalisation of that in Model 8, we will concentrate on the later version of the wage equation in the remainder of this section.   In general terms, the wage equation is of the form (in logs)

$$\alpha(L)\Delta \ W_t = \beta(L)\Delta Z_t + \delta \ (E/P - \delta V)_{t-1} + \epsilon \Delta P_{t+1}^e + n_t \tag{6}$$

In this equation, W is average wages, E is average earnings, and P the consumer price index, with the usual conventions that ΔZ and V are sets of variables which determine the rate of change of wages and the level of real earnings respectively. The elements of these vectors will occupy the rest of our present discussion. The part which we draw attention to however, is that (6) above is a fairly general model, which contains a number of alternatives within it. Thus if the V vector includes a proxy for union power, a measure of income out of work (e.g. the average level of real unemployment benefit) the capital-labour ratio and the level of real import prices, then this part of (6) alone gives the model of real earnings levels popularised by Layard and Nickell (1986), (which in turn incorporates the model used by Minford (1983)). Such models of the level of real earnings can then be imbedded in wage inflation models like (6) using the two-stage estimation for error correction models described earlier in Chapter 2.

In arriving at the preferred form of (6), we adopted a catholic interpretation of the components in ΔZ and V, and proceeded to test for statistical evidence favouring their inclusion. The main results of this exercise are reported in Hall and Henry (1987a and 1987b). In V we allowed a potential influence from a proxy union power (given by the union markup as estimated by Layard and Nickell (1986)), real unemployment benefits, unemployment, real import prices, tax rates (both employer taxes and direct taxes), productivity as measured either by the capital-labour ratio or output per head, and real company profits. In ΔZ we allowed effects from changes in unemployment and productivity. By testing among these alternatives the resulting, quite parsimonious, model for wage inflation was obtained, using IV estimation.

$$\Delta \ln WAGERATE_t = 0.00158 + 0.985 \Delta \ln CPI_{t+1}$$
$$(0.45) \qquad (6.9)$$

$$- 0.937 \Delta \ln AVHMF_t - 0.306 RES_{t-1} \qquad\qquad (7)$$
$$(6.9) \qquad\qquad\qquad (4.2)$$

$$- 1.272 (\Delta UPC_{t-1} - \Delta UPC_{t-3})$$
$$(1.9)$$

$$+ 0.233 \Delta \ln WAGERATE_{t-2}$$
$$(3.0)$$

$$- 0.089 \Delta \ln WAGERATE_{t-3}$$
$$(1.3)$$

IV; SEE = 0.012; DW = 1.97

where UPC = UNEMP/(UNEMP + EMP), and UNEMP is the level of unemployment, EMP is level of employment. In turn RES is defined as

$$RES = [\ln (AVEARN/CPI) - (- 1.049 + 1.103 \ln PRODS$$
$$- 0.859 \ln AVHMF - 0.495 UPC)]$$

which is the equilibrium term dependant upon average earnings (AVEARN), prices (CPI), smoothed productivity (PRODS), average hours (AVHMF) and unemployment. The smoothed productivity variable is

$$PRODS = \sum_{i=0}^{7} \ln (21500 * OGDP/EMP)_{t-i}/8$$

where OGDP is the output measure of GDP.

Additional Instruments used were lagged wages, hours and unemployment.

In this equation price inflation expectations are assumed to be formed rationally, and the procedures for estimating such an equation are noted below. The variable in average hours (AVHMF) acts as a cyclical correction to the average earnings series used in the equation. Before commenting on the estimation of the equation we may also note that many of the variables which have been proposed as potential determinants of real earnings have been eliminated by our empirical search in obtaining (7) above. In particular we decisively find against the use of the capital-labour ratio as Layard and Nickell (1986) advocate. Also, we find the evidence to be against including profits (as recommended by Caruth and Oswald (1987)), and real import prices, proxies for union power and the level of real income out of work (as recommended by Layard and Nickell (1986) and by Minford ((1983)). Details of the empirical tests underlying the derivation of this are given in Hall and Henry (1987a and 1987b), which suggest that although (7) is a relatively sparse formulation, it is a preferred one on statistical grounds to more elaborate models.

Finally we may note that in estimating (7), two issues which have already been extensively discussed, were involved. The first is that, as is evident, (7) was estimated as a two-step error correction model. The first step cointegration exercise was then used to derive the preferred specification against alternative models of real earnings levels. The second issue concerns expectations modelling. Here we assume rationally formed expectations, and estimate (7) by replacing expected inflation by actual future inflation, dealing with the resulting dependence between equation error and regressor variables by instrumental variables.

(ii) Prices

The price equations in Model 8 and 9 have a similar form, in that they are standard mark-up equations on labour and material costs, with allowance for productivity and taxes. The consumer and wholesale price equations (CPI, and PWMF respectively) are the two major price equations in the model, though import and export prices also have an important role to play in influencing model properties.   We will only be discussing the CPI and PWMF equations here though, taking the equations in Model 9, and comparing these with those in Model 8.

In both cases the CPI and PWMF equations are estimated using a two stage estimation procedure used elsewhere, separately identifying the level or equilibrium part of the equation before identifying its dynamics. The estimated price equations are shown next.

$$\Delta \ln CPI_t = 0.0035 + 0.1587 \; \Delta \ln CPI_{t-1}$$
$$(2.7) (2.1)$$

$$+0.076 \; \Delta \ln [(WS + EC + \overline{NIS})/EMP]_t (8)$$
$$(1.9)$$

$$+0.509 \; \Delta \ln PWMF_t + 0.067 \; \Delta \ln PWMF_{t-4}$$
$$(9.1) (1.4)$$

$$+0.004 \; \Delta COMPTAX_t - 0.266 \; RES_{t-1}$$
$$(3.4) (4.1)$$

$$OLS \; ; \; R^2 = 0.86 \; ; \; SEE = 0.0054 \; ; \; DW = 1.8 \; LM(8) = 3.65$$

In this equation WS is total wages and salaries, EC is total receipts from employers contributions and NIS receipts from the National Insurance Surcharge.   EMP is total employment.   The other variable in the equations is an average rate of indirect tax (COMPTAX), defined as the sum of (weighted) average VAT rate and other customs and excise duties, i.e.

$$COMPTAX = (\overline{VATRATE} \cdot SVAT4) + (\overline{OCERATE} \cdot SOCE4), \text{ where}$$

$$SVAT4 = \sum_{i=0} SVAT_{t-i}/4, \quad SOCE4 = \sum_{i=0} SOCE_{t-i}/4$$

and SVAT is the share of consumers expenditure subject to VAT, and SOCE the share of consumers expenditure subject to customs and excise duties. The average rates of VAT and customs and excise duties are taken to be exogenous.   The levels or equilibrium part of the equation is RES, which in turn is given by

$$RES = \ln CPI - [\ 1.345 + 0.571 \ln PWMF$$
$$+ 0.345 \ln (WS + EC + \overline{NIS})/EMP$$
$$- 0.091 \ LOEM8 + 0.007 \ COMPTAX\ ]$$

where LEOM8 is an eight quarter moving average of labour productivity in the manufacturing sector.

Turning to the wholesale price equation, (PWMF), the estimate for this is as follows.

$$\Delta \ln PWMF = 0.443 \; \Delta \ln PWMF_{t-1}$$
$$(3.8)$$

$$+ \; \Sigma \; a_i \Delta \ln PM_{t-i} \qquad\qquad (9)$$

$$+ \; \Sigma \; b_i \; \Delta \ln UNLC_{t-i}$$

$$- \; 0.0480 \; [-1 + 0.244 \ln (PWMF \, / \, UNLC)_{t-1}$$
$$(0.5)$$

$$+ \; 0.0226 \ln \left(\frac{PWMF}{100 \; PMGEO \, / \, EFFRAT} \right)]_{t-1}$$

2SLS ; SEE = 0.00955 ; DW = 1.7.

In this equation UNLC is the unit labour cost variable. The PWMF
equation is also an error correction model, with dynamic effects given
by an Almon lag on import prices (PM) and labour costs. The weights for
these two terms were $\Sigma \; ai = 0.285$, and $\Sigma bi = 0.216$.

One interesting feature of this pair of equations is that import
price changes affect consumer prices only indirectly via their effect on
wholesale prices, which then feed into consumer prices. This induces a
degree of sluggishness in the response of domestic prices to changes in
foreign prices, such sluggishness explaining in part why UK price
inflation was slow to decrease in the 1981-1985 period. Earlier models
of the CPI (notably NI model 8) were more responsive to import price
variables, though these were rejected in favour of the version described
by (8) and (9) above.

(iii) The Exchange Rate
Much of the background to this, and the estimation procedures have been
discussed in Chapter 1, so we will be discussing only a few

additional points here.

The general form of equation used for estimating the real exchange rate is

$$\ln E_t = \alpha o + \alpha_1 \ln E_{t-1} + \alpha_2 \ln E^e_{t+1} + \alpha_3 (rd-rf)_t$$
$$+ \alpha_4 (rd-rf)_{t-4} + \alpha_5 \ln \left(\frac{X/Mt}{X/M_{t-1}} \right) + \alpha_6 \ln (^X/M)_t .$$

where E is the real exchange rate, $(rd-rf)$ the real interest differential (short rates) and $^X/M$ the trade balance. The equation includes as special cases:

(a) $\alpha_1 = \alpha_4 = \alpha_5 = \alpha_6 = 0$, and $\alpha_2 = \alpha_3 = 1$ gives the uncovered interest parity condition arising from perfect capital mobility.

(b) $\alpha_6 = 0$, $\alpha_3 = -\alpha_4$, the equation yields a _flow_ model of capital mobility, so that $\Delta(rd-rf)$ produces permanent changes in the flow of international capital.

(c) $\alpha_6 = 0$, $\alpha_3 = -\alpha_4$ produces a stock view of capital movements, so $\Delta(rd-rf)$ yield transitory capital flows, but no change in steady state levels.

We have already discussed how such an equation may be estimated by Wickens (1982) method for dealing with unobserved expectations of next periods real exchange rate (E^e_{t+1}) using Full Information estimation

methods. The preferred equation estimated in this way, is reproduced as
(10), which includes a difference in the trade balance.

$$E_t = 0.344 \; E_{t-1} + (1 - 0.344) \; E^e_{t+1} + 0.007 \; \Delta \; (rd-rf)_t \qquad (10)$$
$$ (7.5) \phantom{E_{t-1} + (1 - 0.344) E^e_{t+1} +} (3.1)$$
$$ + 0.272 \; \Delta \; (^X/M)_t$$
$$ (10.3)$$

$$\hat{\sigma} = 0.005, \; Dw = 2.09$$

Equation (10) gives a preponderant weight on the forward exchange rate
(it actually approximates 0.7) making the initial part of the solution
dependent upon the <u>timing</u> of the solution period.   Experimentation
however, shows that this dependence is not severe, as we illustrate in
Chapter 5.

E. The Trade Balance

Although the model provides for disaggregated import and export
equations (manufacturing, food and basic goods, and services) we will be
concentrating upon the equations for manufactures in this section.
Apart from their intrinsic importance, the equations for manufactures
provide concepts and results which are common to other sectors.   Where
necessary we will refer to important differences which occur between the
sectors.

The equation for exports of manufactures as it appears in Model 9
is shown below.

$$\ln QXGMA_t = 3.55 + 0.735 \ln \overline{WTM}_t - 0.333 \ln PRPEX5_{t-1} \qquad (11)$$
$$(4.8) \quad (3.6) \qquad\qquad (3.7)$$

$$- 0.391 \ln \overline{WTM}_{t-1} + 0.206 \ln QXGMA_{t-1} + 0.218 \ln QXGMA_{t-2}$$
$$(1.7) \qquad\qquad (1.8) \qquad\qquad (2.4)$$

$R^2 = 0.96$ SEE $= 0.0484$ LM(8) $= 7.5$ DW $= 2.1$

The equation is interpreted as a demand equation dependent upon an activity variable, world trade (WTM), and a relative price variable, (PRPEX5). Two things are important to note in assessing this equation. The first is the apparantly low values for the estimated elasticities in the equation. For WTM the long run elasticity is 0.59 while that for the relative price term is -0.58. The second thing to note is that this is a common finding. For example similar orders of magnitude were obtained in the export of manufacturing equations used in Model 8 estimated with a shorter data set. Also, as Anderton and Dunnett (1987) reveal, other UK models have similar results. The respective elasticities in the equation used by the London Business School for instance are 0.58 (world trade) and -0.33 (relative prices) (see Anderton and Dunnett (1987)).

Although the activity elasticities tend to similar orders of magnitude for other categories of exports in the model, their response to relative prices is rather different. Thus exports of services have a price elasticity of -1.4, whereas for exports of food and basic goods it is zero.

Turning now to the imports of manufacturing equation, this is also

represented by a demand function, this time dependent upon domestic
expenditures, import prices relative to domestic prices of manufactured
goods, and a specialisation index.

The estimated equation is

$$\Delta \ln QMMF = - 0.287 - 0.245 \, \Delta \ln QMMF_{t-1}$$
$$ (2.6) \quad (2.4)$$

$$- 0.515 \, \Delta \ln QMMF_{t-2}$$
$$(4.3)$$

$$+ 1.630 \, \Delta \ln QTFE2 + 1.009 \, \Delta \ln QTFE2_{t-2}$$
$$(5.0) \qquad\qquad\qquad (2.7)$$

$$- 0.271 \, \Delta \ln RELP_{t-1}$$
$$(1.0)$$

$$+ 0.532 \, \Delta \ln RELP_{t-2}$$
$$(2.1)$$

$$+ 0.197 \, \ln (OMF/OGDP)_{t}$$
$$(1.5)$$

$$+ 0.328 \, \overset{7}{\underset{i=0}{\Sigma}} \ln (\overline{WTM} / \overline{WIP})_{t-i}/8$$
$$(2.5)$$

$$- 0.171 \, [\ln QMMF_{t-3} + \ln RELP_{t-3}$$
$$(2.7)$$

$$- \ln QTFE2_{t-3}]$$

$$R^2 = 0.41, \; SEE = 0.042, \; DW = 2.2, \; LM(8) = 7.77.$$

(12)

In this equation imports of manufactures (QMMF) are determined by
weighted domestic expenditures (defined further below), relative prices
(RELP), the ratio of manufactures to GDP (the output measure, hence
OGDP) and a specialisation index WTM/WIP where WTM is world trade in
manufactures and WIP is world industrial production.   The weighted
domestic expenditure variables is QTFE2 which in turn is defined as

$$QTFE2 = QCE + QDST + QEX + 0.33 \, QPAC,$$

where QCE is aggregate consumption, QDST is total stockbuilding, QEX is exports excluding oil exports and QPAC is current spending by government. This definition embodies judgements (based on input-output weights) of differential import propensities between different categories of expenditure. Thus current spending by government has an import propensity of one-third and the import propensity of investment spending is set at zero. The remaining variables are then defined in the following way. RELP is a tariff adjusted unit value index of manufacturers imports in sterling deflated by the wholesale price index. The specialisation index has already been defined. We may also note that it represents a move to growing world specialisation in production, as the ratio of world trade rises relative to production.

In terms of overall properties, the import equation is constrained to produce unit elasticities with respect to demand and relative prices in the long run. Again in comparison with other import equations in the model the price elasticities are not representative. Imports of other goods for example have a price elasticity of -0.2, whereas for imports of services it is zero.

F.   The Monetary Sector

(i)   An overview

The monetary sector of the model seeks to explain some of the main financial transactions between the sectors of the economy. Starting with the public sector the public sector's borrowing requirement is by

definition financed by bank lending to the public sector, by debt sales
to the private sector, by issuing currency and by borrowing from the
overseas sector, the latter being treated as exogenous. The PSBR is
determined by the income and expenditure sectors of the model.
Behavioural equations for the banking sector are designed to leave bank
lending to the public sector as a residual item. Debt sales to the non-
bank private sector are given by equations for the stock of national
savings and the stock of other public sector debt which depend upon
relative interest rates and wealth. The change in currency is given by
an equation dependent upon the consumption expenditure. These
categories are treated as demand determined.

The identity for the change in the broad money supply (sterling M3)
introduces only one further element to be explained - bank lending to
the private sector - as the remaining small elements in the identity are
exogenous.

Bank lending to the private sector is divided into six components,
of which bank lending to other financial institutions, loans for house
purchase and the Issue Department's transactions in commercial bills and
bank purchases of new issues, are given by rules of thumb or treated as
exogenous. Bank lending to the personal and company sectors are given
by behavioural equations.

In the equation for bank lending to the personal sector, this is
assumed to be a demand equation, dependent on interest rates, real

disposable income, and the change in the net acquisition of financial assets by the personal sector, used here to proxy changes in personal wealth.   Bank lending to industrial and commercial companies is a transactions demand equation.   It depends on real output with a significant effect from the real borrowing requirement of this sector. There is also an effect from relative interest rates, including foreign rates, which are included to capture switching between domestic and foreign sources of borrowing.

There are two other demand equations in the model, the demand for currency which is a simple distributed lag on total consumers' expenditure, and the demand equation for narrow money (M1), embodying forward-looking behaviour and buffer stock behaviour.

(ii) Some selected equations.

(a) The demand for narrow money (M1)

The equation for the narrow money aggregate (M1) also incorporates forward-looking behaviour in its planned magnitudes.   Moreover, it is explicitly based on the 'buffer stock' approach to the demand for money which, in essence, sees overall demand as comprising two components: a planned and an unplanned component.   The latter is assumed to depend on unanticipated movements in nominal income, and interest rates.

More specifically, we assume the agent minimises the cost function.

$$C_t = \sum_{}^{\infty} D^t (a_0 (M-M^*)^2 + a_1 (\Delta M)^2)_t$$

where M* is the long-run demand for money and D is the discount factor.
As described in Chapter 1 the first-order condition for this is

$$(1-\frac{(1 + D + a)}{D} L+ \frac{L^2}{D})M_t = - \frac{a}{D} M^*_{t-1}$$

where $a = a_0/a_1$. A forward solution is derived in familiar fashion by
factorising the LHS of this equation. We assume the long-run demand for
money is given by

$$M^* = C_0 P + C_1 Y - C_2 r$$

where P is the price level, Y disposable income, and r is the interest
rate. The demand for money then is equal to

$$M = M^p + M^u$$

where M^p is given as the solution to the above cost-minimisation
exercise and M^u is the unanticipated component dependent upon
innovations in prices, output and interest rates. The model in full is
then

$$M_t = \lambda_1 M_{t-1} + \alpha(P-P^e) + \beta(Y-Y^e) + \sigma(R-R^e)$$

$$+(1-\lambda_1)(1-\lambda_1 D) \sum_{s}^{\infty}(\lambda_1 D)^S(M^*_{t+s})$$

with M* as given above, and the P, Y, R processes given by the time
series representations,

$$P = \mu(L)P_t + V_t$$

With $P^e = \hat{P}$, and similarly for Y^e and R^e.   The result when the backward/forward restrictions is applied is given in table 4.

Table 4. Buffer stock model M1

Constant	M_{t-1}	Y^e	P^e	R^e	$(P-P^e)$	$(Y-Y^e)$	$(R-R^e)$	SEE	DW
-0.05	0.83	0.046	0.04	-0.019	0.57	0.28	0.065	1.44	2.4
(1.1)	(20.8)	(3.2)	(3.4)	(4.7)	(2.4)	(3.0)	(4.1)		

(b) Bank Lending equations

The final item concerns the econometric results for bank lending, and here we will emphasise bank lending to industrial and commercial companies (ICC). The results will be those in Model 8, interest in bank lending equations per se having declined given the problems in accounting for movements in sterling M3, and its virtual demise as a target in governmental monetary policy in the UK.

The approach taken here is detailed in Cuthbertson (1985).   The general form of the model is

$$\theta_1(L)\ QBL = \theta_2(L)\ QGDP + \theta_3(L)R + \theta_4(L)(ICCBR/P)$$

where QBL is the real level of bank lending to ICCS, QGDP is real GDP, R is a vector of interest rates to be described below, and ICCBR/P is the real level of the borrowing requirement of ICC's.

As is evident, the model is a fairly eclectic model involving transactions, precautionary and risk aversion elements from the literature on asset demands. Thus the level of output in the equation signifies that bank advances are substitutes for money held for transactions purposes, and thus will depend upon the level of turnover in the firm (proxied by output). Similarly precautionary elements are introduced via relative interest rates effects. Such effects are allowed here using bank lending rate relative to the local authority interest rate (RBL - RLA), and, because ICCs may borrow in foreign markets, a representative interest rate is included in the equation (actually the 3 month euro dollar rate REU). Finally "buffer stock" type factors in the demand for lending are proxied by including the net borrowing requirement of ICC in the equation.

The estimated equation used in Model 8 is given next, and as is clear it is estimated as an error correction form of equation.

$$\Delta_4 \ln QBL_t = \underset{(3.8)}{0.069} + \underset{(9.9)}{0.86} \ \Delta_2 \ln QBL_{t-1} + \underset{(9.3)}{0.99} \ \Delta \ln QBL_{t-3}$$

$$+ \underset{(2.0)}{0.15} \ \Delta_4 \ln QGDP_t - \underset{(3.6)}{0.06} \ \ln (QBL/QGDP)_{t-4}$$

$$- \underset{(0.7)}{0.001} \ \Delta RBL_{t-2} - \underset{(3.0)}{0.002} \ \Delta RBL_{t-5} + \underset{(2.9)}{0.008} \ (RLA - RBL)_t$$

$$+ \underset{(0.5)}{0.001} \ (RLA - RBL)_{t-2} - \underset{(0.3)}{0.0001} \ \Delta REU_{t-2}$$

$$+ \underset{(1.9)}{0.0003} \ \Delta(ICCBR/p)_t + \underset{(2.0)}{0.0002} \ \Delta_2(ICCBR/p)_{t-2}$$

$R^2 = 0.95,$ SEE $= 0.0143,$ LM(4) $= 4.2$

Generally the equation performs fairly well, with coefficients which accord with a-priori conventions. As is usual in such equations however, there is some lack of precision in some of the interest rate effects, and in particular, the results suggest little influence from overseas interest rates.

3.   Conclusions

This chapter has reviewed some of the considerations which led to the econometric specifications used in recent forms of the National Institute model. It has also provided a representative set of econometric results for some of the major items in those models, with the aim of imparting the flavour of the model, without providing all of the results concerned. In subsequent chapters we will be providing extensive accounts of the properties of these models when they are used in simulation (deterministic and stochastic), dynamic tracking and optimal control exercises.

MODEL SOLUTIONS, DYNAMIC TRACKING AND MECHANICAL FORECASTS

1. Introduction

This chapter considers problems involved in the solution of a large non-linear model. This topic falls naturally into two sections: first, the solution of conventional non-linear models without any forward-looking expectations terms, and second the special problems posed when we introduce rational expectations into a large non-linear model.

When considering the solution of traditional backward-looking models it might be thought that there are no outstanding problems of any great interest. It is true that a battery of solution techniques have been evolved which have been used very successfully for many years. However, while we have a set of analytical results for the performance of these techniques in a linear framework no great attention has been paid to the possible complications which might arise in the context of a non-linear model. The second part of this chapter considers some of these problems and conducts some experiments to investigate the effect of re-ordering and re-normalising a large non-linear model.

The final part of this chapter considers the solution of a non-linear model with consistent forward-looking expectations. A new solution technique is proposed and tested. The problem of terminal conditions is then described and finally a number of illustrations of dynamic experiments on the models are reported.

2. Solving large non-linear models

The large economic models which are currently used for forecasting are
typically both highly simultaneous and non-linear. Because of the
complexity of the models an analytical technique for solving them is
quite impractical. It is common practice therefore to resort to a
numerical algorithm for model solving. Of the two main categories of
algorithms, the Newton and Gauss-Seidel methods, Gauss-Seidel has been
almost universally adopted for application to large models. This is
because it is computationally easier and convergence to a solution is
almost invariably much faster. A disadvantage of the Gauss-Seidel
method, which has not been widely recognised by model builders, however,
is that for a non-linear model it does not converge on the nearest
solution from the initial starting point but it converges on a solution
which is defined by the normalisation and ordering of the equations in
the solution procedure. A non-linear model will in general exhibit
multiple solutions and so when such a model is solved by Gauss-Seidel,
care must be taken to ensure either that the solution is in fact unique
or that if it is not, then the model is converging on a 'desired'
solution.

This section will first outline the Gauss-Seidel solution technique
and indicate how this technique fixes the achieved solution to a
specific one in the multiple solution case. The final part of the
section will report on an exercise carried out to investigate the
importance of ordering and normalisation in the National Institute's
macro economic model.

A. The Gauss-Seidel solution technique

We first state an n equation linear model in the following notation

$$0 = A_i Y_i + B_i X_i \quad , \quad i = 1, \ \ldots , n \tag{1}$$

so that there are n endogenous variables (Y), m exogenous or predetermined variables (X), and A_i, B_i are suitably dimensioned vectors. If n is large and the model is highly simultaneous, it will be hard to solve this sytem analytically. The Gauss-Seidel method proceeds by first assigning starting values to the Y vector. In practice these are often the actual values of the Ys in the previous quarter. The method uses these values to solve the equations, one equation at a time. After each equation is solved the solution value is used to replace the initial guess for that variable in the Y vector. So if $\bar{Y}$ is the initial guess and Y^* is the new value, for any equation

$$Y_j^* = A_K Y_K^* + A_M \bar{Y}_M + B_i X \tag{2}$$

$$K = 1, \ \ldots, J-1$$
$$M = J+i, \ \ldots, n.$$

When the whole model has been solved a check is made according to some convergence criteria on $|\bar{Y}_i - Y_i^*|$; if the two estimates of each Y are satisfactorily close a solution to the model has been found, if not then the Y^* are redefined as $\bar{Y}$ and the process is repeated for another iteration. A more complete exposition of the Gauss-Seidel method may be found in Faddeev and Fadeeva (1963); an early example of its application to econometric models is Norman (1967).

In the linear case described above we know that if a solution exists it is unique and that a solution will exist if all the equations are linearly independent. The Gauss-Seidel technique in practice is not guaranteed to find such a solution even when it exists and is unique. The crucial factors in the success of the Gauss-Seidel approach are the order in which the equations are solved (this is referred to as the ordering of the model) and the normalisation of the equations.

There are a number of variants on the basic Gauss-Seidel technique which have received attention recently. (A good survey of the recent literature may be found in Hughes-Hallett (1981)). If we restate (1) in a more compact form as

$$AY = B \tag{3}$$

Then the iteration procedure may be characterised as

$$Y^{S+1} = GY^S + C \tag{4}$$

with some arbitrary Y^O. The various iteration procedures may be nested within this framework by varying the construction of G and C. If we define $A = (P-Q)$ then $G = P^{-1}Q$ and $C = P^{-1}B$. The way the A matrix is split determines the exact form of the iteration procedure. The simplest procedure is the Jacobi iteration which defines

$$P = \begin{bmatrix} A_{ij} & \text{if } i = J \\ 0 & i \neq J \end{bmatrix} \tag{5}$$

The Gauss-Seidel iteration is produced by setting

$$P = (D-E)$$

where $D = \begin{bmatrix} A_{ij} & \text{if } i = J \\ 0 & \text{if } i \neq J \end{bmatrix}$ and $E = \begin{bmatrix} -A_{ij} & \text{if } i < J \\ 0 & \text{if } i > J \end{bmatrix}$ (6)

The successive overrelaxation iterative method is defined by

$$P = \frac{1}{\alpha} D(I - \alpha D^{-1} E) \tag{7}$$

where D and E are defined above.

A particularly important variant on these techniques allows for the incorporation of a damping factor in the following way

$$Y^{(S+1)} = Y(GY^{(S)} + C) + (1 - Y)Y^S \tag{8}$$

When this is applied to the Gauss-Seidel iteration (6), the resulting technique is often called fast Gauss-Seidel. The importance of this development is that while (4) can only be shown to converge if the spectral radius of G < 1 (see Young, 1971), (8) can be shown to converge on the much weaker assumption that the real parts of the eigenvalues of G are all greater ($Y<0$) or less ($Y>0$) than one (see Hughes-Hallett, 1981).

To make some of these ideas a little clearer, Figure 1 gives a simple two-dimensional example of the Gauss-Seidel technique.

Figure 1.

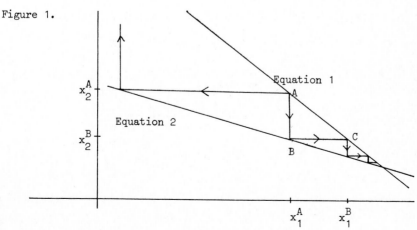

In Figure 1 an initial value is assigned to x_2 of x_2^A and x_1 of x_1^A. The first equation is then solved for x_1 using x_2^A; this yields x_1^A (at point A). This value is used to solve the second equation to yield x_2^B (at point B). The new value of x_2^B is then used to solve the first equation again and this finds x_1^B at point C. The solution procedure then converges in the direction of the arrows towards the solution. But if the equations had been arbitrarily normalised in the reverse way so that from point A equation 2 had been solved first for x_1 the algorithm would have moved away from the solution towards $\bar{A}$ and would have diverged indefinitely.

So far all that has been said is simply the well-known properties of Gauss-Seidel when applied to linear models. In the case of non-linear models the Gauss-Seidel algorithm also has the property of selecting one solution as defined by the model normalisation to the exclusion of other, even nearer, solutions. This is again easy to appreciate by the use of a two-dimensional diagram (Figure 2).

Figure 2.

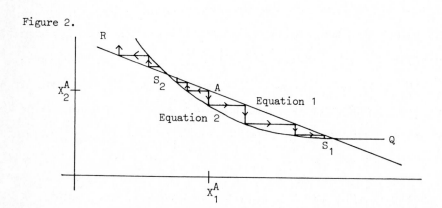

The first point which is made evident by Figure 2 is that as soon as any equation in a model becomes non-linear the possibility exists of there being no solutions, a unique solution, or multiple solutions. The type of non-linearity displayed in Figure 2 is a mixture of linear and log-linear equations which is a typical occurrence in the large models.

If the initial starting point for the Gauss-Seidel technique is point A in Figure 2 and the normalisation is equation 1 solved for x_1, then the convergence will be towards solution S_1 even though there is a closer solution S_2. If the normalisation is reversed, the algorithm will converge on S_2 from any starting point between S_1 and S_2. A normalisation which converges on S_1 will converge from anywhere between S_2 and S_1 and from any point between S_1 and Q, but it will diverge if the starting point is between S_2 and R. So there are some starting points which make a particular solution unattainable for any normalisation. (At R one normalisation converges to S_2, the other diverges.)

In a model which exhibits the possibility of multiple solutions this property of Gauss-Seidel of fixing on one solution is highly desirable. It means that when we carry out simulations of the model we are unlikely to reach different solutions in different time periods; it also means that when we shock the model we will almost certainly track changes in a solution rather than jump from one solution to another, which would give meaningless results.

Gauss-Seidel is therefore a useful technique for practical model use as it provides a high probability of yielding one model solution even in the case where multiple solutions exist. Its main disadvantage, however, is that by 'locking' on one solution it actually hides the existence of all other possible solutions. This means that if model users do not conduct a fairly systematic search for other solutions, then the solution used in forecasting may be an arbitrary one given by the particular ordering and normalisation chosen.

In general terms there are three broad categories of possible solutions. First the solution, even in a non-linear model, may be unique. Second, other solutions may be found, but they may be economically meaningless. Third, there may be more than one solution which could be taken as a viable economic solution to the model. Of these three it is only the final possibility which presents any serious problems to the model user. If there are a number of model solutions within what might be termed the 'reasonable' solution domain, then it is important that the model user is aware of this fact and that a conscious choice has been made as to which solution should be chosen by the Gauss-Seidel algorithm. If such a choice has to be made, a sensible procedure would be to choose that solution which produces the best tracking performance for the model over its estimation period.

This section has examined the broad properties of Gauss-Seidel as a solution technique. It has raised certain questions about model ordering and model solution which ideally should be investigated before any model is used for forecasting. The next section reports on illustrations of these questions using the National Institute's economic model.   The important question is not simply whether more than one solution exists (given the geometry of the model this is almost certainly the case), but if there exists another solution which is achievable from a given starting point, is this solution a rival to the first one?

B.   Reordering the National Institute's Model

Given the proof that Gauss-Seidel will converge if the spectral radius of G is less than unity, the ordering of an equation in a linear system only affects the speed of convergence.   In the case of a non-linear system there is no general convergence proof and it is possible that some orderings could either diverge or even move towards different solutions in the case where multiple solutions exist.   The effect of a large-scale reordering of a big non-linear model is not therefore well understood.   Will the speed of convergence simply deteriorate as different orderings are tried or may divergent orderings or even multiple solutions be discovered?   As a way of investigating these questions a computer program was written to investigate the effect of reordering the National Institute's Model.   The solution program sets up a vector which defines the ordering to be used to solve the model, and a central 'computed GOTO' statement controls the order in which each equation is called in the model coding.   This means that large numbers of orderings can be searched in a single computer job.   However, the large number of equations in the macro model means that it is quite impossible to try all possible orderings.   [There are 274 variables in the National Institute model]. In fact not all equations are treated as separate entities but some blocks of equations are so closely related (e.g. the GDP Identities) that, for ordering purposes, they are treated as a single unit. Nonetheless, there are 131 separate ordering units, most of which are in fact single equations. This produces 6.944 times 10^{219} possible orderings. If it took seven seconds of computer time to search each ordering, a complete check on all the orderings would take something of the order of 2.7 times 10^{211} computer years. Given the enormous number of possible orderings, a complete search is thus totally infeasible. The search pattern of the orderings used must be explained at some length, partly to define the limits of the search which has been undertaken, and partly to show how the search has been focused around the ordering normally used in forecasting and model simulations. It is desirable that the search should be based around the normal model ordering, to investigate the effects of making small or local changes to that ordering.

The ordering search takes the normal ordering pattern as its starting place. It picks the first equation and moves this equation down the ordering one equation at a time until the equation reaches the last position. In addition, after each ordering is tried the exact reverse ordering is also tried. After the first equation reaches the end, the process is repeated with the second equation and so on until all equations have been shuffled. For the purposes of this search a multiple solution is defined as a solution in which any variable differs from the base solution by 2.5 per cent. This is a fairly large margin, but even the normal convergence criteria of 0.02 per cent can give rise to solutions which differ by nearly 1 per cent. For this part of the search, divergence of an ordering is defined as non-convergence after 50 iterations of Gauss-Seidel. This does not mean that the ordering may not converge eventually, but allowing the iteration limit to go above 50 would greatly reduce the number of orderings which it is possible to search. [Below, we report on an extended search of some divergent orderings.]

The shuffling procedure just defined has been applied to the National Institute's economic model, involving some 34,322 different orderings. Of these 15,764 orderings failed to converge within the 50 Gauss-Seidel iteration limit. The remaining 18,558 orderings all converged on the same solution. An investigation of the speed of convergence was also undertaken, and this revealed that the normal model ordering took thirteen Gauss-Seidel iterations to converge while the fastest ordering converged in seven Gauss-Seidel iterations.

While it is impossible to assert that reordering the model cannot locate an alternate solution, other than the basic one, the above investigation covered a wide range of alternatives, and suggests very strongly that reordering does not produce a different solution.

Finally, we are left with the problem of the divergent orderings. It is possible that these orderings are simply divergent orderings. It is also possible that they are actually converging very slowly to the same solution, or that they are converging on a different solution sufficiently far away to be unattainable within the iteration limit. It is obviously not practical to examine all the divergent orderings over an infinite number of iterations. An ordering which appears divergent may well ultimately converge, so an open verdict must be returned on any ordering which cannot be shown to converge. Nonetheless, some of the divergent orderings were subjected to a more extensive search which involved up to 900 Gauss-Seidel iterations. This revealed that of the first 130 divergent orderings found in the initial search, all eventually converged on the same basic solution, so that none of them were truly divergent.

An alternate, or perhaps complementary, line of approach is to investigate the effects of changing the initial starting point on the final solution. In a complex model such as the National Institute's this is not, however, simple. For example, if all the endogenous variables were given an initial value of 10, then the model itself would fail to run simply because 10 would be an absurd value for some of the variables. The approach we have adopted is a more serious alternative, and this scales the starting values of the endogenous variables. That is to say, normally the last quarter's value is taken as the starting value for the current quarter's solution. In the alternative solution this value is multiplied by a scaling factor which effectively moves the starting value along a ray projected from the origin. It was discovered that the model would run with a scaling factor within the range of 0.5-1.5; outside this band the model failed. Starting values were chosen over this range in steps of 0.25 and, in addition, a number of orderings

were tried in combination with these starting values. Once again all
combinations of starting values and orderings which were tried
eventually converged on the same basic solution.

The ordering of a large model is clearly crucial to its rate of
convergence and the efficient use of a Gauss-Seidel type solution
procedure. It does however seem that the reordering of a model is
unlikely either to locate a second solution or to prevent the ultimate
convergence of the solution procedure.

C. Renormalising the National Institute's Model

The problem of the normalisation of the equations of a large model is
not such a difficult one as that of reordering in most cases. This is
simply because most models have a quite definite natural normalisation
in the sense that there is a clear dependent variable in each equation.
Indeed, given the sparseness of many of the equations, re-normalising a
model can be very difficult indeed. Nonetheless, as an illustration of
how this might be done, a sub-block of the National Insitute's Model 7
equations were re-normalised. The block consisted of the following four
equations, in schematic form:

$$E = f(PWMF, X_E)$$
$$PWMF = g(PM, X_{PWMF})$$
$$PM = h(M, X_{PM})$$
$$M = i(E, X_M)$$

where E is the effective exchange rate, PWMF is wholesale prices, PM is
import prices, M is the value of imports and X_J are the other elements
in each equation.

These four equations were re-normalised so that:

$$PWMF = f^{-1} (E, X_E)$$
$$PM = g^{-1} (PWMF, X_{PWMF})$$
$$M = h^{-1} (PM, X_{PM})$$
$$E = i^{-1} (M, X_M)$$

The model was then solved with these four equations replacing the
original four.   Under this condition the model diverged and eventually
failed.   So, as we would expect from the earlier arguments, re-
normalising the model has a profound effect, actually rendering the
solution procedure unworkable.

3.   Solving non-linear models with consistent and rational expectations

Following the seminal paper by Lucas (1976), it has become increasingly
evident that one major weakness in conventional macro models lies in the
modelling of expectations.   As Currie (1985) has pointed out, when we
model the economy we are faced with a problem which is almost unknown in
the natural sciences;   that the individual elements of the economy are
actually intelligent agents, able to alter their modes of behaviour if
they expect a change in the economic climate (either government policy
or some exogenous external shock).   This important feature of the real
world cannot, in principle, be modelled by relying solely on backward-
looking behaviour (of the adaptive expectations type for example).
Instead we must explicitly identify the informed nature of expectations
about the future.   Earlier chapters have described how this problem may
be confronted when estimating dynamic equations.   In this section, we
turn to the allied problem of deriving model solutions with rational, or
model consistent, expectations.

Formally, when we assume rational expectations in a large model, this implies that the expected outcome and the model's forecast of that outcome coincide. Such an assumption renders the solution techniques outlined in the previous section inoperable and a new set of solution procedures have to be developed. We describe some solution procedures below. Then the problem of terminal conditions will be considered, and a number of practical alternatives will be explored.

A. Rational expectations and non-linear models

Before embarking on the details of model simulation and solution, there is an important conceptual problem which must be considered. The theoretical literature on rational expectations has concentrated almost entirely on small linear models. Within this framework it is accepted, almost without real consideration, that a rational individual will be interested in forming an estimate of the expected values of all relevant variables. That is to say, he will use an unbiased estimate of the conditional mean of the probability distribution. Now as the deterministic forecast of a linear model with normally distributed error processes coincides with the conditional mean of the probability distribution of the model, the deterministic model solution may be used to convey this assumption. Unfortunately this is not the case for a non-linear model. The deterministic forecast of a stochastic non-linear model is not the mean of the probability distribution of the model. If the model represents a non-linear mapping from the error terms to the endogenous variables then the deterministic forecast may have no well-defined place on the probability distribution. This train of reasoning leads us towards carrying out stochastic simulations to estimate the

mean forecast of the model. There is, however, a further complication.
The expected values of a non-linear model do not comprise a single
coherent forecast, in the sense that the implicit, or explicit, non-
linear identities in the model will not be maintained by the expected
values.   Thus the expected real exchange rate will not equal the
expected nominal exchange rate deflated by the expected relative price.

The empirical rational expectations macro models which exist at
present are not fully rational as described above.   Possibly a more
descriptive term would be to describe them as consistent expectations
models.   These models are solved on the basis that all plans are made
using values of future variables which are consistent with the model's
solution (see e.g. the Liverpool model. Minford et al (1984)).   The
relationship between this procedure and the assumption of rational
expectations is perhaps tenuous.

These problems are perhaps most easily presented by stating a
general non-linear model in the following form. Let

$$Y_t = f(Y_i, Y_j^e, X_k, B, \Omega) \tag{9}$$

$$i = 0, \ldots, t , j = t+1, \ldots, T , k = 0, \ldots, T$$

where Y is a set of N endogenous variables, with Y_i being lagged
endogenous, and Y_j^e future expected endogenous variables.   X is a set of
M exogenous variables, B is the full parameter set of the model and Ω
is the variance-covariance matrix of all stochastic terms in the model
(both parameters and error terms).   In traditional macromodels the terms

in Y_j^e, the future expected endogenous variables, may be viewed as having been substituted out of the model by some explicit sub-model. So if

$$Y_j^e = g(Y_i, X_k, Y, \phi) \tag{10}$$

$$i = 0, \ldots, t \;, \; j = t+1, \ldots, T \;, \; k = 0, \ldots, T.$$

where Y are parameters and ϕ is a covariance matrix of stochastic terms, then we may substitute this function into equation (9) to eliminate the future terms in endogenous variables. The model may then be solved in the traditional way. However, this procedure fails to explicitly identify the expectations formation procedure so there is a loss of estimation efficiency. Further, if, due to some regime change, there is a shift in either the functional form of (10) or its parameters, then as these parameters are lost in the combined reduced form, all the parameters of the backward-looking model may change. However, if we deal explicitly with equations (9) and (10), any change in expectations formations mechanism is isolated in (10) and the structure of (9) will be invariant to this form of structural change.

Perhaps the simplest form of solution to this problem would be to derive an explicit model for expectations formation (10), and then use a complete structural model in the form of (9) and (10) together. Certainly if we had a good idea of how expectations are actually formed the ideal situation would consist of explicit models of expectations formation. However, in the absence of such information, a second best assumption is often taken to be the rational expectations hypothesis. Under this assumption it is assumed that expectations will coincide with the actual model forecast. According to this assumption,

$$Y_h^e = f(Y_i, Y_j^e, X_k, \beta, \Omega) \tag{11}$$

$$h = i, \ldots, T, \quad i = 0, \ldots, h, \quad j = h+1, \ldots, T, \quad k = 0, \ldots, T$$

In fact most implementations on large models do not fully conform to (11) as the solution is carried out in a deterministic fashion so that Ω is ignored. As already stressed, in the case of a non-linear model the deterministic forecast will differ from the mean (or expected value) of the model's density function. So under the REH assumption the usual procedure is to define

$$Y_h^e = f(Y_i, Y_j^e, X_k, \beta) \tag{12}$$

$$h = 1, \ldots, T, \quad i = 0, \ldots, h, \quad j = h+1, \ldots, T, \quad k = 1, \ldots, T$$

We will call an explicit expectations mechanism such as (10) an expectations model solution, a deterministic model solution such as (12) a consistent solution, and a stochastic solution such as (11) a fully rational solution.

Carrying out a specific explicit expectations model solution involves no special problems, the standard model solution programs are quite able to cope with these models. The problems raised by consistent solution, however, have been the subject of much recent attention in the literature, and we will describe some of these next.

B. Consistent solutions

There are a number of techniques used for solving models with consistent expectations.   The first to be used widely was the Fair (1979), Anderson (1979) iterative technique.   A more recent approach using optimal control is the Holly and Zarrop (1983) penalty function method.

An approach from the engineering literature is the multiple shooting technique (Lipton et al., 1982).   Finally there is the iterative technique outlined in Hall (1985).   All these techniques address the same problem, although the relationship between them is not always clear.   This section will show how they can all be viewed as special cases of the Hall approach, each being a particularly efficient technique in certain circumstances.

For this we will discuss the problem of model solution within an explicitly linear framework.   This is done simply so that matrix notation may be used, and none of the conclusions to be drawn are dependent on the assumption of linearity.

We begin by stating a general linear deterministic simultaneous model as

$$\alpha(L)Y_t = \beta(L)X_t \qquad\qquad (13)$$

where $\alpha(L)$ and $\beta(L)$ are matrix lag polynomials, Y is a vector of N endogenous variables and X is a vector of M exogenous variables. Now if we want to solve this model over a fixed time period, 1 ... T, we may restate the solution problem in a more explicit framework as

$$AY' = BX' + CZ' \qquad\qquad (14)$$

where Z is a suitable set of initial and terminal conditions. It is worth actually writing out in full the lefthand side of (14)

$$
\begin{bmatrix}
\alpha & \alpha(L^{-1}), \alpha(L^{-2}) & & & \alpha(L^{-(T-1)}) \\
\alpha(L) & \alpha & \alpha(L^{-1}) & & \cdot \\
\alpha(L^2), & \alpha(L) & \alpha & & \cdot \\
\alpha(L^3) & & \alpha & & \cdot \\
\alpha(L^4) & & & \alpha & \\
\cdot & & & \cdot & \\
\cdot & & & & \cdot \\
\alpha(L^{T-1}) & & \cdot & \cdot & \cdot & \alpha
\end{bmatrix}
\begin{bmatrix}
y_1 \\
y_2 \\
y_3 \\
\cdot \\
\cdot \\
\cdot \\
\cdot \\
y_T
\end{bmatrix}
\qquad (15)
$$

If the full A matrix is actually lower triangular, having only zeros above the leading diagonal, then the model contains no consistent expectation terms, and it may be solved in the usual way, one period at a time. However, when the upper triangle is not empty, one of the special approaches mentioned earlier must be employed.

The approach outlined in Hall (1985) is simply to deal directly with the equation system set out in (14) and (15). So we may normalise the model by defining $A = D - E$ (see section 2A), and then use any of the standard iterative techniques (Gauss-Seidel, Fast Gauss-Seidel, etc.) to solve the model.

Both the Fair-Anderson and the penalty function techniques make use of a separate split in the A matrix, before the normalisation procedure is made. Both techniques begin by defining $A = (P - U)$, where P is the principal diagonal and all the lower triangular elements of A and U are minus the upper triangular elements of A. We can then rewrite (14) as

$$PY' = UY' + BX' + CZ' \tag{16}$$

This isolates all the lead terms and they can then be treated separately.   This is done by defining a new vector, Y^e, where in solution $Y^e = Y$ by consistency.   The model may then be stated

$$PY' = UY^{e'} + BX' + CZ' \tag{17}$$

The Fair-Anderson procedure begins by setting arbitrary values for Y^e, solving (17), as a model without consistent expectations, and then updating the estimate of Y^e with the solution values.   This procedure iterates until $Y = Y^e$.

The penalty function method proceeds in a similar fashion to achieve consistency by viewing the variables Y^e as control variables and minimising a function $\Omega = \Sigma(Y - Y^e)^2$ using standard optimal control algorithms.   This function has a minimum when $Y = Y^e$ and consistency is achieved.

The advantage of both these techniques is that the actual model solution procedure is reduced to a period-by-period problem without any consistent expectation terms entering.   The added cost of this is obviously the extra iteration procedure in the Fair-Anderson technique, and the cost of the optimal control exercise in the case of the penalty function approach.   In effect, both very sensible procedures to adopt, providing the upper triangle of A is very sparse.   As A becomes more dense, the saving remains much the same, while the costs can rise enormously.

The relationship between (15) and the multiple shooting techniques
is a little less obvious; any of the above techniques would proceed by
normalising the model on the principle diagonal and proceeding from
there. The multiple shooting technique however normalises the model on
any lead terms first. In terms of (15) this is rather like moving any
rows with non-zero upper triangle elements down the model until the non-
zero elements are on the diagonal. The model is then normalised on this
new leading diagonal. This leads to some variables being determined
twice. The initial period variables are then chosen so as to make the
terminal values of the endogenous variables conform with the terminal
conditions.

A simple example makes this more clear. Suppose we have an
equation

$$E_t = E_{t+1} + \alpha X_t \tag{18}$$

We renormalise this equation to give

$$E_{t+1} = E_t - \alpha X_t \tag{19}$$

This equation can now be used to solve the whole path of E_t, given E_0
and X_t. So E_0 is chosen so that E_T, the terminal value, is equal to the
terminal condition.

The advantage of the multiple shooting technique is that it emphasises the importance of model normalisation and suggests ways in which the normalisation can be improved. The disadvantage is that it is only very special cases where renormalisation is actually possible. If a single equation can be renormalised as a single unit, as in the case of (18), then the approach is quite straightforward. However, most cases would involve renormalising whole blocks of the model and this would not generally be feasible. An employment equation which includes expected output cannot be renormalised as a single unit for example.

Examples

Little attention has been paid to the solution of non-linear models on the basis of fully rational expectations as we defined them above. Fair (1984) mentions the problem, and points out that the expectations variables must be updated using stochastic simulations, to give an estimate of the expectation of the model, rather than deterministic model solutions. To recap, there are three types of solution: an expectations model solution, where an extrapolative model of expectations formation is used, a consistent solution based on the model's deterministic solution, and a rational solution which uses the stochastic expectations of the variables.

Table 1 provides a comparative example of all three solution procedures on a version of NIESR Model 8 which contains sixteen future expected variables. These variables occur in the three stockbuilding and three employment equations. For the expectations model solution simple fourth-order auto-regression equations were used. Expectations under this assumption are therefore formed from a simple univariate time series model.

The three solutions methods provide quite different sets of results, as we would expect, although they are all reasonably close to the actual path of the economy. Purely on a basis of tracking performance there does not seem to be a strong argument for preferring one procedure over another.

Table 1. The three model solution procedure

QCE	Actuals	1	2	3
8102	34383	34544	34550	34985
8103	34297	34526	34548	35006
8104	34421	34584	34612	34698
8201	34263	34509	34526	34678
8202	34605	34499	34552	34958
8203	34949	34928	35402	35393
8204	35573	35137	35302	35389
8301	35505	35452	35682	35795
QDK				
8102	8818	8973	8977	9133
8103	8846	8866	8868	9028
8104	9001	8872	8873	9022
8201	9443	9289	9292	9513
8202	9220	9178	9181	9452
8203	9600	9407	9412	9716
8204	9643	9427	9436	9751
8301	9985	10067	10066	10378

Table 1 (cont)

QEX	Actuals	1	2	3
8102	15279	15385	15385	15370
8103	15659	15743	15743	15744
8104	15824	15540	15540	15546
8201	15701	15507	15507	15528
8202	15948	15695	15695	15694
8203	15246	15729	15727	15786
8204	15768	15746	15743	15819
8301	15777	15918	15911	16008

QM				
8102	13378	13644	13685	13911
8103	14807	13613	13647	14019
8104	14475	13461	13465	13751
8201	14357	13925	13933	14273
8202	14793	13868	13940	14410
8203	14187	14333	14486	14984
8204	14227	14522	14745	15157
8301	14686	14704	14849	15273

UNEMP				
8102	2417	2501	2486	2515
8103	2555	2760	2720	2768
8104	2629	3074	3037	3093
8201	2688	3249	3197	3247
8202	2773	3363	3262	3295
8203	2866	3358	3188	3196
8204	2949	3382	3116	3098
8301	3026	3372	3063	3015

QGDP				
8102	48406	48365	48462	48684
8103	48297	48880	48927	49233
8104	49207	49125	49119	49270
8201	49593	49305	49323	49592
8202	49668	49587	49699	50062
8203	49397	49868	50075	50421
8204	50724	50285	50551	50742
8301	51923	51816	51854	52031

CPI				
8102	110.2	108.2	108.2	104.1
8103	113.0	111.3	111.3	107.1
8104	115.5	114.0	114.0	111.8
8201	118.7	116.1	116.2	114.0
8202	120.2	116.0	116.2	110.5
8203	121.8	116.8	117.1	111.6
8204	123.4	117.1	117.8	114.7
8301	125.5	116.8	117.9	115.2

Table 1 (cont)

1) The expectations model solution

2) The consistent expectations solution

3) The rational expectations solution

QCE = Real Consumers Expenditure   QDM = Real Investment

QEX = Real exports   QM = Real Imports

UNEMP = Unemployment   CPI = Consumer Price Index

C. Specifying terminal conditions for a model with consistent expectations

Before it is possible to solve a model which involves future
expectations in a consistent way, a suitable set of terminal conditions
must be supplied.   There has for some time been confusion over the
distinction between terminal conditions and transversality conditions,
with some researchers suggesting that the two are formally equivalent.
We will argue here that in fact this analogy is false and that in
practice terminal conditions can have no choice theoretic backing but
must ultimately be 'ad hoc'.

The proper analogy for an empirical macro model appears to be that
we may interpret terminal conditions as transversality conditions if we
were to solve the model over an infinite horizon.   This is obviously
impractical.

A better interpretation of the terminal conditions is that they should force the model solution to be on the infinite time horizon solution path at period T (where T is the finite solution period). So if we define $\bar{Y}$ to be the solution path of the model solved over an infinite time horizon subject to a set of transversality conditions, then if we solve the model over the finite period 1, ..., T subject to $Y_T = \bar{Y}_T$, the finite solution Y^1, i = 1,..., T, will be equal to the infinite time solution path for the first T periods. So we may achieve part of the infinite time horizon solution path without solving the model to infinity.

The obvious difficulty here is that we cannot know what $\bar{Y}$ is until an infinite model solution has been achieved. However, bearing in mind this interpretation of the terminal conditions, we are able to make a more precise interpretation of the various suggestions which have been made. In particular the Minford and Matthews (1978) suggestion that equilibrium values should be used, is based on the idea that they are using a market clearing model which quickly moves towards its equilibrium. So after a few time periods it is assumed the infinite time solution path should be the steady-state equilibrium. Similarly the Holly and Beenstock (1980) suggestion of projecting constant growth rates as a terminal condition may be seen as suggesting that the infinite time solution path is characterised by steady growth rates. The Fair (1979) idea of testing the terminal condition by extending the solution period, until no significant change occurs in the early part of the solution period, may also be seen as a way of fixing the terminal conditions on the infinite time solution path.

In the Institute model we have four optional forms for the terminal condition. These are:

1)   Setting the terminal conditions to exogenous data values.

2)   Setting the terminal conditions so that they lie on the previous year's growth path.

3)   Setting the terminal conditions so that the levels of the variables are projected flat.

4)   Setting the terminal conditions to project a constant rate of growth from the final quarter of the solution period.

Table 2 gives details of model solutions carried out under the four different options.   It would seem that the form of the terminal conditions can have quite important consequences for the overall solution path.   Although, as Fair suggests, the early parts of the run are not substantially affected by the form of end point condition selected.

The picture is rather different when a forward-looking exchange rate equation is added to the model. (See Chapter 1 for an account of this model).   In this case it proved almost impossible to solve the model except with fixed terminal conditions.   It now seems that it may not, in practice, be possible to solve a model with certain forms of forward-looking equations with anything other than a fixed terminal condition.   The reason for this may be seen if we set out a linear model using matrix notation as

Table 2. Four sets of terminal conditions

QGDP	1	2	3	4	Actual	QS	1	2	3	4	Actual
7901	49,064	49,065	49,064	49,064	48,838		69,688	69,689	69,688	69,688	70,166
7902	51,306	51,308	51,307	51,307	51,163		70,082	70,085	70,083	70,083	70,395
7903	50,360	50,362	50,360	50,361	51,021		70,309	70,315	70,310	70,311	71,435
7904	50,320	50,324	50,321	50,321	50,397		70,429	70,440	70,432	70,433	71,754
8001	50,928	50,935	50,930	50,931	49,769		70,460	70,481	70,466	70,467	71,253
8002	50,374	50,386	50,377	50,378	49,233		70,396	70,434	70,406	70,409	71,112
8003	50,374	50,394	50,379	50,381	48,837		70,317	70,381	70,333	70,338	69,917
8004	50,415	50,447	50,423	50,426	48,803		70,242	70,352	70,270	70,279	68,518
8101	50,386	50,445	50,401	50,406	49,336		70,191	70,382	70,240	70,255	67,508
8102	50,578	50,683	50,605	50,613	48,406		70,156	70,490	70,241	70,268	66,179
8103	50,982	51,154	51,026	51,040	48,297		70,122	70,694	70,268	70,314	65,997
8104	50,755	51,013	50,818	50,841	49,207		70,071	70,995	70,302	70,379	65,863
8201	50,826	51,392	50,973	51,015	49,593		69,929	71,633	70,361	70,497	65,921
8202	50,857	51,819	51,110	51,185	49,668		69,683	72,684	70,449	70,683	66,152
8203	51,134	52,495	51,470	51,590	49,397		69,379	74,170	70,569	70,958	65,532
8204	51,459	53,173	51,837	52,016	50.724		69,063	76,036	70,702	71,313	64,840

QGDP = Real GDP   QS = Real stock levels

Table 2. (cont)

EMP	1	2	3	4	Actual	CPI	1	2	3	4	Actual
7901	22,742	22,742	22,742	22,742	34,063		79.3	79.3	79.3	79.3	80.4
7902	22,855	22,855	22,855	22,855	23,138		81.6	81.6	81.6	81.6	83.0
7903	22,902	22,903	22,902	22,902	23,178		84.2	84.2	84.2	84.2	88.6
7904	22,891	22,893	22,891	22,892	23,186		86.8	86.8	86.8	86.8	91.5
8001	22,939	22,941	22,939	22,939	23,091		88.1	88.1	88.1	88.1	95.2
8002	22,910	22,915	22,911	22,911	22,950		90.4	90.4	90.4	90.4	99.3
8003	22,975	22,984	22,978	22,978	22,672		93.2	93.2	93.2	93.2	101.7
8004	22,993	22,008	22,997	22,998	22,366		95.9	95.9	95.9	95.9	104.0
8101	22,923	22,949	22,930	22,932	22,095		98.3	98.3	98.3	98.3	106.5
8102	22,914	22,960	22,926	22,930	21,845		100.6	100.6	100.6	100.6	110.2
8103	22,956	23,035	22,976	22,983	21,718		104.0	104.0	104.0	104.0	113.0
8104	22,902	23,032	22,936	22,947	21,680		108.3	108.5	108.4	108.4	115.5
8201	22,905	23,161	22,982	23,003	21,627		111.9	112.2	112.0	112.0	117.7
8202	22,878	23,343	23,029	23,068	21,498		115.2	115.6	115.3	115.4	120.2
8203	22,852	23,607	23,098	23,167	21,291		119.3	120.3	119.6	119.7	211.8
8204	22,876	23,997	23,232	23,347	21,213		123.3	125.2	124.0	124.1	123.4

EMP = Employment   CPI = Consumer price index

$$AY' = BX + U$$

where Y is a stacked vector of N endogenous variables for T periods $(Y_{i1} \ldots Y_{iT}, i = 1, \ldots, N)$, A is an NT x NT matrix of parameters, X is a similar stacked vector of MT exogenous variables and B is a similar NT x MT vector of parameters. If Y_T includes a suitable set of terminal conditions then the model may be solved to give

$$Y' = A^{-1}BX + A^{-1}U$$

if A is non-singular. This means that the rows of A must not be linear combinations of each other. However, with many rational equations such linear combinations may easily be created. To take a simple example suppose we have an equation

$$E_t = E_{t+1} + BX_t \tag{20}$$

and we use the terminal condition

$$E_T = E_{T-1} \tag{21}$$

In matrix notation we may express these two equations as

$$\begin{bmatrix} 1 & -1 \\ -1 & 1 \end{bmatrix} \begin{bmatrix} E_{T-1} \\ E_T \end{bmatrix} = \begin{bmatrix} B \\ 0 \end{bmatrix} (X_{T-1})$$

Clearly the A matrix here is singular, and so (21) will not provide a suitably strong condition to allow a solution. It is also true that for equations like (20) the Fair suggestion of extending the solution horizon becomes unworkable. We can express (20) as

$$E_t = \sum_{i=t}^{T-1} BX_i + E_T \qquad \text{for any } T>t,$$

so that no matter how far in the future the terminal date occurs, its effect on E_t will not decline. Equations such as (20) with unit forward roots are unfortunately not uncommon in exchange rate and pricing theory generally.

D. The use of models in forecasting

Forecasting with an econometric model is widely regarded as something akin to art, and mechanical forecasts given by the unadulterated dynamic solution of an estimated econometric model are not attempted. Such mechanical solutions are, typically, the preserve of textbook accounts of predicting with an econometric model. Practical forecasting, it is often urged, must eschew mere mechanical procedures. According to Klein 'It is performance in repeated forecasting of a wide spectrum of economic magnitudes that really puts econometric methods to the supreme test, and elaborate forecasting procedures have to be employed in order to meet this challenge.' (Klein, 1983, p. 165; our emphasis added). The sort of elaboration - in effect augmenting the dynamic solution of a model - which Klein refers to is well known. It includes correction for systematic behaviour in single equation residuals, data revisions, actual and anticipated changes in legislation, and non-modelled effects such as those of the miners' strike. All of these examples suggest that the pure mechanical solution of a model could be improved by intervention.

The intention of this section is to construct a counter-argument to this view. We will argue that a model which is itself a good representation of the data can be used to produce acceptable purely mechanical forecasts. In support of this claim we will use the National Institute's Models 6 and 8 to recreate a set of recent forecasts abstracting from all 'ad hoc' model intervention. We will use exactly the same values for the exogenous variables as were used in the production of the published forecasts. The objective is to see how reasonable the resulting forecasts would have been if we had simply relied on the model in the production of the forecast.

There are a number of points of interest in this exercise. First, given that Wallis (1984) has shown that the NIESR model is one of the most clearly data coherent models of those in use in the UK, it is of interest to see if the model can meet such a challenge in a satisfactory manner. Second, in Wallis (op. cit.) a start has been made in terms of considering the effects of removing 'ad hoc' adjustments from models used for a published forecast. This section extends this work by considering the exercise for a succession of published forecasts. Finally, we make a number of points about the construction of the model-based forecasts which are of some importance.

(a) Model intervention and published forecasts

At the present time all the published forecasts in the UK which are model-based are produced with a considerable degree of intervention. Perhaps the most often cited justification for model intervention is the problem caused by data revision. Data is continually being revised, and it is quite impossible to continually re-estimate a large model on the latest set of data. So in general, while a model will have an expected value of zero for its error term on its estimated data set, this need not be true with respect to a more recent revised data set. Furthermore, there may be a reason for intervention owing to ancillary information which, though not part of the model, is related to variables in the model. The most common example here is survey and anticipations data; investment intentions, for example, are widely used. Both of these broad types of intervention are extensively practised, are defensible procedures and, the evidence shows, improve actual forecasting performance (Klein, 1983, p. 166).

Less justified, but equally widely practised, are subjectively based interventions. Among such interventions are those made to ensure a particular outcome for an endogenous variable because this is thought more 'acceptable'. Although such intervention may be made on grounds of hunch (or probably with an eye on what other forecasters are producing), one subtle justification for this might be that econometric models are invariably estimated by single equation methods. Thus dynamic model solutions may be altered in the belief that the model is misspecified, and, in particular, does not allow for possible inter-equation effects.

Whilst the former set of interventions may be regarded as justifiable, and the latter less so, the important point about interventions of either sort is their bearing upon the possibility of treating forecasts as a _test_ (possibly the ultimate test) of the realism of a model. Again according to Klein, ex-ante forecast performance is the 'bottom line of applied econometrics' in that 'econometric models are unfailingly judged by their predictive ability in genuine forecast situations'.   Indeed he goes on to argue that an 'acceptable' forecasting performance is a sine-qua-non of an econometric model, if this is to be taken seriously for use in evaluating policy alternatives and assessing underlying theory (Klein, 1983, p. 164).   Two absolutely crucial things are evident from this.   The first is that if forecast performance can be used to test anything, it is the forecasting activity as a whole including the solution to the model, residual and other interventions, and exogenous variable forecasts.   This prompts the question of how forecasts may be used to gauge the reliability of the model as such (and the economic theories on which it is based).   As a qualification to the present discussion, it is important to recognise the multiple activity involved in the use of econometric models.   Models are used to produce forecasts.   But, because they are structural models based on behavioural propositions about economic agents, they are also used to provide insights into the responses of the economy to policy changes and other shocks.   Ideally, there would be a close correspondence between these two activities; a good model would not only forecast accurately, but would give reliable information about the consequences of policy changes.   In the present, far from perfect, state of econometric modelling things are more complicated.   At one extreme, it is possible that a model based on weak theoretical/behavioural propositions, could nonetheless forecast tolerably well, with the judicious use of interventions in that model's dynamic solution.   In this case it would be a mistake to infer, from the forecasting record alone, that the model offered reliable guidance on the effects of changes in economic policy for example, or on the response of the economy to shocks.

(b) Model based forecasts

So far we have mentioned 'model based' without defining precisely what this term means. Consider a general statement of a non-linear model

$$F (Y, X, \Theta, e) = 0 \tag{22}$$

where Y is a set of contemporary and lagged values of endogenous variables, X is a set of known exogenous variables, Θ is a set of parameters assumed also to be known and e is a set of single equation error terms assumed to be normally distributed $N(\emptyset, \Sigma)$ (where Σ is the covariance matrix of the error terms).

Within the context of equation (22) it is not entirely clear what the pure model based forecast is. We distinguish three alternatives and the later numerical work will present parallel results for all three. These are:

(i) The zero residual deterministic forecast

This is given simply by taking the estimation assumption of a zero mean residual and ignoring the existence of the covariance matrix of the error terms. This form of solution is defined by

$$F (Y, X, \Theta, 0) = 0 \tag{23}$$

(ii) The constant residual deterministic forecast

We argued in section 2 that, if only because of data revisions, the actual expected value of the equation error terms will not be zero. Given this, it seems that (23) is actually a rather naive concept of a pure model solution as it ignores the fact that the error process is an integral part of the model. Given this fact, we propose, as our second mode of model solution, a structure where the error terms are set at their average value for the last eight quarters of the available data. This is still a very simple rule, and more complex ones are clearly possible, but it has the advantage of adjusting the scaling of the model to the latest data revisions. Formally we express this mode as

$$F(Y, X, \Theta, \bar{e}) = 0, \qquad\qquad\qquad (24)$$

$$\bar{e} = \frac{1}{8} \sum_{i=0}^{7} e_{-i}, \qquad\qquad\qquad (25)$$

where the initial period of the solution is 1.

(iii) The stochastic solution

The last two solution modes have ignored the fact that the error terms are not known with certainty. If the model were linear this would not be a damaging omission as the deterministic forecast of either (21) or (22) would coincide with the model's expected value under a suitable assumption about the mean of e. In the case of a non-linear model this will no longer generally be true. The deterministic model solution has no well defined location on the density function of the endogenous variables. As argued in Wallis (1985) and Hall (1984) the deterministic model solution may be quite misleading as a guide to the location of the centre of the density function. The third solution mode uses stochastic simulation (described in chapter 6) to calculate an estimate of the expected value of the model, conditional on the error terms being distributed as $N(\bar{e}, \Sigma)$ where $\bar{e}$ is defined in (25). So we may express this as

$$E\ [F\ (Y,\ X,\ \Theta,\ \bar{v}) = o]\ ,\quad v \sim N\ (\bar{e},\ \Sigma) \tag{26}$$

where E is the mathematical expectation operator.

Along with an estimate of the mean of the model's density function, stochastic simulations also provide an estimate of the higher moments of the distribution. These are not without interest in their own right, but they are not the central issue here, and we will not report estimates of the variance or other moments. From the point of view of this section, the central interest of the stochastic runs is that we know the mean of the density function to be a good measure of location, even in the case of highly skewed distributions. If the mean is close to the deterministic runs, this shows that using the, much simpler, deterministic solution method does not sacrifice any important information. However, if we find this not to be the case then the argument for deterministic model runs may be considerably weakened.

(c) Practical details of the model solutions

The published forecasts which are analysed here are the August 1983 and November February and May, 1985 forecasts. The first of these is reported, because it is possible to compare forecasts with outturns.

The remaining examples all are based on a model with rational expectation formation.

In implementing the various solution modes (i), (ii) and (iii) above, a number of practical details must be dealt with, and explained. The solutions presented in the next section will be true ex-ante solutions in that they are based on the actual forecasts of the exogenous processes (X) which were used to produce the forecast published in the National Institute Economic Review. The relevant published forecast will also be presented with each set of solutions for comparative purposes. Where specific adjustments were made because of some special, well defined, factor, such as the miners' strike, we have maintained the treatment used in the published forecast even where this turned out to be quite wrong. All other 'ad hoc' model interventions have been removed and substituted with the error processes generated by (i), (ii) and (iii). Where endogenous sections of the model were exogenised in the published forecast we have re-endogenised the relevant sections in our model based runs. We recognise that some researchers might argue that such interventions represent policy choices of the government. Nonetheless, whenever there is any doubt at all about the underlying motive of the forecaster, we have chosen to treat the intervention as 'ad hoc' and to remove it.

Finally, we note some of the details of the various stochastic runs. The error terms used in the generation of the stochastic replication have been drawn from a multivariate normal distribution with mean e (defined in (25)). They have been constructed using the McCarthy algorithm which takes a vector of univariate normal random numbers (in this case generated by the Box-Mueller algorithm), and transforms them into a vector of multivariate random shocks which asymptotically approximate the model's true error covariance matrix. Further details of these techniques may be found in Chapter 6.

(d) Numerical results

Overview

In evaluating the results in tables 3-6 one is faced with the problem that there is no unambiguous and simple way of describing them. No summary statistic exists which shows closeness, nor is there any objective test of reasonableness. Any evaluation must therefore be somewhat subjective. Nonetheless, we believe that the overwhelming conclusion which the detailed results suggest is that any of the three definitions of mechanical model solutions could easily have been presented as an acceptable forecast. The important feature we would stress here is that, when used in a reasonably pure form, the model has not produced any sets of numbers which could immediately be dismissed as absurd. This result contrasts strongly with the more generally held view, set out earlier, that large models, when used mechanically, produce obviously unacceptable forecasts. And it supports the finding of Wallis (1984) that the use of a common set of exogenous variables with mechanical residual adjustments produced comparatively little change in the NIESR published forecast. This result was not found to be true of any of the other UK modelling group forecasts examined by the

Macroeconomic Modelling Bureau.

Two things seem to follow from this. The first is that these published forecasts seem, in a relative sense, to be less dependent upon particular forms of intervention (residual and otherwise) and more dependent upon its econometric model. The second point concerns the usefulness of mechanical versus judgemental forecast comparisons. It is widely believed not only that a variety of interventions are an indispensible part of producing a 'good' forecast, but that the forecast itself is much better as a result. McNees (1975) for example compared the forecast performance of 'mechanical' forecasts produced by Fair with non-mechanical large model forecasts, and found decisively in favour of the non-mechanical approach. These comparisons seem fraught with problems, not least being that the models themselves differ from each other, so the comparisons are not merely between mechanical and non-mechanical methods of forecasting. It would seem necessary, at least, to conduct the exercise with mechanical and non-mechanical ex ante solutions of the same model as we have done. The performance of each may then be evaluated ex post once sufficient time has elapsed.

August 1983

We are particularly interested in an analysis of a forecast made in August 1983 since this allows full comparison with data outturns over the entire forecast period. This forecast was made using a previous vintage of the National Institute's model, [Model 6, described in Britton (ed.) (1983)].

The results in table 3 make the same assumptions as in the published forecast for policy settings and exogenous variables. Qualitatively the results are broadly similar, in that we conclude that all three model runs produce 'sensible' answers. (It should be noted that the need to use the 1975 price-based data means that the 'actuals' must be derived by scaling the last available 1975 based data by the growth rates obtained from the 1980 based data.)

Broadly speaking, the results suggest that if the model had been run without subjective intervention, then the overall shape of the forecast would have changed to give somewhat higher output and lower inflation. As can be seen, this accords well with what actually transpired.

All three model runs produce higher GDP forecasts than that originally published, the constant residual case (ii) producing an end of period value of 111.3. For the stochastic case the figure was 111.8 and the zero residual simulation is the most optimistic at 114.6. All model runs are closer to the outturn than the published forecast.

Turning to total consumption, all three runs perform well and track the increases that occurred. On the trade side, the export profiles are broadly similar, whereas the rise in imports, not captured by the published forecast, is tracked reasonably well by the automatic residual and stochastic runs.

Table 3. August 1983 Forecast

0   Is the published forecast
i   Deterministic solution with zero resiuals
ii   Deterministic solution with constant residuals equal to the average of the last eight quarters
iii The expected value of stochastic solution to case ii
iv   Outturns

Date	GDP					C					I				
	0	i	ii	iii	iv	0	i	ii	iii	iv	0	i	ii	iii	iv
1983															
2	108.0	108.0	108.0	108.0	107.5	18760	18760	18760	18761	18665	5071	5061	5066	5095	4995
3	109.0	111.5	109.0	108.9	109.3	18690	18667	18733	18630	19002	5141	5125	5138	5146	5088
4	109.8	113.7	110.3	110.2	110.5	18829	19056	18956	18794	19060	5177	5148	5171	5167	5220
1984															
1	110.1	113.2	109.7	110.0	110.4	18806	18679	18717	18666	18967	5236	5210	5222	5214	5632
2	110.3	114.4	110.3	111.1	110.3	18772	18937	18877	19007	19183	5259	5247	5270	5238	5409
3	110.3	114.0	110.3	111.1	110.8	18701	18932	18956	19007	19113	5257	5266	5270	5247	5385
4	110.6	115.0	111.3	111.8	111.7	18857	19179	19179	19158	19333	5249	5269	5277	5259	5361
1985															
1	110.4	114.6	111.3	111.8	112.9	18759	19066	19082	19137	19230	5258	5297	5314	5300	5520

Table 3. (cont)

Date	E 0	E i	E ii	E iii	E iv	WS 0	WS i	WS ii	WS iii	WS iv	M 0	M i	M ii	M iii	M iv
1983															
2	8103	8103	8103	8081	8120	113.8	263.1	229.0	158.8	-195	9253	9254	9254	9330	9288
3	8307	8383	8332	8335	8047	174.2	397.0	265.7	161.2	253	9301	8840	9360	9359	9319
4	8380	8414	8405	8396	8478	235.6	798.0	457.3	425.3	290	9406	9080	9543	9508	9788
1984															
1	8494	9503	8529	8502	8695	248.0	791.8	349.7	342.4	-451	9505	9022	9547	9542	9810
2	8547	8527	8580	8549	8632	310.4	949.8	401.2	413.0	-378	9579	9196	9698	9742	10158
3	8603	8545	8634	8600	8616	295.3	738.8	269.3	340.9	-180	9581	9160	9731	9778	10208
4	8659	8554	8686	8650	9220	193.0	837.0	362.7	460.6	414	9614	9265	9864	9899	10681
1985															
1	8715	8577	8747	8717	9160	177.5	736.0	361.3	381.2	-172	9598	9219	9900	9936	10567

Date	PSFB 0	PSFB i	PSFB ii	PSFB iii	PSFB iv	EMP 0	EMP i	EMP ii	EMP iii	EMP iv	UNEMP 0	UNEMP i	UNEMP ii	UNEMP iii	UNEMP iv
1983															
2	1890	2979	3549	3024	2423	20915	20915	20915	20915	21182	3092	3092	0392	3092	3101
3	2225	2520	3622	3055	2784	20882	21137	20958	20954	21229	3128	2881	3056	3060	3115
4	2109	2405	3579	3073	3122	20846	21169	20956	20953	21323	3141	2827	3039	3042	3106
1984															
1	1935	2702	3659	3010	2985	20801	21129	20899	20907	21348	3164	2842	3075	3067	3178
2	1919	2535	3553	2996	2566	20752	21141	20870	20904	21347	3192	2806	3083	3050	3199
3	2098	2650	3536	3033	2590	20696	21103	20828	20872	21376	3225	2819	3104	3063	3260
4	2068	2674	3330	2875	1951	20649	21110	20824	20872	21401	3250	2788	3089	3043	3267
1985															
1	2123	2748	3232	2601	1953	20583	21076	20795	20848	21402	3293	2796	3098	3047	3309

Table 3. (cont)

	AVEARN					PWMF					CPI				
Date	0	i	ii	iii	iv	0	i	ii	iii	iv	0	i	ii	iii	iv
1983															
2	128.2	128.9	128.5	128.2	128.8	255.9	255.9	255.9	255.9	256.5	238.0	238.0	238.0	238.0	237.0
3	130.7	131.2	130.2	129.9	130.6	260.7	260.8	259.4	260.6	259.2	241.5	240.6	241.0	241.1	239.5
4	132.7	139.8	133.5	133.8	132.9	267.4	266.0	264.5	265.1	262.2	245.7	242.5	244.5	244.1	241.9
1984															
1	135.2	134.9	134.0	134.8	134.5	274.8	271.4	270.3	271.0	266.5	250.5	246.4	249.0	248.2	245.5
2	137.4	137.6	135.4	136.9	135.9	280.7	274.4	275.4	275.3	270.7	255.1	248.4	252.9	251.0	248.4
3	140.2	139.1	138.6	140.4	136.3	286.7	274.4	279.6	278.8	273.5	259.4	252.3	256.4	254.5	249.8
4	142.9	138.7	140.2	141.7	140.0	292.8	276.9	284.0	282.8	276.7	263.4	253.8	259.4	258.0	253.2
1985															
1	146.0	141.2	143.8	145.5	142.6	299.1	280.7	288.7	287.6	282.8	267.3	255.3	261.9	261.0	258.7

	COMP					EFF					EX				
Date	0	i	ii	iii	iv	0	i	ii	iii	iv	0	i	ii	iii	iv
1983															
2	1.06	1.06	1.06	1.06	1.07	84.5	84.5	84.5	84.5	84.4	1.56	1.56	1.56	1.56	1.55
3	1.06	1.11	1.09	1.08	1.08	85.7	87.6	86.3	87.8	85.0	1.57	1.62	1.59	1.58	1.51
4	1.04	1.13	1.05	1.05	1.06	83.3	87.6	84.9	86.6	83.3	1.51	1.62	1.52	1.51	1.47
1984															
1	1.03	1.12	1.03	1.03	1.05	81.0	86.2	83.4	85.6	81.8	1.48	1.59	1.45	1.45	1.45
2	1.04	1.13	1.02	1.01	1.04	80.4	86.4	83.7	85.8	79.9	1.47	1.60	1.42	1.40	1.40
3	1.04	1.14	1.01	1.00	1.01	80.0	87.6	84.0	86.4	78.1	1.47	1.62	1.38	1.37	1.30
4	1.05	1.14	1.00	0.99	0.97	79.8	88.1	84.7	87.3	75.0	1.47	1.63	1.34	1.34	1.21
1985															
1	1.06	1.13	0.99	0.98	0.93	79.5	87.3	84.9	87.8	72.0	1.46	1.61	1.30	1.30	1.12

Table 3. (cont)

Definitions:

GDP   Gross domestic product at factor cost
I   Gross fixed investment
E   Exports
AVEARN Average earnings
CPI   Consumer price index
EFF   Sterling effective exchange rate
EMP   Employment (total, UK)
PSFB   Public sector financial deficit

C   Consumers' expenditure
WS   Stockbuilding
M   Imports
PWMF   Wholesale price of manufactures
EX   Exchange rate sterling/dollar
COMP   Competitiveness
UNEMP   Unemployment UK

The forecasts of unemployment and employment are one area where there are noticable differences between the forecasts. The poor unemployment forecast is attributable to errors in forecasts of exogenous labour supply however, not to errors in the model forecast of employment.

Moving on to prices, we can see that the model captures the slowdown in the rate of inflation rather better than the published forecasts. There is, however, an important exchange rate effect at work here, with all mechanical forecasts for the effective exchange rate (the model exchange rate equations) being noticeably overpredictions, producing lower wages and prices in these runs.

A qualification to the comparison of forecasts with outturns is in order. Such comparison, never easy, is especially difficult for 1984. Since one can hardly have expected the model to have predicted the effects of the miners' dispute, which lasted throughout the year, a fairer comparison than that between the forecast and events as affected by the strike is that between the forecasts and what events would have been if the strike had not happened. But, since no exact estimates of the effects of the strike are possible, we have not attempted to adjust the outturns in the tables. It should also be borne in mind that the forecast published in August 1983 was conditional on 'unchanged policies'; since policies subsequently did change, it is not strictly appropriate to compare the forecast directly with what actually happened.

Despite these caveats we conclude that the mechanical model runs (i), (ii) and (iii) are also vindicated in an <u>ex post</u> sense: they are, if anything, closer to what actually happend than the published forecast.

November 1985, February and May 1986 Forecasts

Model 8, unlike the previous example, incorporates a range of expectations variables and is solved using consistent expectations and in this section we use these as the basis of a comparative exercise such as described above. Again in this exercise, all exogenous variables have the same values as used in the published forecast, and all residual adjustments have been removed and replaced either with zero residuals or with the average residual over the last eight data periods. The model has then been used in a purely mechanical fashion to reproduce the forecast. The resulting differences are shown in tables 4, 5 and 6.

Table 4. <u>A comparison between the published November 1985 forecast and</u>
          <u>mechanical model forecast</u>

	Output GDP (1980=100)		Annual inflation (CPI)	
	M	P	M	P
1985 IV	109.4	111.2	4.7	4.7
1986 IV	110.2	112.4	0	3.4
1987 IV	112.1	113.9	4.5	3.8
1988 IV	113.7	113.9	8.1	3.1
1989 IV	115.5	116.6	11.8	3.4
1990 IV	118.0	118.2	16.6	4.8

	Employment (millions)		Consumption (£ billion, 1980)	
	M	P	M	P
1985 IV	21.42	21.37	37.5	37.5
1986 IV	21.52	21.43	38.5	38.5
1987 IV	21.71	21.47	39.3	39.1
1988 IV	21.91	21.58	39.9	39.7
1989 IV	22.17	21.61	40.4	40.3
1990 IV	22.58	21.64	41.0	40.8

Note: M is the mechanical model solution; P is the published forecast.

Table 5. <u>A comparison between the published February 1986 forecast and
a mechanical model forecast</u>

	Output GDP (1980=100)		Annual inflation (CPI)	
	M	P	M	P
1985 IV	110.9	110.9	4.7	4.7
1986 I	111.3	111.8	2.4	3.2
1986 II	112.1	111.4	2.7	3.6
1986III	112.7	112.0	4.3	3.7
1986 IV	112.2	112.2	7.1	4.2
1987 I	112.8	112.3	12.7	4.9
1987 II	113.9	113.2	17.0	5.5
1987III	114.7	113.9	18.4	4.8
1987 IV	114.8	114.5	18.3	3.7
1988 I	115.1	114.8	16.9	3.2

	Employment (millions)		Consumption (£ billion, 1980)	
	M	P	M	P
1985 IV	21.38	21.23	37.5	37.5
1986 I	21.52	21.25	37.8	37.8
1986 II	21.61	21.29	38.2	38.1
1986III	21.72	21.37	38.6	38.3
1986 IV	21.80	21.41	38.9	38.4
1987 I	21.89	21.40	38.9	38.5
1987 II	22.01	21.46	38.9	38.7
1987III	22.16	21.56	39.0	38.9
1987 IV	22.25	21.60	39.1	39.2
1988 I	22.34	21.65	39.1	39.4

Note: M is the mechanical model solution; P is the published forecast.

Table 6.   A comparison between the published May forecast and a
mechanical model forecast

	Output GDP (1980=100)		Annual inflation (CPI)	
	M	P	M	P
1986 I	111.5	111.5	4.4	4.4
1986 II	112.8	111.8	4.2	4.7
1986III	113.7	112.4	2.9	4.2
1986 IV	113.7	112.9	1.2	3.4
1987 I	114.2	113.0	0.7	3.3
1987 II	114.9	113.8	0.7	3.4
1987III	115.6	114.4	1.3	3.5
1987 IV	116.0	115.0	1.0	3.2
1988 I	116.4	115.4	2.8	3.1

	Employment (millions)		Consumption (£ billion, 1980)	
	M	P	M	P
1986 I	21.48	21.35	38.0	38.0
1986 II	21.61	21.42	38.5	38.5
1986III	21.75	21.50	38.9	38.8
1986 IV	21.85	21.55	39.4	39.1
1987 I	21.96	21.57	39.6	39.3
1987 II	22.09	21.65	40.0	39.6
1987III	22.23	21.76	40.4	39.8
1987 IV	22.33	21.82	40.8	40.1
1988 I	22.44	21.89	41.0	40.4

Note: M is the mechanical model solution; P is the published forecast.

There is clearly a close correspondence on the real side between
the published forecast and the mechanical forecast in all three tables.

The forecast for inflation in the November and February published
forecasts differs substantially from the model solution. This is
primarily because the terminal condition used in these model runs was
causing a substantial devaluation in the exchange rate beyond what was
actually known to have occurred.

Conclusions

It is quite widely believed that macroeconomic models cannot be used for
forecasting except with a substantial additional element of judgement.
This view may derive from experience of models which, without
'judgemental' intervention by the user do indeed produce forecasts which
seem totally implausible (or even fail to produce solutions at all).
This exercise has shown that this is far from being true of the
Institute's model. Forecasts produced by 'mechanical' operation of that
model are shown to be plausible and, indeed, not very different from
those actually published by the Institute.

    This being true, one can begin to use forecasting performance as a
test of the model as such, as well as a test of the judgement of the
forecasters who use it (although even in a mechanical forecast much
depends on the forecasts of exogenous variables like world trade or
policy changes). Assessment of forecasting performance can be made only
when a long run of outturn data is available for statistical analysis.
Here we have presented one example of a mechanical forecast as it might
have been made in August 1983 set alongside the outturn figures up to
the beginning of 1985. No firm conclusions can be drawn from this

single instance.   All one can say is that, on this occasion, a
mechanical forecast using the Institute's model would have been not only
(<u>ex ante</u>) a 'plausible' forecast, but even, in some respects at least,
(<u>ex post</u>) a reasonably accurate one.

STOCHASTIC ANALYSIS IN NON-LINEAR MODELS

1. Introduction

By their very nature even large models are stochastic, simply because no description of the world can ever be so complete that the models fit the data perfectly. So the full specification of any general econometric model must include a set of error terms attached to equations which are not actually identities. For a linear model, as long as the error terms are normally distributed with zero mean, the stochastic part of the model has few practical consequences. Ignoring the error terms completely gives a deterministic forecast which is identical to the mean forecast of the stochastic model, and which is optimal on almost any criterion. However, as soon as the model becomes non-linear this is no longer the case. There is then no general analytical relationship between the deterministic solution and the solution to the full stochastic model. This section will explore the consequences of the stochastic nature of large models both from an analytical standpoint, and with the aid of stochastic simulations.

Stochastic simulation is a numerical technique which allows us to investigate the uncertainty which is inevitably associated with any large econometric model. Because such models are generally non-linear and highly complex, an analytical investigation of the effects and importance of their stochastic nature is impossible. Stochastic simulations bypass the analytical problems by simply performing large numbers of model simulations. Each simulation differs from the others because of the addition of a set of shocks to the model. These shocks may be added to the equations, the parameters, or even the exogenous variables. All the simulations are collated, and it is then possible to calculate a range of statistics from the simulated data such as the mean, the standard deviation, and the higher moments. As the number of simulations becomes large these estimates should provide a good guide to the performance of the model.

This chapter is divided into four main parts: section 2 will deal with the general background of stochastic simulation, describing some of the techniques and giving some new analytical results about the relationship between a deterministic model forecast and its underlying density function. Section 3 will use the techniques of stochastic simulation on two of the National Institute's models (6 and 7) under a variety of assumptions about the models' stochastic processes. Section 4 will use some of the results of section 2 to test whether the model falls within an important class of bijective functions, defined in section 2. Finally, section 5 will consider the problem of calculating the moments of the simulation properties of a model. A new algorithm for performing this calculation will be presented and illustrated.

2. A general background

A. The importance of the stochastic nature of models

Any behavioural equation of a macro model is by its very nature stochastic. The equation will not fit its data set perfectly and it can

provide only a partial explanation of the past. There will always
therefore be some degree of uncertainty about the general specification
of the equation, the actual values of its parameters and the importance
of any error term. Typically, when an econometric model is used either
for forecasting or simulation the stochastic nature of the model will be
ignored. All the error terms will be set, at least initially, to zero,
and the parameter estimates will be taken as known with certainty. It
is natural to ask what the standard error of the deterministic forecast
is, and stochastic simulation can provide this answer. However, a much
more important problem lies in the meaning of the deterministic forecast
itself. It is well known that if the model is non-linear then the mean
of the forecast will differ from the deterministic solution value. It
has recently been pointed out (Hall (1984) and Wallis (1984)) that for
some types of non-linearities, the deterministic forecast may be quite
meaningless and highly misleading as to the model's true forecast. A
simple example can demonstrate this.

Let $\quad Y = \alpha X + u$ $\hspace{11cm}$ (1)
$\qquad W = \beta Y + v$, and
$\qquad Z = Y.W$

where u, v are stochastic error processes, α, β are parameters, and X,
Y, W, Z are variables. The reduced form solution is

$\qquad Z = \beta \alpha^2 X^2 + 2\alpha\beta\ Xu + \alpha Xv + \beta u^2 + uv$ $\hspace{5cm}$ (2)
$\qquad Y = \alpha X + u$ $\hspace{9.5cm}$ (3)
$\qquad W = \alpha\beta X + \beta u + v$ $\hspace{8cm}$ (4)

The equations for Y and W are simple linear equations, so assuming $E(u)$

= E(v) = 0, the expected value of Y and W will be equal to the deterministic model forecast. This is not true for Z however, as the term in u^2 will be positive no matter what sign u takes. So the deterministic forecast, which sets $u^2 = 0$ will be an extreme point on the probability distribution of the term u^2. Any error at all will make $u^2 > 0$ and so the deterministic forecast is a highly biased and misleading indication of the stochastic model forecast.

It will be shown below that there are three broad classes of models. First, there are linear models, the deterministic forecast of which is equal to the mean of the stochastic linear model, also all endogenous variables will be normally distributed around this point (assuming normal error processes). Second, there are non-linear models which represent a bijective mapping from the error terms onto the endogenous variables. A bijective mapping is a unique one-to-one mapping in both the function and its inverse. (The quadratic term discussed above is not bijective as its inverse is not a one-to-one function.) The deterministic forecast of such a model can be shown to be the median of a generally skewed probability distribution. In this case the median, the mode and the mean of the probability density functions of the model are different. Forecasting the median seems a reasonable option especially considering some undesirable properties of the mean and the mode, discussed below. Finally, the third category is a non-linear model which is non-bijective. In this case the deterministic forecast has no well defined place on the probability density functions of the model. It can even lie at some highly unrepresentative extreme point, as shown by our illustration above.

The example given above shows that a fairly simple form of non-linearity, which certainly exists in most large models, can give rise to non-bijective terms in the reduced form. So without considerable work to define and investigate the shape of the probability function of such models, there is great difficulty in interpreting their deterministic properties. Stochastic simulations are useful therefore in defining and quantifying the uncertainty associated with a model forecast or simulation. But far more important, they allow us to have a firm basis for interpreting the results of a deterministic model run. If we know that the deterministic forecast is close to the mean value, and that the probability distribution is near to being normal, then the model may be used in the conventional way with some confidence. Until we have that information a serious problem of interpretation exists.

B. A decomposition of the errors and some technical details

By slightly extending the analysis of the decomposition of forecasting errors presented by Bianchi and Calzolari (1982) we may set up a formal framework for analysing the forecasting errors of a large macro-model. Let the general economic model be:

$$Y = Y(X, A, U) \qquad (5)$$

in usual notation. It is useful to then define the deterministic model forecast as

$$\hat{Y} = \tilde{Y}(\hat{X}, \hat{A}, 0) \tag{6}$$

where $\tilde{Y}$ is the functional form estimated, and $\hat{A}$ is the estimated set of coefficients. Now by definition the model's error may be written as $\hat{Y}-Y$. We may now define:

$$\bar{Y} = Y(\hat{X}, A, 0) \tag{7}$$

as the forecast of Y, given by the true parameters when the true functional form is known, but the exogenous variables are estimated. In turn,

$$\tilde{Y} = \tilde{Y}(\hat{X}, A, 0) \tag{8}$$

is the forecast of Y given by the true parameters, but using the estimated functional form and the estimated exogenous variables, and

$$Y^* = Y(X, A, 0) \tag{9}$$

is the forecast produced by the true model structure and parameters and with the true exogenous variables. So we may write

$$\hat{Y} - Y = \hat{Y} - \tilde{Y} + \tilde{Y} - \bar{Y} + \bar{Y} - Y^* + Y^* - Y = [\tilde{Y}(\hat{X},\hat{A},0) - Y(\hat{X},A,0)] \tag{10a}$$
$$+ [\tilde{Y}(\hat{X},A,0) - Y(\hat{X},A,0)] \tag{10b}$$
$$+ [Y(\hat{X},A,0) - Y(X,A,0)] \tag{10c}$$
$$+ [Y(X,A,0) - Y(X,A,U)] \tag{10d}$$

The overall error term is therefore divided into four parts. The first considers the error caused by incorrect parameter estimates, the second by misspecified functional form, the third by incorrectly forecast exogenous variables, and the fourth gives the contribution of the true error term of the model. This decomposition is carried out in terms of actual errors rather than variances. This means that the question of covariances between the four components does not arise. Nonetheless, a practical application of this formula would encounter some problems in distinguishing between the components, particularly the error due to incorrect parameters and functional misspecification. The formula does, however, provide a useful framework for considering these four components of model error, and for examining what model users actually do in practice.

In calculating the model variance we essentially set the first three terms to zero, and look only at the fourth term. The forecasting variance of the model is usually calculated on the basis of known exogenous variables and the assumption of a correctly specified structural form. It therefore comprises the first and last terms. An overall estimate of the reliability of a model's forecast should properly contain terms one, two and four, while the estimate of the reliability of a forecasting group should contain all four terms. It would be possible to add a fifth term to allow for deliberate model intervention on the part of the forecasters, a fairly common practice, but this may be subsumed into the $\hat{X}$ - X term by considering some of the Xs to be the intercept adjustment variables.

There is in fact some conceptual overlap between terms (10a) and
(10b) in that the parameter estimates and the functional form are
closely interrelated. However, by distinguishing the two we are able to
isolate an important omission in much of the work on stochastic
parameters. This is that the vast majority of the parameters of any
macro model are not estimated but are arbitrarily set to zero. By
shocking only the estimated parameters of the model, we implicitly
relegate the zero restrictions to be part of the functional form which
is assumed to be correct. The error decomposition presented above
allows us to reintroduce these restrictions at a later stage along with
the possibility of other more general functional misspecification.

Structural errors and additive errors

Despite the fact that most large models are non-linear, they are
generally estimated by single equation linear techniques, typically OLS.
This is done by subjecting the variables to various transformations,
e.g. by taking the log of a variable. When the equations are coded into
the computer, the dependent variable is transformed back into the
original variable. This means that a random error added to the end of
such an equation will not play the same role, or have the same
properties as the estimation residual. An example will make this clear.
If an equation of the form

$$\Delta \log(Y) = \alpha \Delta \log(X) + U$$

is estimated, then this will be coded as

$$Y = EXP(\log Y_{-1} + \alpha \Delta \log(X) + B) + A \tag{11}$$

where A will be an added residual used for shocking the equation and B will be an error term, normally set to zero, which will represent the estimation error term.

The National Institute's model is coded in precisely the form shown above with both an A and B residual explicitly in the equation. Of course other forms of non-linearity are treated analogously. It is possible therefore to apply random shocks to either the A or the B residuals.   Intuitively the B or structural residuals are more appealing, but this depends really on the estimation assumption of normality, and there is no general reason to expect the B residual to be normally distributed rather than the A.

Univariate and multivariate residual shocks

The distinction between structural (B) and additive (A) residuals has been made above, but when we apply shocks to either of these sets of residuals we must also decide whether these shocks are to be univariate or multivariate ones.   Univariate shocks are simply random normally distributed shocks which have a given variance but are completely independent of each other. Multivariate shocks will also generally be normally distributed with a given variance, but they will also have some covariance structure between the individual shocks.   In its simplest form we might allow for the fact that the error terms of different equations have some non-zero covariances. As an extension we might also allow for covariance of the error term over different time periods.

The main argument for considering the covariances of the error

terms in a model which has been estimated by OLS (which assumes the zero
covariance in the equation error terms) is that we know the estimation
assumptions are not actually fulfilled. Our equation must be subject
either to simultaneous equation bias, or to omitted variable bias, or
both, and the covariance structure of the error terms will contain a
great deal of information on this misspecification. For example, if
current income was incorrectly omitted from the consumption function,
then the covariance of the error term in the consumption equation and
the other income generating equations should pick up this omission.

There are currently three main techniques used to generate additive
residual shocks which follow the covariance structure of the error terms
of the whole model. Only one of these techniques can be used for large
models however. The simplest technique is the Mariano and Brown (1981)
approach. They use observed residuals from an N period model run to
carry out N static, one period, replications. This limits the number of
replications to thirty or forty at the most as well as only allowing the
calculation of the one quarter ahead static error bounds. A more useful
technique is Nagar (1969). This uses an estimate of the full covariance
structure of the model to apply shocks to the residuals. The problem
here is that the covariance matrix must be estimated from observed
residuals, so that there must be more data points available than
equation residuals. This will not generally be the case for a large
model and so the initial covariance matrix cannot be defined. The
final, and more useful, technique is the McCarthy (1972) algorithm.
This approach generates a vector of shocks by using the formula,

$$S = T^{-\frac{1}{2}} r U$$

where S is the vector of random shocks, r is a 1 x T vector of random numbers which are distributed N(0,1), and U is a T x M matrix of disturbances from T observations of M true structural equations.

This technique, therefore, only requires a set of equation errors over T periods. T may be any length, although the properties of S only tend to those of the true structural errors as T tends to infinity. This then gives an asymptotic estimate of the true covariance matrix. The McCarthy technique has also been extended to take account of serial correlation in the error terms, although this extension will not be used here.

Handling parameter uncertainty

As noted above, the variance of the forecast errors is made up from two sources; the variances of the true error term (U), and the parameter uncertainty, represented by the covariance matrix of the parameters. In stochastic simulation exercises it is relatively easy to take account of the variance of U, but it is extremely difficult to make proper allowance for the variance of A when the model is large. It is, of course, easy to shock the parameters by applying normal random shocks within the parameters' estimated standard error. This procedure is, however, not satisfactory, as it ignores the covariances between the parameters in an equation as well as the covariances of parameters across different equations. When these covariances are ignored there is

a significant possibility that all the shocks in an equation may be
applied in the same direction, causing the dependent variable to change
by an enormous amount, possibly even changing sign. This need happen to
only one equation for the model to fail to solve. Making allowance for
the parameter covariance is therefore vital as this will mean that, on
average, if one parameter fails then another will move in a compensating
fashion so that the level of the dependent variable is maintained within
'sensible' bounds.

There are three main techniques used to deal with the problem of
stochastic parameters, none of them being entirely satisfactory. These
techniques are:

(i) Stochastic simulation and re-estimation (see Schink, 1971)
This technique involves adding random shocks to the error term of the
model to generate new values for the endogenous variables. These new
values are then used to re-estimate the entire model, and carry out a
forecast run. This process is then repeated many times so that the
forecast errors can be calculated. This technique is almost completely
satisfactory in the sense that it generates sets of parameter values
which take full account of the covariances between the parameters
themselves, and between the parameters and the error terms. The
disadvantage is, of course, that it is almost infeasible to consider 500
or 1000 replications of this technique for a large model.

(ii) Monte Carlo on coefficients (see Cooper and Fischer, 1974)
This involves applying shocks to the parameters as well as to the random

errors of each equation. The disadvantage here is that in the case of a large model, where system estimation techniques are impractical, it is very hard, if not impossible, to carry out the necessary decomposition of the parameter covariance matrix. The normal technique used here when dealing with a large model is simply to ignore the cross equation covariances, and deal only with the within equation covariance of the parameters. This clearly represents an important loss of information.

(iii) Analytical simulation of coefficients (see Bianchi and Calzolari, 1980)

This technique involves an analytical formula for parameter uncertainty, which involves the partial derivative of the parameters with respect to the endogenous variables. These partial derivatives are evaluated by using finite differences which involves many model simulations. The analytical formula also involves an estimate of the variance/covariance matrix of the parameters.

It seems that the only feasible method in the case of a large model is to use procedure (ii) and follow the assumption of Cooper and Fisher (1974), Fair (1980), and Haitovsky and Wallace (1972), and assume that the cross equation covariances are all zero. It is recognised that this is an undesirable assumption, but there seems no practical alternative.

Antithetic errors

Stochastic simulations are a special application of the general technique of Monte Carlo experimentation, and in many cases a considerable improvement in the efficiency of the estimates of parameters of interest can be achieved by employing one of the variance reduction techniques. The main approach used here is the application of antithetic errors. This simply means that the sets of residual shocks are generated in pairs, the second of each pair having the same value as the first, but the opposite sign. The advantage of doing this can be illustrated by considering a simple linear model expressed in reduced form.

$$Y = \bar{Y} + AU$$

where $\bar{Y}$ is the deterministic value of the endogenous variable Y, U is an error term $\sim N(0, \sigma)$, and A is a reduced form coefficient. We would normally perform stochastic simulation by choosing many values of U, calculating Y for each value of U then calculating the mean and variance of Y. Consider the choice of two error terms U_1 and U_2, then

$$Y = \bar{Y} + (AU_1 + AU_2)/2$$

as $E(U_1) = E(U_2) = 0$, then $E(Y) = E(\bar{Y})$

and $VAR(Y) = \dfrac{A}{4}(VAR(U_1) + VAR(U_2) + 2COV(U_1, U_2))$

Now generally the errors are generated independently so the $COV(U_1, U_2)$ = 0, but if we set $U_2 = -U_1$ we produce a perfect negative correlation between U_2 and U_1 which substantially reduces the variance of our estimate of Y. Calzolari (1980) compares the efficiency of the estimates using standard independent errors and antithetic errors, and shows that the use of antithetic errors could produce estimates with the same accuracy as between 500 and 50,000 times as many model replications with non-antithetic errors.

The use of antithetic errors can also provide exact information about the type of model which is being investigated. For example, a frequent question is whether the model is linear. In this case, if we apply one pair of antithetic errors we can answer this question exactly, as in the case of a linear model we have

$$Y = \bar{Y} + (AU_1 + AU_2)/2$$

which implies $Y = \bar{Y} + U_1(A - A)/2 = \bar{Y}$

A linear model will produce a mean value from one pair of antithetic shocks which exactly equals the deterministic forecast. There is therefore no need to carry out statistical tests; if $Y \neq \bar{Y}$ after one pair of antithetic shocks, the model is non-linear.

C. Interpreting the deterministic solution

When we are faced with the problem of having to choose a single point forecast from a skewed probability distribution there is no single point on the distribution which should be chosen in all circumstances. Instead, the optimal predictor will depend on the specific loss function of the forecaster (see Dunham and Jackson, 1921). For example, with a quadratic loss function,

$$S_1 = \sum_{i=1}^{N} (x - a_i)^2 \tag{12}$$

where a_i $i = 1, ..., N$ is a set of real numbers then S_1 may be minimised with respect to x by setting x equal to the arithmetic mean of the a_i.

In a forecasting context if x is a point forecast and the a_i are all possible outcomes, then the optimal forecast is the mean of the probability distribution of the a_i.

The quadratic loss function is perhaps the most immediately appealing choice but it is by no means the only one. A clear alternative is to minimise the absolute error of the forecast. So that

$$S_2 = \sum_{i=1}^{N} \left| (x - a_i) \right| \tag{13}$$

This function will take a minimum value when x is equal to the median of the distribution of a_i.

Both loss functions (12) and (13) consider the whole range of possible errors. A more restrictive loss function might be to maximise the probability of picking the correct value, i.e.

$$S_3 = - \left| \text{Max PR} (x - a_i) = 0 \right| \tag{14}$$

This function will be minimised when x is set equal to the mode of the a_i.

Clearly in the case of a normal distribution all three loss functions will deliver the same point estimate. The final function (S_3) is in general unappealing, as it gives no weight to the shape of the density function and, in a highly perverse case, could lead to extreme boundary forecasts. When considering the other two functions it may be argued that it is desirable to penalise large errors with a proportionately greater weight than small errors, so at first sight we might prefer the quadratic function.

There is, however, one highly undesirable property of the mean which makes it difficult to present as a coherent forecast. This is that the mean forecast of the model is likely to violate any non-linear identities in the model. We can see quite easily that linear identities will hold in the mean forecast as

$$E(\Sigma x_i) = \Sigma E(x_i) \tag{15}$$

But we know that

$$E(XY) = E(X).E(Y) + COV(XY) \tag{16}$$

So any relationships which involve deriving a variable from the product of two other endogenous variables, which are not independent of each other, will not hold in expected values. This is not a trivial problem as most large macro models have many such identities. In particular the nominal value of a variable is often derived as the product of the real quantity of the variable and its price. In general we would not expect the price of a good to be independent of the quantity traded. The co-variance of the two will be non-zero, so we should not expect the mean value of a good to be equal to the mean quantity multiplied by the mean

price. Such relationships abound in any model and we will describe this
problem as one of model coherency.

The concept of coherency may be defined more precisely in the
following terms; suppose a model consists of M endogenous variables Y_M,
N exogenous variables X_N, L error terms U_L (L < M) and a parameter
vector $\emptyset$ so that endogenous variables which are generated by identities
do not have error terms. So we may write the model as L behavioural
equations and M-L identities

$$f_i\ (Y,\ X,\ \emptyset) = U_i \qquad i = 1,\ldots,L$$
$$f_j\ (Y,\ X,\ \emptyset) = 0 \qquad j = L+1,\ldots,M$$

A particular vector $\tilde{Y}$ is said to be coherent if there exists a vector $\tilde{U}$
such that

$$f_i\ (\tilde{Y},\ X,\ \emptyset) = \tilde{U}_i \qquad i = 1,\ldots,L$$
$$f_j\ (\tilde{Y},\ X,\ \emptyset) = 0 \qquad j = L+1,\ldots,M$$

Note that in general if $\bar{Y}$ is the vector of mean values of Y, no vector
of error terms will exist which are capable of satisfying this.

There are, of course, a number of alternatives which could be used
to derive a coherent forecast based on the expected values of the model.
One would derive the expected values of the behavioural equations and
then calculate any identities on the basis of these values. There are

two objections to this: first if the identity feeds back into the model, then the value calculated will not be the same as the value used in the model.   Second, if we report the means because our loss function is quadratic, then to impose the identities is to behave sub-optimally. This point raises the second major objection to requiring coherency; it may be that rather than abandon the mean forecast we should actually abandon the coherency requirement. Part of the popular appeal of large models among forecasters is that they ensure that a large number of accounting identities are simultaneously observed. This may, however, be a mistake if the forecaster is simply interested in minimising his squared forecast error.   However, if a forecasting group places some weight on the coherency of its forecast, then it may well be that the use of mean forecasts is too simplistic.

The importance of non-linearities in large econometric models should not be underestimated.   The interpretation of the stochastic nature of the endogenous variable is rendered particularly difficult by this problem. While we appear to have a good deal of information about the density function of the error terms of the model, the only information usually available on the endogenous variables is the deterministic forecast. Generally we have no way of even knowing where the deterministic solution lies on the density function.

For the univariate case a number of results can be established using the following theorem (see Hoel, 1962, page 383).

Theorem 1

If the continuous variables x_1, x_2, ..., x_k possess the frequency function $f(x_1, x_2, ..., x_k)$ and the transformed variables $u_i = u_i(x_1, x_2, ..., x_k)$, $i = 1, 2, ..., k$ yield a one-to-one transformation of the two coordinate systems, the frequency function of the u's will be given by the formula

$$g(u_1, u_2, ..., u_k) = f(x_1, x_2, ..., x_k)|J|$$

where

$$\frac{1}{|J|} = \begin{vmatrix} \dfrac{\partial u_1}{\partial x_1} & \cdots & \dfrac{\partial u_1}{\partial x_k} \\ \cdots\cdots\cdots \\ \dfrac{\partial u_k}{\partial x_1} & \cdots & \dfrac{\partial u_k}{\partial x_k} \end{vmatrix}$$

and where the x's on the right are replaced by their values in terms of the u's by solving the relations $u_i = u_i(x_1, x_2, ..., x_k)$ for the x's.

For brevity throughout the rest of this book we will refer to a function which satisfies the above conditions as a bijective function.

If

$$Y = g(x, U) \quad \text{where } U \sim N(0, \sigma) \tag{17}$$

and the frequency distribution of U is $f(U_i)$, then for a bijective function the frequency distribution of Y is given by

$$h(Y) = f(U) \frac{dU}{dY} \qquad (18)$$

The mode of this distribution is given as the maximum of the frequency function, so

$$\frac{dh(Y)}{dY} = [f'(U) \frac{dU}{dY} \cdot \frac{dU}{dY} + f(U) \frac{d^2U}{dY^2} \cdot \frac{dU}{dY}] = 0 \qquad (19)$$

Now if $\tilde{U}$ is the mode of the distribution of U, then

$$f'(\tilde{U}) = 0 \qquad (20)$$

But unless $\frac{d^2U}{dY^2} = 0$, equation (19) will not be zero at $\tilde{U}$, which implies that the mode of Y is at some value other than $y = g(x + \tilde{U})$. If the second derivative $\frac{d^2U}{dY^2} = 0$, then the function g must be linear.

It is extremely difficult to prove anything about the properties of the identities when using the mode but it seems likely that, at least, the non-linear identities will not hold for the mode of the variables. The above result may be generalised quite easily to the multivariate case although there will then be special cases where the mode and the deterministic solution coincide. The argument that we should actually report the most likely forecast of the model (i.e. the mode of the distribution) is clearly appealing. It does, however, have the major practical disadvantage that the mode is computationally almost impossible to locate.

So far we have argued that in the case of non-linear models the deterministic forecast is neither the mean nor the mode of the probability distribution.   It has not yet been made clear if the deterministic forecast has any well defined place on the probability distribution.   In fact, in the univariate case, the deterministic forecast can generally be associated with the median of the distribution.   If we again take the model (17) and assuming g is bijective, define $\bar{U}$ to be the median of U such that

$$\int_{-\infty}^{\bar{u}} f(U) \, dU = \frac{1}{2} \tag{21}$$

Now if we evaluate

$$\int_{-\infty}^{\bar{y}} {}^{= f(x,\bar{U})} h(Y) \, dY = \int_{-\infty}^{\bar{u}} h(Y) \frac{dY}{dU} \, dU \tag{22}$$

$$= \int_{-\infty}^{\bar{u}} \left(\frac{dY}{dU}\right)^{-1} f(u) \frac{dY}{dU} \, dU$$

$$= \int_{-\infty}^{\bar{u}} f(u) \, dU = \frac{1}{2}$$

So $\bar{y} = f(x, \bar{U})$, is the median of the distribution of y. As $\bar{U} = 0$ for the assumed error process of the model this implies that $\bar{Y}$ is the deterministic forecast.

This result cannot however be carried over into the multivariate case directly as there is no generally accepted idea of a multivariate median.   It is necessary therefore to define a generalisation of the median concept to the multivariate case.   The basic idea of the median point is that it is a point which divides the density function into regions of equal area.   In the univariate case half the area of the

density function lies on each side of the median. The natural extension
of this is that a point in $R^N(\bar{Y}_1 \ldots \bar{Y}_N)$ is a median if all the areas
under the following integrals of the density functions are equal to $\frac{1}{2^N}$.

$$\int_{-\infty}^{\bar{Y}_1} \ldots \int_{-\infty}^{\bar{Y}_N} h(Y_1 \ldots Y_N) \, dY_N \ldots dY_1 = \frac{1}{2^N}$$

$$\int_{\bar{Y}_1}^{\infty} \ldots \int_{-\infty}^{\bar{Y}_N} h(Y_1 \ldots Y_N) \, dY_N \ldots dY_1 = \frac{1}{2^N}$$

$$\vdots \qquad\qquad\qquad \vdots \qquad\qquad\qquad\qquad (23)$$

$$\int_{\bar{Y}_1}^{\infty} \ldots \int_{\bar{Y}_N}^{\infty} h(Y_1 \ldots Y_N) \, dY_N \ldots dY_1 = \frac{1}{2^N}$$

This effectively divides up the multivariate density function into 2^N
segments of equal area.

    This definition is not in fact new as it may be shown to be
equivalent to that proposed in Kendall and Stuart (1969) and Haldane
(1948).

    "The extension of the median to the multivariate case is not
    entirely straightforward.   The median of a univariate distribution
    is usually taken to be a pair of values each being the median of
    one univariate marginal distribution."
    (Kendall and Stuart, 1969, page 39)

Because there are 2^N segments defined by the integrals above, this means that

$$\int_{-\infty}^{\bar{Y}_1} \int_{-\infty}^{+\infty} \int_{\infty}^{+\infty} h(Y_1 \ldots Y_N) \; dY_N \ldots dY_1 = \sum_{i=1}^{\frac{2^N}{2}} \frac{1}{2^N}$$

$$= \frac{2^N}{2} \cdot \frac{1}{2^N} = \frac{1}{2} \tag{24}$$

So the above definition simply locates the vector of Marginal Medians.

If we now assume that the error process of the model $U_1 \ldots U_N$ is made up of a set of independently distributed errors with median values $\bar{U}_1 \ldots \bar{U}_N$, such that for any i

$$\int_{-\infty}^{\bar{U}_i} f(U_i) dU_i = \int_{\bar{U}_i}^{\infty} f(U_i) dU_i = \frac{1}{2} \tag{25}$$

Then it is possible to show that $\bar{Y} = h(X\bar{U})$, the vector of endogenous variables given by the model solution with median error term values, is a multivariate median in the sense defined above, if the mapping h is bijective. This can be shown by evaluating these integrals at $\bar{Y}$

$$\int_{-\infty}^{\bar{Y}_1} \ldots \int_{-\infty}^{\bar{Y}_N} h(Y_1 \ldots Y_N) dY_N \ldots dY_1$$

$$= \int_{-\infty}^{\bar{U}_1} \ldots \int_{-\infty}^{\bar{U}_N} h(Y_1 \ldots Y_N) |J| dU_N \ldots dU_1$$

where $\dfrac{1}{|J|} = \begin{matrix} \dfrac{\delta U_1}{\delta Y_1} & \ldots & \dfrac{\delta U_1}{\delta Y_N} \\ \cdot & & \cdot \\ \cdot & & \cdot \\ \cdot & & \cdot \\ \dfrac{\delta U_N}{\delta Y_1} & \ldots & \dfrac{\delta U_N}{\delta Y_N} \end{matrix}$

$$\tag{26}$$

$$= \int_{-\infty}^{\bar{U}_1} \cdots \int_{-\infty}^{\bar{U}_N} f(U_1 \ldots U_N) |J|^{-1} |J| dU_N \ldots dU_1$$

and as the U_i are independent

$$= \int_{-\infty}^{\bar{U}_1} f(U_1) dU_1 \int_{-\infty}^{\bar{U}_2} f(U_2) dU_2 \cdots \int_{-\infty}^{\bar{U}_N} f(U_N) dU_N$$

$$= \frac{1}{2^N}$$

A similar process will allow the evaluation of all the other $2^N - 1$ conditions, which then demonstrates that the deterministic model solution using the median values of the error term maps onto a point which is a multivariate extension of the concept of a median point.

The loss functions outlined in equations (12)-(14) gave no weight to the coherency of the forecast. Functions S_2 will yield an optimal forecast of the median points of the distribution which will automatically be internally consistent. The quadratic function S_1 will, however, violate internal consistency and so it may be unacceptable for some purposes. The quadratic function can, however, be modified to explicitly take account of the desire on the part of the forecaster for internal consistency, in the following way

$$S_4 = \sum_{i=1}^{N} (x - a_i)^2 + \Omega D \tag{27}$$

where $D = 1$ if x is not internally consistent,

$D = 0$ if x is internally consistent,

Ω = the cost of being inconsistent.

This function is no longer continuous and so simple analytical techniques cannot be used. If, however, we set $D = 1$ and minimise S_4 (as ΩD is simply a constant and drops out of the optimisation) the solution value for x will be the mean value of a_i and we can evaluate S_4 to give S_4^*. Now if we choose x so that it is internally consistent (one point is the median forecast), we can evaluate S_4 at this point to yield $\hat{S}_4$. Clearly for some Ω sufficiently large $\hat{S}_4 < S_4^*$ and an internally consistent forecast is the result of the quadratic loss function. However, as the median forecast is not the only internally consistent forecast of the model, $\hat{S}_4$ may not be a true minimum. A similar argument may be made with respect to the loss function of equation (14) (S_3).

The case for reporting the conditional mean of a non-linear model seems to be very weak. It rests on the assumption of a quadratic loss function which either gives no weight to the internal consistency of a forecast, or gives a weight of sufficiently small size that it does not affect the optimal solution. Such a situation is not impossible of course, but we would take the view that most forecast producers (as well as forecast consumers) put a relatively high weight on the internal consistency of the forecast. It may well be argued that the deterministic model forecast is generally the optimal choice when a point forecast has to be made. However, when dealing with skewed density functions, no single point estimate can ever convey very much detail about the underlying density function.

3.   An application of stochastic simulation

A.   A brief survey

Table 1 gives summary details of a number of studies of stochastic simulation conducted over the last 15 years.   The first important feature to note is the steady increase in the number of replications being used.   Before 1975 the largest number of replications was 300 but most studies used much less, typically 50 or fewer.   Since 1975 the number of replications has increased dramatically, partly due to the development of more efficient computers.   But this development is also due to a growing awareness among researchers that very large numbers of replications are required before results become reliable.   This has been paralleled by a growing use of variance reduction techniques, in particular antithetic errors.   It is also worth noting that apart from two early studies on fairly small models (Muench, 1974 and Cooper and Fischer, 1974) only two researchers have applied shocks to the coefficients of a large econometric model (Hall, 1984 and Fair, 1984).

As an illustration of the importance of a large sample in this type of work Figure 1 shows the distribution of numbers produced by one of the standard normal random number generators.   A sample of 500 random numbers is far from being a satisfactory sample;   it is not until the sample size is expanded to close to 10,000 that the distribution begins to look normal.   Clearly the fact that such large samples are needed to produce good estimates of the underlying probability distribution in such a simple case, indicates that the model runs involving less than 500 replications are highly unreliable.

Table 1. A Survey of Some of the Existing Studies

Authors	Model(s)	Number of behavioural equations	Estimation Technique	Dynamic or Static	Number of Time Periods	Number of Replications	Method
Nagar (1969)	Brookings (U.S.)	112	OLS	Dyn.	38	20	Nagar
Sowey (1973)	Australian Reserve Bank 1	24	OLS	Dyn. and Stat.	31	20	McCarthy
Fitzgerald (1973)	National Income Forecasting 7 (Aust)	14	OLS	Dyn.	13	80	Nagar
Bianchi Calzolari	G. Fua (Italy)	18	OLS	Dyn. and Stat.	15	100 200 10,000	McCarthy
Bianchi and Calzolari (1980)	Klein-Goldberger revised (US)	16	2SLS	Single Period	1	200,000	Nagar
Fair (1980)	Fair (US)	29	2SLS	Dyn.	15	1,000	Nagar
Fair (1984)	Fair (US) ARUS VARIUS VAR2US LINUS	108 10 5 5 12	Various	Dyn.	8	approx 250 each	Nagar
Hall (1984)	NIESR MODEL 7	88	OLS IV	Dyn.	8	1,000	McCarthy
Corker Ellis & Holly	LBS MODEL	155	OLS IV	Dyn.			

Table 1. (cont)

Authors	Model(s)	Number of behavioural equations	Estimation Technique	Dynamic or Static	Number of Time Periods	Number of Replications	Method
Green, Lieben- berg & Hirsch (1972)	O.B.E. (US)	56	2SLS and OLS	Dyn.	100	50	McCarthy (up to T-1)
Fromm, Klein and Schink (1972)	Brookings (US)	118	OLS	Dyn.	100	50	McCarthy (up to T-1)
Evans, Klein & Saito (1972)	Wharton (US)	47	2SKS	Dyn.	100	50	McCarthy (up to T-1)
Cooper and Fischer (1972)	a) FRB-MIT Penn b) St. Louis US	a) 66 b) 5	a) OLS b) OLS	DYn.	52	10,20	McCarthy
Cooper and Fischer (1974)	St. Louis (US)	5	OLS	Dyn.	68	20	McCarthy
Muench Rolnick Wallace & Weiler	a) FRB-MIT (US) b) Michigan (US)	a) 75	a) OLS	Dyn.	a)12	3000	Naive
Calso- lari (1980)	Klein- Goldberger revised (US)	16	2SLS	Dyn.	1, 6 and 9	1,000 1,000	Nagar
Fisher & Salmon	NIESR	86	OLS IV	Dyn.	8	500	McCarthy
Salmon (1983)	LBS	155	OLS	Dyn.	8	250	McCarthy

Notes:
1)   MR - model residuals SD structural disturbances
2)   Bianchi et al (1976) and (1980) and Calzolari (1980) used annual modes, all the others were quarterly
3)   Muench et al (1974), Cooper and Fischer (1974), Fair (1984) and Hall (1984) shocked the coefficients as well as disturbances. Fair (1980), Bianchi and Calzolari (1980) did this in some of their experiments.
Source : Fisher & Salmon (1983)

Figure 1.

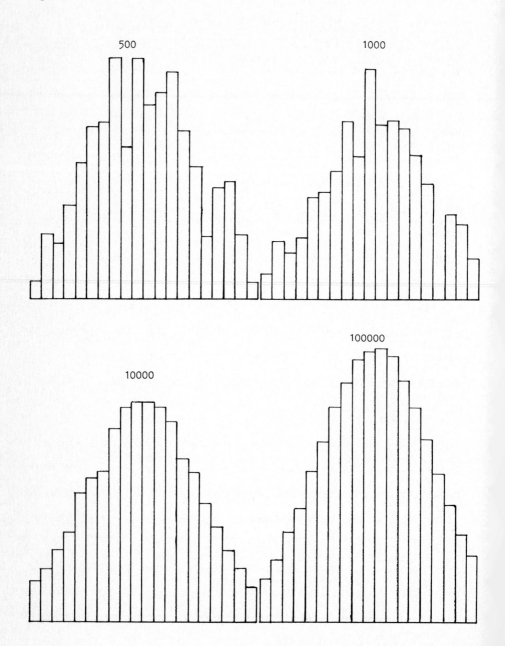

B. Some results

This section will use two versions of the National Institute's non-
linear macro model to illustrate the type of information which may be
provided by stochastic simulation. The two versions are Models 6 and 7,
both being similar sized quarterly forecasting models.

Sections (i) and (ii) will present estimates of the model standard error
(derived from 10(d), the additive error term) and the forecasting
standard error (derived from 10(d) and 10(a) the uncertain parameter
term). These two sections will differ in that section (i) will apply
univariate shocks to the estimated (B) structural residuals, while
section (ii) will apply multivariate shocks to the additive (A)
residuals. Section (iii) will then look at the question of structural
misspecification (10(b)) using multivariate shocks applied to the
structural residuals (B). Finally, section (iv) will show the effect of
making automatic residual adjustments on the forecasting standard error
to offset any simple misspecifications in the equation.

(i) Stochastic simulation under the estimation assumptions
This section will present two sets of stochastic simulation results, one
for an estimate of the model error term and one for the forecasting
error term, under the set of assumptions which lie behind the single
equation estimation of the model. These assumptions are, that the
structural residuals (B in equation (11)) are normally distributed with
zero mean and a variance given by the estimation equation, and that
there is zero covariance between the residuals of different equations.
As the equations are coded there is also an assumption of zero serial

correlation in the errors. Most equations are actually estimated on the assumption of no serial correlation in the error terms and LM and Durbin-Watson statistics are used to support this assumption. Occasionally, however, an equation will be estimated explicitly on the basis of an auto-regressive error process, but the coded version of the equation will be a transformed version of this equation which will not exhibit autocorrelation.

The first set of results provides an estimate of the model error term under this set of assumptions by carrying out 1000 simulations of the model, adding univariate normal errors to the structural residuals of each behavioural equation. In all the simulations presented in this section the individual replications are actually constructed as antithetic pairs of replications. This simply means that an initial replication is carried out using a vector of random shocks. The next replication does not generate a new random vector but takes the same random vector and reverses the sign of each element. The replication is then carried out on the basis of this altered set of shocks. So the 1000 replications actually consist of 500 symmetric pairs. The advantage of doing the simulations this way is that because the shocks are symmetric a much more efficient estimate of the deviation of the deterministic and mean forecast is achieved.

The simulations have been carried out in a dynamic forecast mode, over the period 1984 I to 1986 I, using the National Institute's February 1984 forecast as a base. This means that the deterministic forecast of the model would be the result reported in the February 1984

Table 2.   An Estimate of the Model Error Term under the Estimation
Assumption

Quarter	Consumption[1]	Exports[1]	Imports[1]	Output[1]	ΔCPI[2]	Effective exchange rate
1	0.011	0.015	0.032	0.015	1.7	0.05
2	0.012	0.015	0.032	0.016	2.0	0.08
3	0.014	0.015	0.031	0.017	2.7	0.09
4	0.016	0.017	0.032	0.018	3.9	0.09
5	0.017	0.021	0.031	0.019	3.9	0.09
6	0.021	0.023	0.032	0.019	4.8	0.10
7	0.020	0.027	0.033	0.020	5.2	0.16
8	0.027	0.029	0.036	0.020	5.7	0.19
9	0.029	0.033	0.036	0.020	6.6	0.20

1 = Standard error/mean value of the variable.
2 = Standard error of the percentage rate of inflation.
Deviation of Mean and Deterministic solution values

$D < 1$, Number of variables (N) = 139
$1 < D < 5$, "   "   = 38
$5 < D < 10$, "   "   = 8
$10 < D$,   "   "   = 4

D = the absolute percentage deviation of the mean from the deterministic
value after eight quarters.

Table 3.   The Forecasting Error on the Estimation Assumption

Quarter	Consumption[1]	Exports[1]	Imports[1]	Output[1]	CPI[2]	Effective exchange rate
1	0.011	0.015	0.036	0.016	1.8	0.05
2	0.012	0.015	0.036	0.018	2.2	0.08
3	0.014	0.016	0.035	0.019	2.8	0.10
4	0.017	0.020	0.036	0.020	4.0	0.11
5	0.018	0.023	0.034	0.032	4.2	0.12
6	0.023	0.028	0.036	0.022	5.2	0.15
7	0.023	0.032	0.037	0.023	5.9	0.19
8	0.031	0.045	0.044	0.032	6.7	0.23
9	0.034	0.04	0.044	0.024	8.0	0.25

1 = Standard error/mean value of the variable.
2 = Standard error of the percentage rate of inflation.

$D < 1$ N = 1 134 $5 < D < 10$, N = 12
$1 < D < 5$ N = 5 37 $10 < D$, N = 6

National Institute Economic Review.   This has been done by using a
'POSTMORT' stochastic simulation option, which is available within the
National Institute's solution program NIMODEL.   In this mode the program
calculates a set of equation residuals which cause the model to
reproduce exactly either an historical base or, in this case, a specific
forecast base.   The stochastic shocks are then applied in addition to
the 'POSTMORT' residuals. The reason for doing this is that in the case
of a non-linear model its general properties (i.e. simulation
properties, dynamic multipliers, variance, deviation, etc.) will vary
with the level of the exogenous variables.   So in assessing such model
properties it is important to assess them around a relevant base.   The
ideal base for a model which is used in forecasting would seem to be a
recent forecast.

This first set of results is reported in table 2.   All the
variables in the main table show the standard error in each quarter
divided by the mean value of the variable, except for the inflation term
(ΔCPI) which gives the standard error of the percentage inflation rate.
The first four terms are real consumption, real exports, real imports
and real output. The lower part of the table shows how the means of the
variables have been affected relative to their deterministic values.
This shows that the mean values of the vast majority of variables (139)
have hardly changed from the deterministic values, some 38 variables
have been changed by the stochastic simulation by between 1 and 5 per
cent, only eight variables have been affected by 5 to 10 per cent and
four variables have been affected by more than 10 per cent, after eight
quarters. Typically, the variables which have been subject to large

deviations are those variables which have unusually large variances due to the fact that they are the difference of two other variables. A typical example is the visible balance which in the eighth quarter has a standard error which is 2.8 times the value of the visible balance itself. This variable is one of the four in the highest category and it illustrates the difficulty of using the deviation of the mean from the deterministic value as a guide to the importance of non-linearity in the model. Such deviations are also a product of the size of the standard error.

Turning now to the standard errors of the variables themselves we can see that there is an obvious tendency for the standard errors to grow over time, as one would expect in a dynamic simulation of this type. Also, as one might expect, the model has much smaller standard errors with respect to the real sectors than the nominal. The standard error on consumption varies from 1.1 per cent in the first quarter to 2.9 per cent after nine quarters, for example, while the standard error of the exchange rate equation varies from 5 per cent in the first quarter to 20 per cent after nine quarters.

We will now move on to consider the standard error of the model forecasts, which includes the effect of parameter uncertainty. For this simulation exactly the same set of standard errors has been used to shock the structural equation residuals as in table 2, but in addition the estimated parameters of the model have also been shocked in accordance with their single equation variance-covariance matrices. This is equivalent to an assumption of a block diagonal variance-

covariance matrix for the model parameters as a whole. Table 3 presents
the results of this exercise.

    In fact it was necessary to exclude the parameters of a small
number of the behavioural equations from the simulation, as the
numerical techniques for generating the random shocks subject to the
covariance matrix actually failed for these equations. Table 3 presents
the results of this exercise. As expected, including parameter
uncertainty always increases the estimated standard errors of the model.
In the one quarter ahead forecast, the standard error generally rises by
between 10 and 20 per cent, but the divergence grows over the simulation
period so that by the eighth quarter it is substantially higher.
Throughout this section a standard set of results will be reported for
each set of stochastic simulations (as in Table 2). But an extra set of
results are reported in table 4. These variables are only reported for
this simulation, as the proportional changes between variable standard
errors is fairly constant over the different simulations. This table
contains variables with some of the largest proportional standard errors
found in the model, and these variables raise an interesting question in
the definition of the model itself. Typically these are variables which
are derived as the difference of two or more other model variables (e.g.
unemployment, the visible balance, or the PSBR). Often the 'primary'
variables have quite respectable standard errors. Table 3 shows that
even after nine quarters the standard error on both exports and imports
is less than 5 per cent. But when the 'secondary' variables figuring in
table 4 are derived by identity, the resulting standard error is very

large, as in the case of the current balance. We could easily specify

the model without these 'secondary' variables and this would have the

effect of producing much lower overall standard errors as well as

removing the variables which have large percentage deviations. So when

cross-model comparisons are being carried out it is important to take

into account this area of ambiguity in the 'secondary' variables.

Table 4. Some additional estimates for the forecasting error on
the estimation assumptions

Variable Q	Investment[1]	Unemployment[1]	Visible balance[1]	Money[1] (M1)	PSBR[1]	CPI (level)[1]
1	0.007	0.031	3.01	0.031	.25	0 017
2	0.012	0.054	4.98	0.054	.38	0.020
3	0.015	0.061	2.75	0.074	.46	0.026
4	0.016	0.062	2.16	0.095	.37	0.038
5	0.015	0.068	3.03	0.117	.50	0.042
6	0.014	0.071	2.85	0.142	.49	0.059
7	0.013	0.071	3.75	0.165	.50	0.069
8	0.014	0.072	3.01	0.190	.46	0.089
9	0.015	0.077	6.04	0.215	.82	0.109

A general point of interest which applies to all the simulations in

this section is that often the standard errors do not rise

monotonically. In table 2 the consumption standard error actually falls

in quarter seven. In table 3 it fails to rise in this quarter, and

indeed throughout all the reported simulations, this variable behaves in

this fashion at this point. This cannot simply be ascribed to small

sample bias, partly because 1000 replications is quite a large sample, partly because it occurs repeatedly in different simulations, and partly because the result has been noted by other researchers (see Corker, Ellis and Holly (1983)). Hendry (1984) has demonstrated that the standard error need not increase monotonically, as there is a term in the formulae for the model standard error which reaches a maximum and which then may decline. If this non-monotonicity is stronger than the rest of the formulae, then the total standard error can indeed behave as it does in the simulations.

(ii) An alternative to the estimation assumption.

This section will relax the assumption made in section (i) that the covariances of the equation residuals are zero. The McCarthy algorithm will be used to carry out two stochastic simulations to estimate the model standard error and the forecasting standard error. As pointed out in the introduction, this section will concentrate on the additive or A residuals. This really amounts to the assumption that, regardless of the way the equations are estimated, the error terms are normal in the coded form of the equation. In fact we have very little information to support either the assumption made in section (i) or this section. There seems no strong a priori reason, for example, to expect the error term in a consumption function estimated in Δ logarithmic form to be normal as opposed to the equation estimated in pure levels.

Apart from the assumption about the covariance of the residual terms, the simulations reported here differ in one other important respect. In section (i) the only equations to which residual shocks were applied were the estimated equations, which therefore, had estimated standard errors. There are, however, some equations in the model, such as the tax sector, which are not estimated because we have independent information on the relevant parameter values, e.g. tax rates, but which do not fit perfectly. In this section we extend the application of residual shocks to these equations also, and apply shocks to all the equations in the model which have non-zero residuals in a single equation residual solution of the whole model.

Table 5 reports the results of the estimates of the model's standard errors produced by these assumptions. The first impression is that the overall results of this exercise are remarkably close to those of table 2, given that they are derived by a totally different procedure. The estimate of the consumption standard error is slightly lower than table 2, while those of exports, imports and output are slightly higher. There is no strong a priori expectation as to which way the change should go, i.e. whether taking account of the covariances of the error terms should increase or reduce the overall size of the standard errors. Generally there seems to be a slight increase in the standard errors, as shown by the summary of deviations presented in table 5. The number of variables which have deviated by less than 1 per cent has fallen, while the number of variables in the higher categories has risen.

Table 6 presents a set of estimates for the forecasting standard error based on the same assumption about error process as above. As in the previous section, the introduction of parameter uncertainty has the expected effect of increasing the standard errors. Once again the effect in the first quarter is very small but it grows over time, so

Table 5. An Estimate of the Model Error Term under the Assumption of Non Zero Covariance in the Error terms

Quarter	Consumption[1]	Exports[1]	Imports[1]	Output[1]	ΔCPI[2]	Effective exchange rate
1	0.013	0.018	0.037	0.013	1.1	0.05
2	0.014	0.018	0.039	0.017	1.9	0.08
3	0.015	0.021	0.044	0.021	2.9	0.10
4	0.016	0.027	0.042	0.025	4.0	0.11
5	0.017	0.030	0.044	0.026	4.4	0.14
6	0.020	0.032	0.045	0.026	4.8	0.16
7	0.019	0.034	0.043	0.026	4.9	0.19
8	0.025	0.040	0.045	0.025	5.5	0.20
9	0.025	0.044	0.042	0.023	6.2	0.22

1 = Standard error/mean value of the variable.
2 = Standard error of the percentage rate of inflation.
Deviation of Mean and Deterministic solution values
      $D < 1$, Number of variables (N) = 155
  $1 < D < 5$, "   " = 55
  $5 < D < 10$, "   " =   7
 $10 < D$, "   " = 12

Table 6. The Forecasting Error under the Assumption of Non Zero Covariance in the Error terms

Quarter	Consumption[1]	Exports[1]	Imports[1]	Output[1]	ΔCPI[2]	Effective exchange rate
1	0.008	0.019	0.031	0.014	1.2	0.05
2	0.011	0.020	0.036	0.017	2.1	0.07
3	0.014	0.029	0.043	0.022	3.1	0.09
4	0.017	0.029	0.045	0.028	4.3	0.10
5	0.021	0.031	0.050	0.029	5.0	0.11
6	0.025	0.031	0.050	0.029	5.8	0.46
7	0.027	0.032	0.046	0.027	6.2	0.16
8	0.034	0.038	0.048	0.025	6.9	0.19
9	0.037	0.042	0.047	0.024	7.5	0.22

1 = Standard error/mean value of the variable.
2 = Standard error of the percentage rate of inflation.
      $D < 1$, N =   129. $5 < D < 10$, N =   7
  $1 < D < 5$, N =   44. $10 < D$, N =   9

that by the end of the period the standard errors are considerably larger.

(iii) An estimate of the degree of misspecification of the model
This section will look at how important is model misspecification in determining the overall errors in a forecast.   This concept is summarised in equation 10(b).   There is no generally accepted way of evaluating this part of the error process.   Fair (1980) uses a set of out-of-estimation sample, single quarter, forecasts to derive an estimate of functional misspecification.   We will use a different, but related, technique here.   The McCarthy technique used in section (ii) takes an observed set of single equation residuals from within the estimation period, and uses this to generate an estimate of the model standard error.   A formal proof of this is provided in McCarthy (1972). If the same procedure is applied to a set of single equation residuals taken from outside the estimation sample, the algorithm will yield an estimate of the model standard error taking account of the basic error term 10(d), the effect of the uncertain parameter estimates 10(a), and the function misspecification 10(b).   The National Institute Model 6 was used for this exercise, since this has more data from the outside estimation sample.   Two sets of stochastic simulations were produced, one using the within estimation sample, the other using residuals from outside the estimation sample.

The   interpretation   of   this   procedure   is   not   entirely straightfoward;   in a formal sense we are setting up the hypothesis

that the model is stable, and not subject to functional misspecification
of a serious nature. We then see if the model's performance outside its
data sample is so much worse than within it, that we can reject this
assumption. The important point to note is that a failure to reject the
hypothesis does not, in itself, imply that the model is well specified.
If the model were completely misspecified in a given sector, say because
two variables were closely colinear in the estimation period, then if
this colinearity continued into the test period, we could not expect to
detect this misspecification. The technique should, however, be useful
in two ways. First it should give a better guide to the actual standard
error of the forecast of the model, conditional on the correct set of
exogenous variables. Second it should point out areas of specific
weakness in the model. This information may be used in two ways.
Either it can be used to focus attention on a part of the model with a
view to improving it, or it may be used as a guide to constructing other
sectors of the model. An example of this is where theory suggests that
a variable might enter an equation, such as real money balances in the
consumption function, but the model has a number of definitions of money
available, M1 or M3, say. If we know that the sector of the model which
generates M3 is subject to a greater degree of misspecification, we
might, in the absence of strong statistical evidence to the contrary, be
well advised to use M1 in the equation.

Table 7 presents a set of estimates based on the McCarthy algorithm
for Model 6, where the equation residuals have been taken from the
period 1979 I to 1980 IV, which is within the estimation period of the

Table 7.   Within Estimation Sample Estimates of the Model Error for

Model 6

Quarter	Consumption[1]	Exports[1]	Imports[1]	Output[1]	CPI[1]	Effective exchange rate
1	0.014	0.040	0.046	0.019	0.007	0.031
2	0.016	0.042	0.045	0.023	0.016	0.045
3	0.016	0.045	0.044	0.025	0.023	0.061
4	0.018	0.047	0.046	0.026	0.028	0.078
5	0.028	0.044	0.042	0.029	0.032	0.082
6	0.029	0.048	0.040	0.030	0.035	0.083
7	0.029	0.053	0.038	0.032	0.036	0.086
8	0.031	0.050	0.037	0.031	0.037	0.090
9	0.034	0.053	0.033	0.033	0.038	0.092

1 = Standard error/mean value of the variable.

Deviation of Mean and Deterministic solution values

    D < 1 ,   N = 137

  1 < D < 5 ,   N = 18

  5 < D < 10,   N =   5

 10 < D   ,   N = 12

regressions.   On the whole, the picture is fairly similar to that
presented in table 5 for Model 7 except perhaps for the exchange rate.
The explanation for this discrepancy would seem to lie in the relatively

erratic behaviour of trade flows during the 1980s, which causes a much larger standard error in the visible balance in the simulation for table 5 than for table 7. The summary of deviations is fairly similar to table 5, with only a very small number of variables showing more than 5 per cent deviation.

Table 8 now presents an identical simulation to table 7 except that the single equation residuals used in the McCarthy algorithm have been drawn from outside the model's estimation period. The single equation residuals in this case have been taken for the period 1981 I to 1983 II. We must, of course, remember that both the simulations presented in this section rely on a relatively small set of residuals, so that the problem of small sample bias is more acute here than elsewhere in the chapter. Considering the table 8 simulation as a whole, the standard errors were generally increased quite considerably. This is demonstrated by the summary of deviation in Table 8. The majority of variables deviated by between 1 and 5 per cent and 32 variables deviated from their deterministic value by over 10 per cent. Of the variables shown in the tables only exports present the anomaly of a sharp fall in standard error out of estimation sample, as opposed to within sample. Among the other variables, consumption, output and the CPI show almost unchanged standard errors, while imports and the effective exchange rate show marked increases in standard errors. The lower part of table 8 gives a set of summary statistics which are akin to the single equation forecasting χ^2 statistic (here calculated with nine degrees of freedom). They are simply the ratio of out of sample

Table 8. Out of Estimation Sample Estimates of the Forecasting Error of
          Model

Quarter	Consumption[1]	Exports[1]	Imports[1]	Output[1]	ΔCPI[1]	Effective exchange rate
1	0.010	0.017	0.057	0.026	0.007	0.058
2	0.017	0.018	0.055	0.029	0.013	0.076
3	0.019	0.018	0.056	0.030	0.017	0.108
4	0.025	0.026	0.056	0.032	0.024	0.136
5	0.027	0.030	0.054	0.034	0.027	0.153
6	0.030	0.039	0.054	0.035	0.034	0.176
7	0.026	0.042	0.055	0.034	0.038	0.189
8	0.029	0.046	0.056	0.031	0.048	0.211
9	0.027	0.049	0.056	0.030	0.055	0.216

Deviation of Mean and Deterministic solution values

$$D < 1 \; , \; \text{Number of variables (N)} = 39$$
$$1 < D < 5 \; , \; " \qquad\qquad " \; = 72$$
$$5 < D < 10, \; " \qquad\qquad " \; = 29$$
$$10 < D \qquad , \; " \qquad\qquad " \; = 32$$

Comparison of the sum of the ratio of the variances for the in and out
of estimation sample runs

	Consumption	Exports	Imports	Output	CPI	Effective exchange rate
Ø	8.5	4.5	15.7	11.9	9.4	29.4

$$Ø = \sum_{i}^{9} \sigma_{i6}^{2} \frac{}{\sigma\frac{}{15}} \text{the sum of the ratios of the variances for each variable in}$$

table 6 and 5.

variable variance to within sample variable variance summed over nine quarters. This indicates the possibility of specification error in the imports sector and strongly suggests some instability in the exchange rate sector. Care must be taken not to associate these statistics with individual equations, however. In the case of the effective exchange rate the increased variance comes almost wholly from an increase in the variance of the balance of goods and services, which is one of its arguments. In turn the increase in the variance of the balance of goods and services is given by the increase in the variance of imports.

On the whole it seems that there is relatively little evidence for general misspecification of the functional form of the model, although this technique does point to the imports sector of the model as being relatively weak. It does suggest, however, that on the whole forecasting errors due to functional form misspecification are comparatively small.

(iv) The effect of model intervention on forecasting error
When models are used in practical forecasting they are virtually never used without some direct intervention in the model by the forecaster. This question was extensively discussed in Chapter 5. But, to re-iterate the main point, there are two reasons for intervention. The first is that the data itself is often revised between the time of producing the forecast and estimating the equations. These revisions often take the form of a systematic move up or down in the recent past data. Given that it is not possible, for practical reasons, to re-estimate the whole model each time a data series is revised, the usual

practice is to make an intercept adjustment in any equation which seems to be consistently failing to track the data. The second justification for direct intervention is that the modeller has information available from outside the estimation data set which may suggest some functional misspecification.   This data may simply be more recent (out of estimation sample) data, or it may be other extraneous information which is not modelled within the equation.   This extra information may again be incorporated within the model, in the simpler cases, as an intercept adjustment.   The effect of such adjustments should be to reduce the size of the model forecasting standard error.

This section will consider the effect of making residual adjustments for the first of these two reasons only: to offset a recent run of bad residuals over the past. Corker, Ellis and Holly (1983) consider a more broad approach to residuals which also includes some elements of the second reason given above.   By concentrating on the first reason for residual adjustments, we are concentrating on the model's properties rather than making an additional allowance for the skill of the forecaster. This gives an estimate of the model's forecasting standard error on the assumption that there are no structural changes in the economy.   In practical forecasting applications, the residuals applied due to extraneous information would be expected to reduce the overall standard error further.   However, if a structural change occurs during the forecast period this would obviously raise the standard error of the forecast, even if some ad hoc residual adjustments were made in an attempt to offset this.

Some authors have taken the presence of runs of errors in single equations as a sign of serial correlation in the error terms (Fisher and Salmon, 1983, for example), and the original McCarthy paper suggested a procedure which would allow the construction of serially correlated error processes. We have not chosen to use this approach. The earlier arguments for model intervention suggested that where equations have been estimated without any apparent serial correlation, but show serially correlated errors using forecasting data (that is, a data set of a different vintage to the estimation data set) the cause may not be serially correlated errors but an inappropriate intercept adjustment. The proposed technique here is to reproduce the second simulation presented in section (ii), except that an automatic intercept adjustment will be made to ensure that the single equation residuals used in the McCarthy algorithm actually have a mean of zero. This approach is much more in keeping with the practice of forecasters, and should provide a closer estimate of the actual standard error of published forecasts.

The results of this procedure are reported in table 9. The intuitive expectation for table 9 is that the standard error should be reduced, and this is generally the case, but there are variables which provide quite striking exceptions. The reason for this is twofold: first, in the table the standard errors are expressed as percentages of means. If the intercept adjustment is substantial then the mean can change substantially, and this may affect the numbers presented. The second reason is that the table reports the forecasting standard error and this is not itself a constant - it will vary with the solution values of the model variables. To make an intercept adjustment is equivalent, therefore, to making a change which actually alters the forecasting standard error itself.

Table 9. The forecasting error with intercept adjustment

Quarter	Consumption[1]	Exports[1]	Imports[1]	Output[1]	ΔCPI[2]	Effective[2] exchange rate
1	0.008	0.017	.029	0.012	1.2	.005
2	0.011	0.017	.035	0.016	2.0	.007
3	0.013	0.019	.041	0.020	3.2	.009
4	0.016	0.025	.043	0.025	4.3	.010
5	0.020	0.029	.045	0.026	5.0	.011
6	0.023	0.028	.045	0.027	5.9	.12
7	0.027	0.033	.042	0.025	6.3	.16
8	0.032	0.038	.046	0.024	7.1	.18
9	0.036	0.044	.046	0.023	8.0	.21

1 = Standard error/mean value of the variable.

2 = Standard error of the percentage rate of inflation.

Conclusion

The results presented in this section may be broadly considered in two parts corresponding to the first and second moments of the probability distribution. With regard to the first moment, it is clear that most of the variables have mean values which are very close to their deterministic values; where the per cent deviation is large, this is almost always associated with the variables which have very large variances, such as the rate of inflation or the visible balance. If a forecast is being presented along with its standard errors, there seems little point in discriminating between the deterministic forecast and the model expectation. However, where a point forecast is presented on its own (the usual case), then the difference between the mean forecast and the deterministic forecast might well be regarded as a cause for concern. For example, in the multivariate additive simulation without stochastic parameters (table 5), the mean level of manufacturing output is 1 per cent higher after nine quarters than the deterministic value. In a statistical sense these are not significantly different, given the estimate of the standard error, but it is often differences of such a magnitude which distinguish different forecasting groups.

As for the second moment, the different techniques used suggest a good degree of uniformity as to the estimated size of model and forecasting standard errors. Parameter uncertainty has been shown to have relatively little effect in the first quarter but this factor grows in importance quite rapidly in a dynamic simulation. It is clear, therefore, that to ignore the stochastic nature of the parameters leads to a very large understatement of the forecasting standard error after the first few quarters of the simulation.

4. Testing if a non-linear model is bijective

In section 2 we established that if a model represents a bijective mapping from the error terms onto the endogenous variables then we can associate the deterministic model forecast with the median of the models' density function. If the model does not satisfy this condition then nothing can be said, in general, about the relationship between the deterministic forecast and the density function. This section will address two questions. First we will outline and demonstrate a testing procedure which will determine whether or not a model satisfies the condition of being a bijective mapping. Second, for the case of a model shown not to be bijective, we will perform a large number of stochastic simulations in an attempt to identify the complete shape of the density function.

A. Testing for bijectivity

The procedure outlined here for testing if a model is bijective, involves carrying out a set of stochastic simulations using only stochastic shocks to the error terms. The simulations are performed using antithetic errors. Because the use of antithetic errors produces a perfectly symmetric set of error terms, if the model is bijective, then from Theorem 1 the distribution of the endogenous variables will be perfectly symmetric around the deterministic forecast. So an equal number of observations will lie below the deterministic forecast as above it. If this is found not to be the case then the model is shown not to be bijective. This is not a statistical test which isaccurate only to some probability level. It is an absolute test in the sense that if the model fails then we know, with certainty, that it is not a bijective model.

Using the stochastic simulations reported in section 3, table 5, the following sets of results have been derived. (See tables 10 and 11. The results for only two variables will be reported as these are fairly typical of the overall results.) The first important feature of the results is that it is not possible to make general statements about the bijectivity of the model as a whole. Some variables are clearly bijective all the time, others are not bijective at all and most variables are bijective for the first few quarters of the run and then become non-bijective as some crucial lagged endogenous variable works its way into the density function calculation. This is not surprising and a simple example may make this clear. Suppose,

$$Y = \alpha_1 Y_{-1} + B_1 Z + U_1 \tag{28}$$

$$X = \alpha_2 X_{-1} + B_2 Y^2_{-1} + U_2 \tag{29}$$

In the first period of the model solution, when all lagged values are predetermined, the final form equation for X is simply (29), and so the function is bijective. In the second period of the solution the lagged values become stochastic themselves, and so the final form equation for X_2 is

$$X_2 = \alpha_2 [\alpha_2 X_0 + B_2 Y^2_0 + U_{21}]$$

$$+ B_2 [\alpha_1 Y_0 + B_1 Z_0 + U_{11}]^2 + U_{22} \tag{30}$$

As the second term is squared in (30), the density function of X_2 is no longer a bijective mapping. As we move further into a model run the chances that the model mapping will become non-bijective increases.

Table 10. The distribution for consumption

Quarter	Below deterministic value	Above deterministic value
1	500	500
2	500	500
3	500	500
4	516	484
5	500	500
6	500	500
7	500	500
8	515	485

Table 10 gives the distribution for consumption. This is a very peculiar result. It suggests that for the first three quarters the median and the deterministic forecast coincide, but in the fourth quarter the median is slightly less than the deterministic value. For the next three quarters they are again identical but in the eighth quarter the two diverge in a similar fashion to the fourth quarter. This result seems to be due to the treatment of tax allowances in the model. These allowances are uprated in line with inflation once every four quarters. The allowances have a strong effect on real disposable income, which is one of the main arguments of the consumption function. This multiplicative uprating seems to be sufficiently non-linear to make the model mapping no longer truly bijective. We may confirm this by exogenising the tax allowances in the model and reproducing the stochastic simulation. When this was done the fourth quarter anomaly disappeared.

Perhaps a more typical pattern is exhibited by the investment sector of the model. Here the model is actually linear for the first quarter, so that the estimate of the density function is perfectly symmetric. In the second quarter non-linear lagged terms remove the linearity, but there is no divergence between the median and the deterministic point until the fifth quarter of the simulation is reached. Once the median and deterministic values diverge they remain apart. The results for this variable are reported below.

Table 11. The distribution for investment

Quarter	Below deterministic value	Above deterministic value
1	500	500
2	500	500
3	500	500
4	500	500
5	406	594
6	485	515
7	452	532
8	508	492

The conclusion to be drawn here is quite unambiguous: the model does not represent a wholly bijective mapping with respect to all the endogenous variables. It is not therefore possible to associate the deterministic forecast of the model with median values of the density function.

B. Estimating the total density function

The crucial question which must be addressed is the interpretion of the deterministic forecast now that we know the model is not bijective. An attempt will be made to answer this question by looking at the shape of

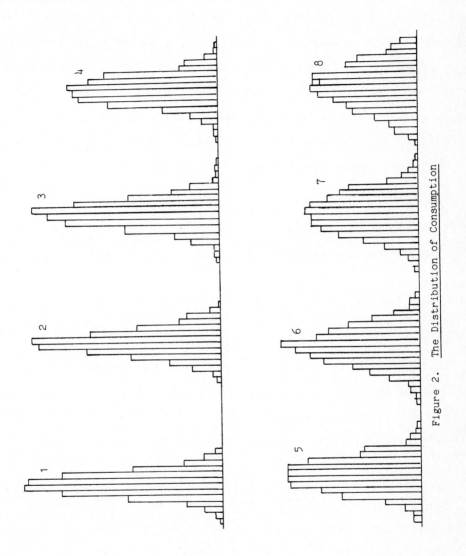

Figure 2.   The Distribution of Consumption

the density function around the area of the deterministic forecast. If we were simply interested in how skewed the density function was, we could address this problem by simply calculating the higher moments of the distribution. But this would tell us nothing about the location of the deterministic forecast on the density function. In order to gain some insight into the problem a large number of stochastic replications (6,000) of the model forecast have been done, and the results have been collated in the form of histograms.

Figure 2 shows the histograms for consumption over the eight quarters of the simulation. The deterministic value actually lies on the boundary between columns 10 and 11; there is a slight suggestion that the distribution is skewed so that the mode actually lies inside column 11. Column 11 is the mode in quarters 2, 3, 4, 6 and 7.

The steady growth over time of the variance of the distribution is quite obvious, but there is no obvious increase in skewness. It seems clear from the figure that while the distribution is not actually normal, it is very close to normal and that there is no evidence of the distribution being very skewed.

Perhaps a more typical variable is Investment. We know from table 11 that the model seems to be bijective for the first four quarters but that it then loses this property. This causes no obvious sign of extra skewness in the density functions which are shown in Figure 3. In the first quarter, the distribution is symmetric, suggesting that the asymptotic density function is actually normal. This is no longer true

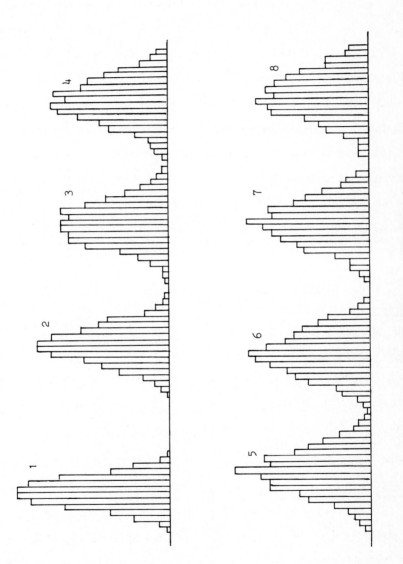

Figure 3.   The Distribution of Investment

from the second quarter onwards. However, in this case it does not seem to be clear in which direction the distribution is skewed.

The mapping from the error terms to the endogenous variables is clearly not always bijective; this is established by the two tables above. The failure of this condition seems to be of very small numerical importance, however, as the density functions are clearly not heavily skewed. If the failure of the bijective condition were important, then we would expect to see very one-sided distributions as in the case of equation (2). As we do not find this, it seems reasonable to conclude that the deterministic forecast of the model either actually is the median of the density function, or is very close to it.

Conclusion

It seems likely that large models in general, and certainly the National Institute's Model 7, do not fully lie within the class of functions which allow us to associate the deterministic forecast with the median of the distribution. However, this failure seems to be of minor empirical importance, and for practical purposes it seems that the deterministic forecast of a model is very close to the median of the distribution.

5. Estimating the uncertainty of a model's simulation properties

A. Introduction

From the point of view of economic policy formation, the main interest in any macro model lies in its simulation properties. It is these properties which determine the policy prescriptions which are given by the model, no matter whether a simple set of policy alternatives are examined or if a more complex analysis involving optimal control is used.   When evaluating a large model an important aspect of its properties, which is often ignored, is the density function of the simulation effects. To say that the deterministic effect of a rise in government expenditure is to raise GDP is of little use until we are able to say what the margin of error surrounding this estimate is.

The original work in this area was undertaken by Fair (1980) and the approach is summarised in Fair (1984). This section will begin by outlining the analytical approach he adopted and it will then go on to discuss his proposed procedure.   The section will conclude with an alternative procedure. It will then give an example of this technique using the National Institute's Model 7.

B. An analytical framework

Let Y_{it} be the set of i endogenous variables in a general non-linear model, X_{nt} be a set of n exogenous variables, Ω represents the variance-covariance matrix of all stochastic elements in the model (error terms and parameters), and B is a vector of parameter estimates. It is then possible to state the model in reduced form as

$$Y_{it} = Y_{it} \ (\Omega, \ B, \ X) \tag{31}$$

The deterministic model solution would be given by ignoring the stochastic parts of the model as,

$$Y^D_{it} = Y_{it} (B, X) \tag{32}$$

Conventional stochastic simulation techniques allow us to estimate the expected value of the endogenous variables conditional on an estimate of the variance-covariance matrix.

$$Y^e_{it} = Y_{it} (\hat{\Omega}, B, X) \tag{33}$$

A model simulation exercise consists in solving the model for some base set of exogenous values (X^1), and then comparing this with another solution carried out on the basis of a different set of exogenous variables (X^2). So the deterministic simulation will be

$$d_{it} = Y_{it} (B, X^2) - Y_{it} (B, X^1) \tag{34}$$

and similarly the expected value effect of the simulation will be

$$d^e_{it} = Y^e_{it} (\Omega, B, X^2) - Y^e_{it} (\Omega, B, X^1) \tag{35}$$

In order to assess the uncertainty of a model's simulation properties we need to investigate the probability density function of d_{it}. As with conventional stochastic simulations, if the model is non-linear we will generally expect d_{it} to differ from d^e_{it}. Also it is clear that when we are dealing with non-linear models, the variance of d_{it} will depend on both the stochastic parameters and the stochastic error terms. It is only in the case of a linear model that the variance of d_{it} is due only to parameter uncertainty. This point can be

easily appreciated by referring back to the simple model of section 2.
The reduced form equation for W, a linear part of the model, is

$$W = \alpha B \; X + B \; U + V \tag{36}$$

A simulation on X would give

$$dW = \alpha B \; (X^2 - X^1) \tag{37}$$

The error terms U, V drop out, and the density function of dW is due
solely to the stochastic nature of α and B. However, the situation is
different for Z, the reduced form equation here is

$$Z = B\alpha^2 \; X^2 + 2\alpha B \; X \; U + \alpha XV + BU^2 + UV \tag{38}$$

So

$$dZ = B\alpha^2 \left[(X^2)^2 - (X^1)^2 \right] + 2\alpha BU(X^2 - X^1)$$
$$+ \alpha V \; (X^2 - X^1) \tag{39}$$

Here both the second and third term include the stochastic variables U
and V so the density function of dZ depends in part on the density
function of U and V. Fair suggests that the stochastic error terms in
the model may be ignored if Y_{it}^e, is close to Y_{it}^D and he carries out his
simulations using only stochastic shocks to the parameters. This
process will, however, yield a biased estimate of the standard error of
d_{it}^e as the part of the variance due to the error terms of the model will
be missing.

(i) The Fair stochastic simulation procedure

The procedure outlined below is set out in Fair (1980) and it makes full

allowance for the stochastic error terms of the model. The applications

reported in Fair (op.cit.) however, make a simplifying assumption which

removed the error terms from the calculation.   The procedure is as

follows:

1.   Given the covariance matrix of the parameters, draw a set of random

      parameters from the distribution (B*).

2.   Using the set of parameters B* and a set of base exogenous

      variables X^1, perform a set of stochastic simulations using the

      covariance matrix of the error terms to derive $\tilde{Y}^{1e}$, the expected

      outcome of the model conditional on B* and X^1.

3.   Using the same set of parameters B* and a new set of exogenous

      variables X^2, perform another set of stochastic simulations, again

      using the same covariance matrix of residuals and derive $\tilde{Y}^{2e}$ the

      expected outcome of the model conditional on B* and X^2.

4.   Compute $\tilde{d}^J = \tilde{Y}^{2e} - \tilde{Y}^{1e}$.

5.   Repeat steps 1 through 4, J times, where J is the desired number of

      trials.

6.   Given the J values of $\tilde{d}$ compute the mean and variance of $\tilde{d}$.

This process in effect nests two separate stochastic simulations within

a larger stochastic simulation.   If J = 1000 and the stochastic

simulation at stages 2 and 3 are both 1000 replications, the algorithm

would require 2,000,000 model solutions.   Because this represents an

enormous burden of computation, Fair actually dropped the stochastic

simulations at stages 2 and 3 in his applied work. For the trials, Fair used his own model, and reported eight individual simulations exercises using 250 replications for each of the eight simulations.

(ii) An alternative procedure

The Fair technique outlined above makes it almost impossible to take full account of the stochastic error processes of the model.   This section puts forward a simpler, more efficient technique which would allow for the full effects of both stochastic parameters and the error terms.   The procedure is as follows:

1.   Given the covariance matrices of the parameters and the error terms, draw a set of random parameters $B*$ and a set of residuals $U*$.

2.   Using the set of parameters and errors $(B*, U*)$, solve the model for a base set of exogenous variables X^1 to give $\hat{Y}^1$, the outcome of the model conditional on $B*$, $U*$ and X^1.

3.   Using the same set of parameters and errors $(B*, U*)$, solve the model for a simulation set of exogenous variables X^2 to give $\hat{Y}^2$, the outcome of the model conditional on $B*$, $U*$ and X^2.

4.   Compute $\hat{d}^J = \hat{Y}^2 - \hat{Y}^1$.

5.   Repeat steps 1 through 4, J times, when J is the desired number of trials.

6.   Given the J values of d, compute the mean and variance of d.

This represents an enormous improvement on computational efficiency as there are no 'inner loops'; using this procedure it becomes quite feasible to carry out a full set of simulations on even quite large models.

(iii) An example of the proposed technique

This section will report on a set of five simulation studies carried out on the National Institute's Model 7. The simulations have all been carried out on the basis of a multivariate set of shocks applied to the equation error term derived by using the McCarthy (1972) algorithm and a set of parameter shocks derived from the actual estimated parameter covariance matrix. One thousand replications were performed in the simulations in antithetic pairs. The simulations were carried out over the period 19842-19861 using the November 1984 National Institute forecast as a base. The five simulation changes were (1) an increase of £400 million (1980 prices) to current government expenditure, (2) a one percentage point decrease in the real UK interest rate (defined in terms of the Treasury bill rate and domestic wholesale prices), (3) a one percentage point reduction in the standard rate of income tax, (4) a one percentage point reduction in the rate of VAT and (5) an increase of 10 index points to the dollar price index (1980=100) of UK oil exports. We will not discuss the base simulation properties of the model in any detail here, these are all standard NIESR simulations and a detailed discussion of the model's simulation properties may be found in Henry and Johns (1985).

Each of the five following tables reports the 8 quarter path of results for one of the simulations mentioned above. The table reports the mean simulation effect on the main model variables followed by the standard error of the effect divided by the mean changes in brackets. The following variables are reported in the tables:

QGDP   Real Gross Domestic Product (Expenditure) at factor cost (1980

            prices £M)

CPI   Consumer Price Index (1980=100)

QCE   Real Consumers' Expenditure (1980 prices £M)

QDK   Total Real Fixed Investment (1980 prices £M)

QEX   Total Real Exports (1980 prices £M)

QM   Total Real Imports (1980 prices £M)

UNEMP   Total UK Unemployment (thousands)

EFFRAT   Sterling Effective Exchange Rate (1980=100)

VISBAL   Balance of Visible Trade (£M)

Table 12 shows the effect of an increase of £400M (1980 prices) in
current government expenditure within the model. Output quickly rises
as does consumption, exports, imports and the price level; the visible
balance, the exchange rate and unemployment all fall. In all cases but
investment the changes over the whole period are much larger than one
standard error. If the standard error divided by the mean (in brackets)
is unity, the standard error is equal to the change in the variable. A
figure of less than half implies a simulation change more than twice the
size of the standard error, and so on. This table indicates that we can
have considerable confidence in both the sign and the approximate size
of the predicted effect of a change in government consumption. As is
typical of dynamic models, the size of the standard error grows over
time, but even after eight quarters the standard errors are considerably
less than the simulation change in the case of most variables. Finally,
the difference between the deterministic simulation and the mean effect
was very small indeed, far smaller than was discovered in Hall (1985)

Table 12. <u>An Increase of £400 million to Current Government Expenditure</u>

Q	QGDP		CPI		QCE	
1	359.9	(0.015)	0.04	(0.290)	42.8	(0.151)
2	429.8	(0.083)	0.71	(0.083)	162.0	(0.191)
3	449.9	(0.051)	0.60	(0.265)	147.3	(0.221)
4	442.1	(0.100)	1.79	(0.179)	153.8	(0.463)
5	472.2	(0.138)	2.09	(0.233)	256.0	(0.398)
6	476.1	(0.180)	2.82	(0.220)	248.4	(0.501)
7	486.7	(0.235)	3.58	(0.225)	251.2	(0.677)
8	505.6	(0.275)	4.28	(0.237)	254.4	(0.743)

Q	QDK		QEX		QM	
1	11.6	(0.043)	4.42	(0.320)	77.9	(0.052)
2	15.4	(0.225)	18.56	(0.352)	166.9	(0.087)
3	31.9	(0.211)	40.47	(0.415)	200.3	(0.087)
4	22.6	(0.475)	68.52	(0.464)	219.2	(0.160)
5	8.5	(1.735)	95.02	(0.498)	263.9	(0.199)
6	-0.8	(22.681)	130.67	(0.499)	269.9	(0.255)
7	-10.9	(2.216)	164.43	(0.516	277.8	(0.340)
8	-9.7	(2.500)	192.58	(0.549)	284.1	(0.393)

Q	UNEMP		EFFRAT		VISBAL	
1	-154.6	(0.003)	-0.39	(0.283)	-123.5	(0.122)
2	-160.3	(0.007)	-1.30	(0.283)	-304.7	(0.195)
3	-168.9	(0.015)	-2.28	(0.311)	-415.1	(0.292)
4	-175.4	(0.023)	-2.79	(0.357)	-454.3	(0.445)
5	-178.4	(0.032)	-3.06	(0.380)	-503.0	(0.476)
6	-183.4	(0.048)	-3.52	(0.367)	-522.2	(0.644)
7	-188.5	(0.068)	-3.57	(0.393)	-484.8	(0.768)
8	-193.5	(0.093)	-3.65	(0.452)	-492.6	(1.007)

Table 13. A One Percentage Point Reduction in UK Real Interest Rates

Q	QGDP		CPI		QCE	
1	-8.5	(0.349)	0.03	(0.137)	-39.9	(0.139)
2	-1.4	(5.571)	0.09	(0.253)	-78.5	(0.108)
3	13.2	(1.013)	0.16	(0.505)	-84.5	(0.149)
4	24.4	(0.870)	0.25	(0.720)	-94.8	(0.185)
5	34.3	(0.896)	0.35	(0.827)	-102.0	(0.242)
6	45.3	(0.999)	0.48	(0.911)	-110.6	(0.303)
7	57.8	(1.080)	0.64	(0.971)	-115.4	(0.377)
8	72.7	(1.155)	0.83	(0.999)	-118.6	(0.457)

Q	QDK		QEX		QM	
1	1.28	(0.0935)	3.9	(0.126)	-17.3	(0.140)
2	15.20	(0.288)	9.3	(0.313)	-34.7	(0.117)
3	23.25	(0.259)	17.0	(0.538)	-36.2	(0.171)
4	26.39	(0.275)	28.5	(0.664)	-37.6	(0.255)
5	25.38	(0.361)	43.4	(0.728)	-37.5	(0.416)
6	22.74	(0.552)	62.4	(0.801)	-37.6	(0.611)
7	18.32	(0.903)	84.4	(0.856)	-35.6	(0.912)
8	14.11	(1.457)	108.5	(0.904)	-32.4	(1.324)

Q	UNEMP		EFFRAT		VISBAL	
1	-0.84	(0.180)	-0.34	(0.083)	0.67	(9.444)
2	-1.72	(0.428)	-0.54	(0.374)	16.14	(1.133)
3	-2.06	(0.884)	-0.77	(0.617)	8.93	(5.457)
4	-2.76	(1.061)	-1.04	(0.735)	-0.41	(191.787)
5	-3.90	(1.048)	-1.31	(0.795)	-11.65	(9.540)
6	-5.56	(0.994)	-1.59	(0.849)	-21.52	(7.385)
7	-7.60	(0.974)	-1.84	(0.878)	-29.49	(6.743)
8	-10.02	(1.001)	-2.12	(0.895)	-53.76	(5.270)

Table 14. A One Percentage Point Reduction in the Standard Rate of
          Income Tax

Q	QGDP		CPI		QCE	
1	15.17	(0.143)	0.003	(0.581)	34.2	(0.141)
2	26.00	(0.126)	0.02	(0.612)	58.6	(0.106)
3	27.34	(0.170)	0.04	(0.619)	57.6	(0.128)
4	34.17	(0.188)	0.08	(0.626)	70.4	(0.120)
5	37.13	(0.220)	0.12	(0.584)	72.9	(0.142)
6	42.58	(0.260)	0.17	(0.565)	78.9	(0.160)
7	49.66	(0.287)	0.23	(0.565)	86.1	(0.175)
8	54.79	(0.324)	0.29	(0.551)	88.8	(0.198)

Q	QDK		QEX		QM	
1	0.60	(0.184)	0.73	(0.384)	14.5	(0.144)
2	-0.62	(1.143)	2.62	(0.449)	27.4	(0.106)
3	-1.57	(1.027)	5.27	(0.535)	30.4	(0.121)
4	-1.66	(1.584)	8.75	(0.569)	38.0	(0.123)
5	-1.17	(3.177)	12.84	(0.567)	41.7	(0.148)
6	-0.74	(6.232)	17.89	(0.596)	46.5	(0.167)
7	1.03	(5.041)	23.28	(0.613)	52.2	(0.189)
8	1.79	(3.250)	28.64	(0.631)	55.8	(0.213)

Q	UNEMP		EFFRAT		VISBAL	
1	0.26	(0.257)	-0.06	(0.341)	-22.6	(0.186)
2	-0.32	(1.331)	-0.17	(0.372)	-46.6	(0.228)
3	-1.94	(0.577)	-0.25	(0.448)	-56.2	(0.356)
4	-3.47	(0.509)	-0.32	(0.467)	-70.5	(0.387)
5	-4.99	(0.488)	-0.38	(0.449)	-77.6	(0.484)
6	-6.32	(0.486)	-0.43	(0.491)	-87.0	(0.621)
7	-7.55	(0.491)	-0.47	(0.491)	-94.8	(0.598)
8	-8.86	(0.503)	-0.52	(0.504)	-104.5	(0.829)

Table 15. <u>A One Percentage Point Reduction in the Rate of VAT</u>

Q	QGDP		CPI		QCE	
1	22.3	(0.455)	-0.72	(0.009)	48.1	(0.472)
2	36.6	(0.486)	-0.80	(0.029)	70.0	(0.520)
3	36.9	(0.691)	-0.83	(0.059)	59.6	(0.820)
4	46.2	(0.773)	-0.96	(0.091)	72.3	(0.917)
5	46.4	(0.791)	-1.07	(0.131)	60.9	(1.022)
6	50.2	(0.806)	-1.17	(0.160)	57.7	(1.150)
7	57.4	(0.794)	-1.25	(0.187)	61.3	(1.185)
8	60.8	(0.823)	-1.32	(0.230)	78.0	(1.199)

Q	QDK		QEX		QM	
1	1.27	(0.341)	1.6	(0.469)	20.7	(0.465)
2	2.80	(0.358)	7.6	(0.368)	36.3	(0.470)
3	3.90	(0.433)	13.8	(0.416)	38.7	(0.635)
4	6.39	(0.431)	20.1	(0.519)	48.3	(0.712)
5	9.23	(0.422)	27.4	(0.582)	48.3	(0.747)
6	11.90	(0.418)	35.0	(0.621)	50.5	(0.790)
7	16.60	(0.387)	42.4	(0.655)	56.4	(0.791)
8	17.74	(0.408)	49.1	(0.703)	60.3	(0.780)

Q	UNEMP		EFFRAT		VISBAL	
1	0.32	(0.596)	-0.14	(0.445)	-35.2	(0.444)
2	-0.67	(1.040)	-0.29	(0.552)	-64.9	(0.495)
3	-2.93	(0.715)	-0.30	(0.824)	-69.9	(0.693)
4	-4.89	(0.757)	-0.29	(1.235)	-83.5	(0.901)
5	-6.99	(0.816)	-0.30	(1.451)	-85.8	(0.985)
6	-8.60	(0.852)	-0.28	(1.650)	-89.5	(1.015)
7	-9.75	(0.887)	-0.29	(1.775)	-99.1	(1.060)
8	-10.75	(0.922)	-0.29	(1.928)	-109.3	(1.264)

Table 16. <u>An Increase in UK Oil Export Prices in Dollar Terms</u>

Q	QGDP		CPI		QCE	
1	-33.1	(0.309)	-0.23	(0.271)	22.9	(0.388)
2	-65.0	(0.385)	-0.73	(0.296)	20.7	(1.357)
3	-92.8	(0.449)	-1.14	(0.333)	-7.6	(6.791)
4	-118.2	(0.503)	-1.46	(0.350)	-24.6	(3.127)
5	-152.7	(0.511)	-1.78	(0.355)	-50.8	(1.965)
6	-197.7	(0.498)	-2.16	(0.369)	-54.6	(2.105)
7	-239.9	(0.503)	-2.61	(0.390)	-49.2	(2.667)
8	-269.6	(0.530)	-3.10	(0.399)	-50.4	(3.034)

Q	QDK		QEX		QM	
1	0.89	(2.011)	-33.1	(0.260)	8.6	(0.258)
2	9.30	(0.546)	-76.2	(0.296)	-5.8	(2.247)
3	22.59	(0.447)	-119.8	(0.319)	-34.8	(0.752)
4	38.53	(0.426)	-169.3	(0.325)	-59.8	(0.729)
5	55.72	(0.418)	-222.9	(0.328)	-85.4	(0.689)
6	61.34	(0.453)	-280.2	(0.343)	-102.4	(0.688)
7	56.81	(0.510)	-329.2	(0.364)	-117.4	(0.711)
8	48.91	(0.624)	-360.4	(0.387)	-130.5	(0.761)

Q	UNEMP		EFFRAT		VISBAL	
1	3.03	(0.295)	2.99	(0.236)	487.0	(0.151)
2	5.89	(0.360)	4.50	(0.261)	592.6	(0.238)
3	7.75	(0.417)	5.05	(0.284)	634.3	(0.298)
4	10.64	(0.445)	5.26	(0.295)	632.0	(0.364)
5	15.30	(0.482)	5.31	(0.303)	620.6	(0.459)
6	22.78	(0.499)	5.43	(0.331)	619.8	(0.594)
7	32.10	(0.500)	5.46	(0.361)	601.9	(0.705)
8	41.05	(0.506)	5.55	(0.377)	598.0	(0.784)

for the base forecast.

Table 13 shows the results for a one percentage point reduction in
the UK real interest rate. In this case we see that the impact effect
on most of the variables is fairly well determined, but by the end of
the eight quarters most variables have a standard error equal to the
simulation effect.   There is therefore considerable uncertainty as to
the sign of change which would occur in most of the model variables
eight quarters after the start of the simulation.

Table 14 gives the result for a change in the standard rate of
income tax. In this case the model's simulation properties are quite
well determined, the increase in output, even after eight quarters, is
much larger than its standard error for example. An interesting result
holds for unemployment where the impact effect over the first two
quarters is highly uncertain, but the longer term effect is much better
determined.

Tables 15 and 16 present a similar picture to table 14 with
comparatively well-determined simulation effects over the whole eight
quarters.

Conclusions

This section has proposed and implemented a new technique for assessing
the simulation properties of large non-linear econometric models. This
allows the calculation of the mean and variance of the effect of a

policy simulation in a large model.   The results obtained using the
National Institute's Model 7 broadly confirm the intuitive belief that
we can have much greater confidence in the simulation properties of our
models than in their ability to produce base forecasts.   The policy
implications here are that much of the value of large structural models
lies in their use as a tool for policy simulations and analysis rather
than as a simple forecasting apparatus.

OPTIMAL CONTROL AND DYNAMIC ANALYSIS OF MACRO ECONOMIC MODELS

1. Introduction

In this chapter we bring together some of the elements of empirical dynamic modelling described in earlier chapters, and consider issues raised by the interpretation of entire model properties. The techniques used will be exclusively concerned with optimal properties of these models, so will concentrate on the use of optimal control techniques. We eschew the use of simulation techniques, though extensive model exercises on National Institute models using simulation methods are reported in Britton (1986). General issues in simulation methodology with empirical results derived from selected vintages of the National Institute model were, of course, reviewed in chapter 5 earlier. For the related investigation of the policy properties of these models however, an optimal control formulation offers a considerable advantage in rendering the policy framework explicit. Not that we necessarily interpret the resulting policy implications in a <u>normative</u> way. Rather we will emphasise the use of simple but plausible objective functions, often capable of reparameterisation, so that sensitivity exercises can be conducted (see section 4 below). The general approach therefore is to use optimal methods as a way of conducting investigations into the dynamic properties of large non-linear models.

The chapter is organised as follows. Section 2 outlines linear theory for the finite horizon, comments on the presence of uncertainty in linear optimisation, and on the problems in deriving solutions in the presence of rational expectations. Following our earlier practice, this survey of the linear case is provided as a basis from which the non-linear case can be judged. The problems in analysing non-linear models is the subject matter of section 3. Empirical examples using versions of the complete National Institute model are presented in section 4. Conclusions are provided in the final section.

2. Linear theory of optimal control: an overview of the finite case

A. Optimal closed loop feedback rules

The most obvious, possibly the standard, case in economics is that of the linear regulator which produces linear feedback rules. It takes the underlying model in the discrete linear form as the following, (perhaps after transformation into first order case),

$$X_{k+1} = AX_k + BU_k, \qquad k = 0, \ldots, T. \tag{1}$$
$$X(0) = X_0$$

where X is a set of state variables, and U a set of controls. The cost function to be minimised is

$$J = \tfrac{1}{2} X_T' S X_T + \tfrac{1}{2} \sum_{k=0}^{T-1} q_k [X_k' Q X_k + U_k' R U_k] \tag{2}$$

Where the weighting matrices Q, R and S are given, symmetric matrices, with Q and S assumed non-negative definite, and R is positive definite. Deriving the optimal trajectory by the use of the discrete maximum principle we define the Hamiltonian

$$H_k = \tfrac{1}{2} q_k [X_k' Q X_k + U_k' R U_k] + \lambda_{k+1}' (A X_k + B U_k) \tag{3}$$

The first-order conditions for optimality require

(a) $X_{k+1} = \dfrac{\partial H_k}{\partial \lambda_{k+1}}$,   (b) $\dfrac{\partial H_k}{\partial U_k} = 0$

and   (c) $\lambda_k = \dfrac{\partial H_k}{\partial X_k}$

together with the terminal condition

$$\lambda_T = S\, X_T \tag{4}$$

Equations (a) and (b) yield

$$X_{k+1} = AX_k - BR^{-1} B' \lambda_{k+1} \tag{5}$$

while from (c)

$$\lambda_k = Q\, X_k + \lambda'\, \lambda_{k+1} \tag{6}$$

These equations define the optimum open loop control. To identify the appropriate closed loop control, we set

$$\lambda_k = P_k\, X_k \tag{7}$$

which when substituted into (5) and (6) above gives

$$X_{k+1} = AX_k - BR^{-1} B' P_{k+1} X_{k+1} \tag{8}$$

$$P_k\, X_k = QX_k + A'\, P_{k+1} X_{k+1}$$

These equations imply that

$$P_k - Q - A' \, [P_{k+1}^{-1} + B \, R^{-1} \, B']^{-1} \, A = 0 \tag{9}$$

for $X_k \neq 0$.

This matrix Riccati difference equation may be solved backwards through time [from k = T to 0], and these pre-computed 'gain' functions used to derive the optimal closed loop control

$$U_k = - \, R^{-1} \, B' \, [P_{k+1}^{-1} + B \, R^{-1} \, B']^{-1} \, AX_k \tag{10}$$

B. Uncertainty in the linear case

If we consider the model outlined in (1) uncertainty will generally enter the model in two possible ways: the addition of an error term with a well defined probability distribution; and because the parameter matrix (A) is only an estimate of the true parameter matrix. If the model is non-linear there is also the general problem of misspecified functional form; when we assume linearity this reduces to the problem of the incorrect imposition of zero parameters which may be treated as an example of the case of uncertain parameters. The case of additive errors is particularly easy to deal with and so it will be discussed first.

Additive error processes

We may restate (1) to include an additive error term quite simply as

$$X_{k+1} = A X_k + BU_k + \epsilon_k \qquad k = 0, \ldots, T \qquad (11)$$

$$X(0) = X_0$$

where $E(\epsilon_k) = 0$, $E(\epsilon_k, \epsilon_k') = \omega$

and $E(\epsilon_k, \epsilon_j) = 0 \qquad k \neq j$.

The vector of error terms has mean zero, covariance matrix ω and is serially uncorrelated. The criterion function (2) must make an allowance for the stochastic term in (11) and the usual assumption is that agents wish to minimise the expected value of (2). Thus the problem is to find U_k, $k = 1, \ldots, T$ which will minimize $E(J)$ subject to (11).

For this case where (11), the model, is linear, and J, the objective function, is quadratic, then an important theorem applies. This is the certainty-equivalence theorem which establishes that under these conditions (together with the assumption the $E(\epsilon, \epsilon')$ and x are independant) the expected value of the random term can be used, and the problem solved as if it were deterministic. So we may set the error terms to zero and proceed as outlined for the deterministic case above.

When either the objective function is non-quadratic or the model is non-linear a more complex procedure must be used. The general approach here is to use a non-linear approximation method (an example of this approach using a macro model of the UK may be found in Bray, 1975). This relies on forming a Taylor expansion of the system around some nominal path U_k^0. The general choice of nominal path is usually the deterministic optimal path. The procedure then forms a second-order Taylor series expansion of the objective function on a first-order expansion of the model equations. This then produces a quadratic-linear problem which may be solved deterministically under the certainty-equivalence theorem. The solution then yields a general feedback rule of the form

$$U_k^1 = U_k^0 + H_k \, [x_k^1 - X_k^0] + h_k \tag{12}$$

The effect of this procedure is to stabilise the solution path around the deterministic solution path U^0; this may be seen either as an advantage or a disadvantage. It clearly produces results which are easy to interpret and understand within the context of the deterministic solution. However, it also severely limits the effects of uncertainty on the solution if the functions are highly non-linear. One alternative which may go some way to meeting this criticism would be to recalculate the set of Taylor expansions around the new solution U^1 and then recalculate a new optimum. This procedure could in principle iterate until the control variables converge on a fixed point.

Multiplicative uncertainty

The model remains essentially that set out in (11) except that now the parameter matrices (A, B) are viewed as simply estimates of the true but unknown parameter matrices. At this stage it is also useful to introduce the notion of active and passive learning within the optimal control framework. In essence passive learning simply means that as we move through time we receive new data about the system and so we can produce better estimates of the parameters of the system. Active learning not only includes the use of new data for re-estimation but it also involves deliberately perturbing the system so that we can gain information in order to better control the system in the future. In engineering applications active learning is clearly an important and useful approach; we can imagine running a power station for a few weeks in a highly erratic fashion so as to completely learn the parameters of the system and to achieve much better control from then on. In macroeconomics active learning is of much less interest partly because the time lags between conducting an experiment and getting the new information are long and partly because the costs of making such experiments are far larger. We will not therefore discuss active learning further here, the interested reader is referred to Kendrick (1981).

The derivation of the feedback rule when the parameters of the system are uncertain proceeds from the dynamic programming principle of optimality. This states that the optimal path from period $T - j$ to .T will consist of the optimal policy for the period $T - j$ and then the optimal path from $T - (j - 1)$ to T. This means that we can build up the optimal path from the final period backwards through time, adding each period's optimal plan to the existing optimal path. In order to state the principle more formally it is useful to introduce the concept of the cost-to-go. The cost-to-go is simply the value of the objective function evaluated from a time period to T. The notation is generally set up in the following way: let C_{t-i} be the cost-to-go with $T - i$

remaining periods. So given our objective function (2)

$$C_{T-T} = C_0 = \frac{1}{2} X_T' \, S \, X_T \tag{13}$$

$$C_{T-(T-1)} = C_1 = \frac{1}{2} X_T' \, S \, X_T + \frac{1}{2} q_{T-1} \, [X_{T-1}' \, Q \, X_{T-1} + U_{T-1}' \, R \, U_{T-1}]$$

and $\quad C_{T-i} = \frac{1}{2} X_T' \, SX_T + \sum_{k=i}^{T-1} \frac{1}{2} q_k \, [X_k' \, Q \, X_k + U_k' \, R \, U_k]$

Now, as we are dealing with a stochastic problem, let the expected cost-to-go be written as $V_i = EC(i)$. The principle of optimality then states that if C_i^* is the optimal cost-to-go for the remaining i periods then C_{i+1}^* may be stated as follows

$$C_{i+1}^* = \underset{U.}{Min} \, \{\frac{1}{2} X_T' \, S \, X_T + \sum_{k=T-(i+1)}^{T-1} \frac{1}{2} q_k \, [X_k' \, Q \, X_k + U_k' \, R \, U_k]\}$$

$$= \underset{U_j}{Min} \, \{\frac{1}{2} q_k \, [X_k' \, Q \, X_k + U_k' \, R \, U_k] + C_i^*\} \, , \tag{14}$$

$$k = T-(i-1)$$

We may then state the optimal expected cost-to-go at period $T - j$ as

$$V_{T-j} = \underset{U_j}{Min} \, E \, \{\dots \underset{U_{T-2}}{Min} \, E\{ \underset{U_{T-1}}{Min} \, E \, (C_{N-J} \mid \Omega^{T-1}) \mid \Omega^{T-2}\} \, \dots \mid \Omega^j\} \tag{15}$$

where Ω^j is the mean and covariance (σ) of the unknown elements. This expression may be solved in a series of steps, starting with the middle expression working outwards. This amounts to solving the expression for the last period and then working backwards through time one period at a time.

So we begin by solving

$$V_0^* = \underset{U_{T-1}}{\text{Min}} \; E(C_{N-j} \mid \Omega^{T-1}) \tag{16}$$

that is the expected cost-to-go in the last period of the solution. Now substituting the objective function (2) into this expression gives

$$V_0^* = E(\tfrac{1}{2} \; X_T' \; S \; X_T) \tag{17}$$

where we now drop the term Ω for notational simplicity and we take expectations to give

$$V_0^* = \tfrac{1}{2} \; X_T' \; E(S) X_T \tag{18}$$

Now we assume that the optimal cost-to-go is a quadratic function of the state of the system given by

$$V_0^* = V + \tfrac{1}{2} \; X_T' \; k_T \; X_T \tag{19}$$

and so by inspection of (19) and (18) we see that

$k_T = E(S) = S.$

Consider the solution for the period T-1 given this result for period T,

$$V_1^* = \min_{U_{T-1}} E \left\{ \tfrac{1}{2} q_{T-1} \left(X_T' Q X_{T-1} + U_{T-1}' R U_{T-1} \right) + V_0^* \right\} \tag{20}$$

so that the optimal cost-to-go at period T-1 is the minimum for the control at T-1 and the optimal cost-to-go for the final period. We may now substitute equation (17) into this expression to get

$$V_1^* = \min_{U_{T-1}} E \left\{ \tfrac{1}{2} q_{T-1} \left(X_{T-1}' Q X_{T-1} + U_{T-1}' R U_{T-1} + \tfrac{1}{2} X_T' S X_T \right） \right\} \tag{21}$$

At this point it is helpful to write this expression out in terms solely of U_{T-1} and X_{T-1} by using the system equation (1). This will give an equation of the form

$$V_1^* = \min_{U_{T-1}} E \left\{ \tfrac{1}{2} X_{T-1} C X_{T-1} + X_{T-1} D U_{T-1} + \tfrac{1}{2} U_{T-1} L U_{T-1} \right.$$

$$\left. + \tfrac{1}{2} \epsilon_{T-1}' F \epsilon_{T-1} + X_{T-1}' G \epsilon_{T-1} + U_{T-1}' H \epsilon_{T-1} \right\} \tag{22}$$

where

$C = q_Q + A'kA$

$D = A'kB$

$L = q_R + B'kB$

$F = k$

$G = A'k$

$H = B'k$

If we take the expectation with respect to all the parameter vectors and the error terms ϵ, we obtain

$$V_1^* = \min_{U_{T-1}} \left[\tfrac{1}{2} X_{T-1} E(C) X_{T-1} + X_{T-1} E(D)U_{T-1} + \tfrac{1}{2} U_{T-1} E(L)U_{T-1} \right.$$

$$\left. + \tfrac{1}{2} E[\epsilon_{T-1}' F \epsilon_{T-1}] \right] \tag{23}$$

We may now minimise equation (23) with respect to U_{T-1} to give

$$X_{T-1}' E(D) + U_{T-1}' E(L) = 0 \tag{24}$$

and so the feedback rule may be stated as

$$U_{T-1} = T X_{T-1}$$

where $T = - (E(L')^{-1} E(D))'$ (25)

In order to evaluate T we must first evaluate k (the Riccati matrix);
we develop a recursion formula for k in each period by substituting the
feedback rule (25) back into equation (23) and then expressing this
equation solely in terms of X_{T-1} so that

$$V_1^* = \tfrac{1}{2} X_{T-1} k_{T-1} X_{T-1} + V_{T-1}$$

where

$$k_{T-1} = E(C) - E(D) (E(L_{T-1})^{-1} E(D))' \tag{26}$$

$$V_{T-1} = \tfrac{1}{2} E(\epsilon_{T-1} F \epsilon_{T-1}) \tag{27}$$

Equation (26) then forms the Riccati equation for k, and the right-hand side of (26) may be expanded in terms of k and this then yields k_{T-1}. In general therefore it is seen to be a difference equation in k, given k_{T-j}, k_{T-j-1} may be calculated. The terminal condition for this recursion is k_T = k = S from (19) and so the whole time path of k may be calculated. The whole problem may therefore be solved by first solving the Ricatti matrix k backwards through time and then using this to derive the feedback rule T in (25) which yields the solution to the problem.

If this problem had not involved stochastic parameters, then equation (24) would not have involved any expectations terms and so we see a simple demonstration of the certainty-equivalence rule that the solution is not affected by a stochastic error term in the quadratic linear case. The reader should note that while equations such as (24) and (25) appear to be simple linear equations in expectations variables the solution given by these equations may be very different to the deterministic model solution. This arises because of the fact that the expectation of the product of two matrices is not the product of the expectation. So, for example,

$$E(D) = E(A'kB) \neq E(A') \cdot E(k) \cdot E(B) \tag{28}$$

and so the deterministic value of D = A'kB $\neq$ E(D). In fact evaluating the expectation of products of matrices is not conceptually difficult as all the necessary information is contained in the covariance matrices of the parameters. The numerical calculation in (28) is of course complex but modern computers can easily deal with this problem. But where the variance's of A and B have to be estimated, and A and B do not have well

defined higher moments, these calculations may be extremely difficult.

C. Rational expectations and the optimal control of linear models

Following the discussion of rational solutions for the general linear

model in chapter 5 (ref.), the equivalent analysis in the case of a

system subject to control is as follows. The model under rational

expectations is now extended to allow for control variables, W, thus

$$
\begin{matrix} z_{t+1} \\ {}_t x^e_{t+1} \end{matrix} = A \begin{matrix} z_t \\ x_t \end{matrix} + B W_t + \varepsilon_t \tag{29}
$$

where z is the (n-m) vector of predetermined, and x^e an m vector of non-

predetermined variables as before. We assume that the non-predetermined

variables are rationally expected variables, where the expectation is

formed in period t. Define the vector of all elements $Y_{t+1} = (Z_{t+1},$

$_t X^e_{t+1})$.

As discussed in section B above, for the kinds of policy design

problem we concentrate upon, the deterministic solution is sufficient.

Providing certainty equivalence holds, the deterministic optimal rule is

optimal for the stochastic case also. Thus to derive the controls for

the deterministic case let $\varepsilon = 0$ in (29) above, and also set $_t x^e_{t+1} =$

x_{t+1}. We then seek to minimise the quadratic cost function

$$
V = \frac{1}{2} \sum_{}^{\infty} R^t (Y' Q Y + 2Y' UW + W' G W) \tag{30}
$$

Subject to (11) above, both $\varepsilon = 0$ and $x_{t+1} = _t x^e_{t+1}$, where R is a

discount factor, and Q, U and G are constant matrices, Q and G are also assumed to be symmetric. Again the solution may be obtained using the maximum principle. So let

$$H_k = \tfrac{1}{2} R^k (Y_k' Q Y_k + 2Y_k' U W_k + W_k' G W_k) + \lambda_{k+1}' (AY_k + BW_k)$$

where λ is the vector of co-state variables. Again, first-order conditions are

(a) $\dfrac{\partial H_k}{\partial \lambda_{k+1}} = Y_{k+1}$,   (b) $\dfrac{\partial H_k}{\partial W_k} = 0$, and

(c) $\dfrac{\partial H_k}{\partial Y_k} = \lambda_k$

This condition yields the model under dynamic control

$$\begin{bmatrix} Y_{t+1} \\ P_{t+1} \end{bmatrix} = K \begin{bmatrix} Y_t \\ P_t \end{bmatrix}$$

where $K = \begin{bmatrix} A - BG^{-1} U', & - BG^{-1} B' \\ UG^{-1} U' - Q, & R - A' + UG^{-1} B' \end{bmatrix}$

where $P_t = R^t \lambda$. The boundary conditions are the zn initial conditions $z(0) = P_2(0) = 0$, and the transversality condition $\text{Lim}_{t \to \infty} R^{-t} P_t = 0$.

The solution may be put into a familiar form, by associating the co-state variables with the predetermined and non-predetermined variables (see Currie and Levine, 1985). So if, $p' = (P_1', P_2')$ where P_1 is associated with z, and P_2 is associated with x, then we can operate as if the model were an augmented RE model, with n predetermined variables (z', P_2') and n non-predetermined ones (P_1', x').

Currie and Levine (op. cit.) show that if K in the dynamic system under optimal control above satisfies the saddle-point property (n eigenvalues have real parts > 1, n eigenvalues with real parts < 1), then according to the transversality condition

$$
\begin{bmatrix} P_1 \\ x \end{bmatrix} = - N \begin{bmatrix} z \\ P_2 \end{bmatrix}
\tag{31}
$$

where $N = M_{22}^{-1} M_{21}$, where M is the matrix of left eigenvectors of k, with its last n rows associated with the unstable roots. From (31) and the condition $\partial H_k / \partial w_k = 0$, the optimal rule may be expressed as

$$
W = D \begin{bmatrix} z \\ P_2 \end{bmatrix}
\tag{32}
$$

where $D = (D_1, D_2) = G^{-1} (U^{1'} - B^1 N_{11}' - U^{2'} - N_{21}, B^{2'} - B^{2'} N_{12} - U^{2'} N_{22})$, and where we have used a partition of the vectors B and U', and the N matrix, to be conformable with $(z', P_2')'$. Notice that we are qualifying the nature of this solution. A fuller discussion of this is postponed until the next chapter. For the present, this 'optimal' rule may be described as the optimal time consistent policy.

Turning now to the stochastic case we seek to minimise E(V) where E is the expected value of V, subject to the stochastic form of the dynamic system (29). We have discussed the circumstances when the resulting optimal feedback rule is the optimal rule for the stochastic case. Further discussion of the nature of the properties of this dynamic solution subject to feedback is postponed to chapter 8, which discusses macro policy and time inconsistency. The results for the optimal rule for the deterministic and the stochastic case are shown to have an important bearing on the analysis of time inconsistency.

3. Optimal control solutions using non-linear models

A. The control problem

In the non-linear discrete case many of the underlying ideas reviewed in the linear case carry over, with the obvious difference that now numerical techniques are needed to derive the required optimal solutions. The general ideas are that with the non-linear system and cost function

$$X_{k+1} = f(X_k, U_k, k) \tag{33}$$

$$V = [\theta_k (X_k, k)] \ \Big| \ \begin{matrix} k = T \\ k = 0 \end{matrix} \ + \overset{T-1}{\underset{1}{\Sigma}} \phi (x_k, u_k, k : q) \tag{34}$$

The first order conditions for obtaining the set of optimal controls are

(a) $\qquad X_{k+1} = \dfrac{\partial H_k}{\partial \lambda_{k+1}}$

(b) $\dfrac{\partial H_k}{\partial U_k} = 0$

and (c) $\lambda_k = \dfrac{\partial H_k}{\partial X_k}$

                                                                        (35)

where H_k is now $\phi(.) + \lambda'_{k+1} f(.)$, and $\phi(.)$ and $f(.)$ are defined in (33) and (34) above. With the end-point conditions, implementation of these steps [(a), (b) and (c)] result in a discrete non-linear, two-point boundary value problem. This must be solved, in general, by numerical or iterative techniques, and the rest of this section reviews some of the problems and the procedures in implementing these.

B. Practical computation

For the purposes of this review of numerical procedures we do not state the necessary end-point conditions to the optimising problem, but concentrate on the problem produced by the non-linearity of the system.

In its most general form, the finite optimising problem may be represented as unconstrained non-linear optimisation, by substituting the system equations (33) into the cost function (34). Then without loss in generality we may restate the problem as the simple non-dynamic optimisation of the non-linear function, i.e.

    Min $Y = M(C)$

where C is now taken to be the vector of all control variables, but over all time periods, i.e. $C = (U_1, \ldots, U_T)$ where U is the vector of control variables. In such a form, the problem becomes a familiar one

of minimising an unconstrained non-linear function, although the

dimensionality of this may be considerable (depending as it does on the

size of the model and the length of optimisation interval).

All the many methods of solving a minimisation problem such as this

proceed along a broadly similar set of steps and may all be classified

under the general heading of hill climbing algorithms. From an initial,

and arbitrary, guess of the optimal solution C^*, say C^1, they attempt to

construct a sequence of vectors C^1, C^2, ..., C^N such that at every point

on the sequence $M(C^J) < M(C^{J-1})$ and as $N \rightarrow \infty$, $C^N \rightarrow C^*$.

The broad steps of achieving this sequence may be outlined as

follows:

1)   set an arbitrary initial value for C^i;

2)   determine a direction of movement for C^i which will decrease the

      value of $M(C^i)$;

3)   determine a step length to change C^i by and evaluate the objective

      function of C^{i+1};

4)   examine some termination criteria; if it is fulfilled, stop. If

      it is not fulfilled, set i = i+1 and repeat the procedure from

      stage 2.

A usual criteria for termination would be that $M(C^{i-1}) - M(C^i) < \epsilon$

where ϵ is some small tolerance. Because of the possibility of the algorithm 'jamming' at some non-optimal point we might also examine

$$\frac{\partial M}{\partial C_K'} \qquad , \quad \text{for } K = 1, T . J$$

or $\left[\frac{\partial M}{\partial C'}\right]' . \left[\frac{\partial M}{\partial C'}\right]$

to see that both of these are close to zero.

Among the hill climbing algorithms by far the most important group are those which base the optimisation procedure on the calculation of derivatives of the objective function. These algorithms are collectively known as gradient methods and they include the Newton method, Davidson-Fletcher-Powell, Steepest Descent, Gauss, and Quadratic Hill Climbing, among many others. The non-gradient, or derivative free methods, are generally of most use when the function to be minimised is extremely irregular. This class includes the Powell algorithm, the non-linear Simplex method and Grid Search methods among others.

(i) Gradient methods
Given a current value C^i the gradient methods all proceed by constructing a sequence where

$$M(C^i - S N \delta) < M(C^i) \tag{36}$$

so that $C^{i+1} = C^i - S N \delta$,

where S is the step length (a scalar), δ is a vector of first partial derivatives of M with respect to the control variables, so

$$\delta = \frac{\partial M}{\partial c^i}$$

The construction of N is the feature which characterises the various gradient methods. The definition is considered below. As for the evaluation of both first and second derivatives, these may be done either analytically or numerically. For analytical calculation the actual formulae for the derivatives must be coded into the computer program. In the case of large models this formulae is often impossible to calculate analytically as the expression will involve differentiation with respect to the whole model. In practice it is often satisfactory to use numerical approximation to the derivatives, so that

$$\frac{\partial M}{\partial c_K} = \frac{M(C_1 \ldots (C_K + \Delta) \ldots C_{TxJ}) - M(C_1 \ldots C_{TxJ})}{\Delta} \qquad (37)$$

where Δ is a suitably small number. This is a 'one-sided' derivative calculation. Improved accuracy can be achieved, at extra cost, by using a two-sided approximation. In choosing Δ two factors should be borne in mind: an accurate derivative requires a small Δ but, if the model is being solved iteratively, there will be some inaccuracy in the model solution itself so Δ must not become so small that the model inaccuracy significantly affects the calculation of (37).

(a) The Newton method

The Newton (sometimes called Newton-Raphson) method is perhaps the most fundamental of the gradient methods. Many other methods are developments of it, or approximations to it, and are often called quasi-Newton methods. The Newton method makes use of the matrix of second derivatives of the objective function with respect to the control variables (the hessian matrix) to set the step size. So in this case

$$N = \left[\frac{\partial^2 M}{\partial C \partial C'} \right]^{-1} \tag{38}$$

and $S = 1$. If the function M were quadratic the Newton step procedure would reach the optimum point in one iteration. In essence the algorithm works by making a series of local quadratic approximations of M, solving this problem and then recomputing the approximation.

In order to give some intuitive understanding of the procedure consider the one control variable case where the minimum is given by C^* and the initial value is C^1. At the optimum point we know that the derivative $\frac{\partial M}{\partial C} = 0 = \delta^*$. We can approximate the second derivative by

$$\frac{\delta_1 - \delta_2}{C_1 - C_2} = \delta^2 \tag{39}$$

In the case of a quadratic function the second derivative is constant and (17) will be accurate for all values of C_1 and C_2. If the derivative at C^1 is δ_1 then we know that

$$\frac{\delta^* - \delta_1}{C^* - C^1} = \delta^2 \tag{40}$$

and rearranging this with $\delta^* = 0$ gives

$$C^* = C^1 - \frac{\delta_1}{\delta^2} .$$

(b) Method of steepest descent

At the current point C^i, the direction which will improve the objective function most rapidly, is given simply by the vector of first derivatives, δ. The method of steepest descent therefore sets N equal to the identity matrix (or minus the identity matrix if the problem is one of maximisation). The important choice therefore becomes the determination of the step size. In this case some variant of the Armijo (1966) step procedure is generally used. This works as follows. A succession of steps are generated using

$$S_i = \lambda B^i \qquad i = 0, \ldots$$

where λ is some given maximum step size and B is a constant, $0 < B < 1$. Some form of grid search may then be used over these step sizes to check for the best step size at each iteration.

The method of steepest descent avoids the costly computation of the hessian matrix but its disadvantage is that convergence can often be slow and there are well-known examples where the algorithm will not reach a maximum.

(c) Method of Quadratic Hill Climbing

The method of Quadratic Hill Climbing (Goldfeld et al, 1966) is a slight extension of the standard Newton algorithm to include a variable step size.   This may improve the performance of the algorithm when the function is non-concave or far from close to quadratic.

(ii) The Quasi-Newton methods

In order to calculate the hessian matrix required by the Newton method either an expensive numerical procedure must be repeated at each iteration or the analytical second derivatives must be calculated and supplied.   The Quasi-Newton methods are a family of algorithms which avoid this necessity by calculating an approximation to the hessian matrix, continually updating this and improving this approximation.

From (40) we can see that

$$\left[\frac{\partial^2 M}{\partial C \partial C'} \right]_i^{-1} = (C^{i+1} - C^i)(\delta^{i+1} - \delta^i)^{-1} \tag{41}$$

so by comparing the parameter estimates and the derivatives at two succeeding iterations we can estimate the hessian at the last iteration. This may be compared with the estimate using E_i and then some correction based on the error can be made so that

$$E_{i+1} = E_i + g(E_i, \frac{\partial^2 M}{\partial C \partial C'}) \tag{42}$$

The precise form of the correction determines the form of the Quasi-Newton algorithm under consideration. One of the most common algorithms in this class is the Davidson-Fletcher-Powell method. Himmelblau (1972) presents a number of correction formulae.

(iii) Derivative-free techniques

Generally speaking optimisation techniques which employ derivatives are faster and more reliable when the function being maximised is well behaved. The derivative-free techniques are recommended for highly non-linear functions or functions which are subject to discontinuities. In principle the reason for this is simple to understand: the gradient-based techniques work by examining the first and second derivatives at a single point, and drawing an inference about the whole surface based on some simple regularity conditions. When a function is either discontinuous or highly non-linear the information given at a single point can be very misleading. The derivative-free techniques generally derive their working information by examining a larger area around a current point on a surface, and so they are less likely to draw very fragile inferences about the shape of the surface being climbed.

The two widely used algorithms in this class are the conjugate gradient method of Powell (1964) and the non-linear Simplex method suggested by Spendley, Hext and Himsworth (1962). The Powell technique works essentially by carrying out a set of linear searches in orthogonal pairs and deriving a direction of movement from this information. The Simplex technique constructs a simplex around some initial point and evaluates the objective function at the vertices of the simplex. It then uses this information to derive its direction of movement.

(iv) Inequality-constrained optimisation

If, in addition to the constraints provided by the model, the optimisation is also subject to a set of inequality constraints, the problem becomes much more difficult. There are basically two approaches to dealing with this problem: the first involves adapting the objective function so as to penalise any violations of the constraint; the second adapts the optimisation algorithm.

When the objective function is adapted the technique is generally known as a barrier method. The idea is to define a barrier function which heavily penalises violation of the constraint but has a near-zero effect when the constraint is satisfied. Suppose we have the following set of inequality constraints

$$G(C) \geq 0 \tag{43}$$

Then we create a set of barrier functions such as

$$B[G(C)] \tag{44}$$

where $B[G(C)]$ is near zero for $G(C) \geq 0$ and is large for $B[G(C)] < 0$. A typical function might be

$$B_i[G(C)] = - \gamma \ln[G_i(C)]$$

where γ is a suitably chosen weighting factor.

The disadvantages of this technique are first, that a good barrier function should be highly non-linear and so will make the optimisation more difficult. Second if the unconstrained optimum were near or on the constraint the barrier function will tend to distort the final solution. If a barrier function is to be used it is often advisable to experiment with dropping all or some of the terms to check which constraints would be actually violated in unconstrained optimisation.

The other approach to inequality constraints is to adapt the direction finding procedure so that the algorithm does not move in directions which violate the inequality constraints. This amounts to deriving an (M, δ) pair in such a way that it will not cause steps out of the feasible region. Algorithms which implement such procedures are collectively termed methods of feasible direction, and a detailed survey of these techniques may be found in Polak (1972). A typical procedure would be to derive the gradient vector and then calculate the derivatives of any close inequality constraints. A linear-programming problem may then be formed which maximises the change in the objective function, given from the gradient vector, subject to not violating the constraints.

4. Optimal control exercises using complete macro models

A. Introduction

The rest of this chapter is mainly devoted to describing the results of applying optimal control methods to large scale non-linear econometric models.   The aim is to illustrate the use of optimal control in analysing the policy implications of models, not the derivation of normative policy rules per sé.   To this end, we invariably set the optimising problem up as a regulator problem, the main features of which, for the linear and non-linear case, were reviewed in sections 2 and 3.   This invariably entails the use of quadratic-type cost functions for the optimisation.   In our applications this does not yield the familiar advantages for such an assumption when used in conjunction with linear models - namely the derivation of linear control rules.   In our examples, however, the use of these quadratic cost functions may be justified in terms of their relevance to the particular problem investigated.   For example, below we illustrate the calculation of a dynamic non-accelerating inflation rate of unemployment [the NAIRU] using optimal control methods.   The relevance of a quadratic cost function to this is clear, it makes the derivation and interpretation of the resulting dynamic solution particularly easy.

The rest of the section describes the results of a number of diverse applications of control theory to macro models, designed to illustrate a number of issues raised in earlier parts of the chapter. First, we illustrate the use of optimal control in the analysis of the policy properties of estimated macro models (section (ii)), and section (iii) illustrates the problem of model uncertainty using optimal control. (Section (C) in Chapter 8 shows the results of optimal policy analysis in a model using rational expectations, in deriving optimal time consistent policies.)

B. Policy trade-offs in optimal control exercises

There are a variety of techniques for studying the dynamic policy properties of an econometric model, the most common being simulations where deviations of endogenous variables from historical or base paths are computed following a change in a policy instrument like government spending, or tax rates, The deviations in the endogenous variables are then attributable to the change in the instrument, and illustrations of the policy implications derivable from models were given in chapter 5. In this chapter, we will use optimal control analysis to provide an alternative evaluation of the policy properties of dynamic econometric models. Though the policy implications of the models are given by the estimated properties of that model, optimal control analysis enables a more sophisticated policy design to be derived, as compared with the less formal analysis provided by simulation exercises. In this section we provide two illustrations of these techniques, both concerned with policy trade-offs.

(i) An optimal interpretation of the Phillips Curve

The optimising exercises are conducted by treating the full National Institute model as a set of known deterministic constraints which define the set of feasible, or possible, values which policy instruments and objective variables may take (see Brooks, Henry and Karakitsos (1983)). The optimisations are also deterministic, and conducted over a six year horizon, this period being taken as a period sufficiently long that its further extension will make no appreciable difference to the recommended initial policy. For these optimal control exercises the objectives are price inflation (ΔP) and unemployment (U), although we also use intermediate objectives like the current balance of the balance of payments and the PSBR. The policy instruments are the average rate of indirect tax (tp), the standard rate of income tax (t) and the level of general government consumption of goods and services (G). The objective function is of the form:

$$J = \sum_t [\alpha_1 (Y - Y^*)_t^2 + \alpha_2 (X - X^*)_t^2 + \alpha_3 (\Delta X)_t] \tag{45}$$

where Y is the set of objective variables, X the set of policy instruments and * indicates a desired value. Several things have to be noted about this form of objective function. Firstly, concentration on inflation and unemployment objectives provides a reasonable representation of macro economic priorities in many developed economies. Secondly, it ignores discounting. This would be a serious weakness in long-run analysis, but here it is a convenient simplification. Thirdly, we include the levels and rates of change of the policy instruments in the objective function. This reflects the emphasis of the present exercise on optimal stabilisation policies. It may be that these instruments are important for other aspects of economic policy not considered here; the relevance of income tax rates to questions of income distribution is one obvious example. Penalising the movement of instruments from their historic levels is a general recognition that other policy - apart from stabilisation - matters. We also incorporate a penalty on the rate of change of each policy instrument on the grounds that changes in policy involve direct administrative costs in themselves.

To produce the optimising runs, a base run is needed. In an informal way, this is described as a 'do nothing' case, i.e. a simulation of the model over the planning horizon where the designated policy instruments are not actively used to achieve an optimal outturn. In order to derive this base run, the model is solved over the period 1978Q2-1984Q1, with the policy instruments fixed at their average value for the period. The instruments involved and their base run values are:

tp = the tax rate of consumers' expenditure. Average value taken as 15
     per cent.
t = the standard rate of income tax. Average value taken as 30 per
     cent.
G = public authorities' consumption. Average value taken as £6,000
     million (1975 prices).

The base solution then is the solution given these values for the policy instruments, with all exogenous variables taking their historical values for the period 1978Q2-1983Q1, and taking forecast values for all subsequent quarters, using the May 1983 National Institute forecast.

Control runs are then generated by optimising the given objective function, by active use of the three policy instruments (tp, t, G). The resulting values for the endogenous variables in the model, including price inflation, unemployment, and the current balance, measured as deviations from the base run, can then be attributed to the changes in the policy instruments (also measured from their base run values). Apart from tp, t, and G, all other variables which might be policy determined are held at their base run values. In particular it is assumed that monetary policy ensures that nominal interest rates are kept at their actual values.

The relative weights on objectives and instruments are given numerical values as shown in the table below. Later we conduct sensitivity analysis, which explores the consequences of changing these weights in a specified way. The final items in the specification of the objective function are the 'desired' values of instruments and objectives. For the instruments we assume that the desired levels of these variables are the same as in the base - or 'do nothing' - run; hence penalising movement of policy instruments away from their historic average value. The desired values of objective variables are chosen as follows: for unemployment a level of 500,000; for the current balance a desired value of zero is taken. For further sensitivity analysis see

Henry, Karakitsos and Savage (1982).

Table 1. Specification of the objective function

Variable	Definition	Desired value	Weight
U	UK unemployed ('000s)	500,000	0.5×10^{-4}
ΔP	Consumer price inflation	0	1.0
CB	Current balance (£ million)	0	
tp	Tax rate of consumers' expenditure	15%	0.9
t	The standard rate of income tax	30%	0.35
G	Public authorities' consumption	6,000 £ 1975, million	0.1×10^{-3}
ΔG	-	0	0.1×10^{-3}
Δt	-	0	50.0 [1]
Δtp	-	0	300.0 [1]

(1) In the second quarter of each year this weight is decreased to ensure tax changes occur annually.

The control exercises reported use the cumulative values of the current balance in the objective function. This may be interpreted as a concern with the terminal state of the optimising problem. On this interpretation policy is directed at inflation and unemployment objectives, but without the cumulative current balances seriously moving further from their historical values over the period. The risk of pursuing domestic objectives by building up problems for subsequent periods is then minimised.

The possibility of costless improvements

Under this heading we discuss two possible fiscal manoeuvres which may produce an output expansion without significant inflation cost and note some empirical evidence bearing on this issue. The policies involved are a reduction in the rate of income tax and a reduction in the rate of indirect tax.

Income tax cuts

The 'free lunch' possibility based on reductions in personal income taxes has been widely discussed (Corden, 1981). A central assumption is that wage inflation depends on the discrepancy between the value of actual and desired net real wages. On this assumption, an income tax reduction, while demand expansionary through familiar channels (increasing net real incomes and expenditures), may reduce wage demands and, hence, inflation. Output expands and price inflation may or may not increase depending upon the net effect of several factors: the effect on prices of a declining exchange rate, the effects on wage settlements of the tightening labour market, and the countervailing effect on wage bargains of the increase in the average retention ratio (the ratio of net to gross wages). If the last mentioned effect is sufficiently large, then the inflationary effects of the expansion in demand may be offset by the increase in net wages compared to their desired or target value.

Indirect tax changes

The underlying analysis of this problem can be illustrated by using an orthodox aggregate demand model for the open economy with wage-price interactions. Initially monetary accommodation is assumed. Then a decrease in the level of indirect taxes will initially decrease price inflation, but this initial change in prices is echoed by feedback from the price inflation effect on wage inflation and from wage inflation to price inflation. Decreases in domestic inflation (with overseas inflation constant) will lead to appreciations in the exchange rate, tending to amplify the effects of the initial tax change. Meanwhile on the real side, increases in real incomes and real balance effects will encourage expenditure, leading to increases in output and employment. These expansionary influences will be moderated, or offset, by the effects of falling unemployment and a worsening trade balance on the rate of inflation. The overall quantitative results will depend upon the strength of certain key relationships; the unemployment effect on wage inflation, the size of the inflation loss term in the consumption function, and so on. Allowing the money supply to adapt as activity changes to ensure that nominal interest rates remain unchanged, will imply that the real interest rate changes as price inflation varies. Increases in real interest rates will lead to decreased aggregate expenditure and appreciations in the exchange rate, while decreases in real interest rates have the opposite effect. The eventual quantitative outcome for unemployment and price inflation could be that each will move in the same direction, or in a more familiar inverse way, depending on the magnitudes of the influences noted above.

The optimal solutions

These possibilities in the responses of the estimated model are now explored in an optimal control exercise. These use the objective function described in Table 1, using the National Institute Model 7 as the set of non-linear constants in the optimisation. The instruments are the fiscal instruments tp, t, and G defined earlier, and the exercise is conducted over the period 1978Q2-1984Q1, although to economise on detail only annual results of the optimisation are reported. This version of the model is a 'backward' looking one in the sense that explicit rational expectations are not assumed. Expected future variables where they enter the model are proxied by lagged actual values.

Table 2. Optimal solution using the objective function from table 1.

Variable Year	1	2	3	4	5	6	Average
U	11	-79	-178	-212	-213	-300	-162
ΔP	0.49	-0.88	-0.16	0.92	0.34	0.03	0.12
CB	76	-18	-164	-111	-48	-216	-80
ΔY	-0.16	0.70	1.40	1.20	1.00	1.90	1.00
PSBR	-328	236	345	-102	87	656	149
ER	0.41	0.25	-0.52	-1.10	-1.80	-2.80	-0.92
tp	1.20	-0.96	-1.10	-0.08	-1.00	-1.70	-0.62
t	1.70	1.70	1.90	2.70	3.20	2.30	2.30
G	22	195	285	263	248	383	233

(for definitions see overleaf)

Definitions:

(1) All figures are annual averages.

(2) Y and ER are given as percentage changes from the base; all other
     variables are given as absolute changes from the base.

U   Unemployment, UK, thousands.

P   Rate of consumer price inflation.

CB   Current balance.

Y   Rate of growth of GDP (expenditure estimate) at factor cost, 1975
     prices.

PSBR Public sector borrowing requirement.

ER   Sterling effective exchange rate.

tp   Tax rate on consumers' expenditure.

t   Standard rate of income tax.

G   Public authority consumption, 1975 prices.

The results shown in table 2 indicate that a significant decrease
in unemployment is possible with very little change in the general rate
of price inflation over the control period using a judicious mixture of
expenditure and tax changes. This result suggests that when policy is
optimally calibrated, the implied trade-off between price inflation and
unemployment is quite shallow. A note of caution is required however in
this interpretation.   The trade-off we describe is between two
variables, but other variables enter the objective function, and these
will change during the optimisation. The ceteris paribus interpretation
we give of the (P, U) trade-off is not strictly valid therefore, though
multi-dimensional trade offs would be cumbersome. But to continue in
the vein of the previous exercise, we next investigate the effects of
altering the relative weight on unemployment in the objective function
(table 3), first by a decrease of 100 per cent from the value in that
table and then an increase of 100 per cent (table 4). The results of
this exercise are shown in tables 3 and 4, and indeed show that the

implied trade-off is fairly shallow. (At least this appears true in the
region of solution values embraced by the results in the three tables.)
Roughly speaking, what this calculation shows is that a fall in
unemployment of 200,000 produces an additional 1 per cent inflation on
average over the six year period of the exercise.

Table 3.   100 per cent decrease in the weight on unemployment

Variable	Year	1	2	3	4	5	6	Average
U		62	113	145	163	173	212	145
P		-0.61	-0.68	-0.68	-0.60	-0.56	-0.62	-0.62
CB		6.60	53	66	21	2.20	97	41
Y		-0.51	-0.74	-0.86	-0.87	-0.86	-1.20	-0.84
PSBR		117	11	-108	-91	-51	-200	-54
ER		0.02	0.69	1.80	2.90	4.00	5.20	2.40
tp		-1.30	-0.93	-0.50	-0.21	-0.05	0.13	-0.48
t		0.28	-0.02	-0.26	-0.47	-0.57	-0.30	-0.22
G		-132	-189	-207	-203	-199	-249	-197

Definitions as table 2.

Table 4.   100 per cent increase in the weight on unemployment

Variable	Year	1	2	3	4	5	6	Average
U		-104	-178	-221	-245	-262	-317	-221
P		0.90	1.10	1.10	0.94	0.88	0.99	0.98
CB		-16	-88	-101	-26	0.80	-158	-65
Y		0.85	1.20	1.30	1.30	1.30	1.70	1.30
PSBR		-186	-31	158	120	42	284	64
ER		-0.07	-1.10	-2.80	-4.30	-5.90	-7.60	-3.60
tp		2.20	1.50	0.82	0.37	0.15	-0.12	0.82
t		-0.51	-0.04	0.34	0.72	1.00	0.64	0.36
G		219	290	310	304	305	377	301

(ii) An optimal version of the NAIRU

A related concept to that of the Natural Rate of Unemployment which has
gained increasing currency in policy debate, especially in the UK, is
the Non-Accelerating Inflation Rate of Unemployment (NAIRU). In most
applications this is taken to be the non-accelerating solution to an
estimated labour market model, and below we note how this concept may be
applied to the relevant equations of a version of the National Institute
model. However, our main argument in this section is implicitly a
general critique of the analysis of macro economic behaviour using the
NAIRU. [See for example the special issue of Economica (1986) for
numerous examples of this.] Our argument is essentially very simple:
the NAIRU analysis is firstly couched in long-run steady states (i.e.
non-accelerating states) and so suppresses dynamic features of models
which may be long-lasting. Secondly, concentration on the labour market
is at best a partial analysis, which ignores substantial influences from
other sectors of the economy. These include sectors such as the
overseas sector and exchange rate, and for an economy with the degree of
openness which the UK has, their suppression is obviously a serious
limitation. These limitations, we suggest, are too high a price to pay
for the advantages of simplicity and the relative ease of interpretation
which such NAIRU analysis affords.

Below we remedy these defects by illustrating the calculation of
NAIRUs for complete macro models with full allowance for the model's
dynamics. These will use National Institute Model 8, a model with

extensive forward-looking behaviour. Two illustrations are then made:
one where backward-formed expectations are applied in the model, and one
with forward-looking rational expectations.

(a) Backward-formed expectations

Chapter 5 describes how the model may be operated with expectations
formed using autoregressive equations for expected variables. In this
mode, we then calculate the NAIRU implied by the model by formulating an
optimal control problem, using central government current expenditure on
goods and services as the sole policy instrument, and the unweighted
objective function

$$W = \sum_{1}^{T} (\Delta \ln CPI - \phi)_t^2$$

where CPI = the consumer price index, and ϕ is some pre-set value for
this. The optimising problem is then the (conceptually if not
computationally) simple one-objective/one-instrument problem, which we
can solve uniquely. The optimisation is subject to the deterministic
form of the whole model over the time interval 1979Q1-1983Q4. In these
experiments ϕ is taken to be 10% and 5% per annum in two separate
optimisations, and can be used to investigate the quantitative nature of
the trade-off between constant inflation and average unemployment
levels. In all the model simulations we report, expectations are
assumed to be formed using predictions from single equation, backward-
looking, time-series models for expected variables. Also the solutions
are each ex-post, using actual values for all exogenous variables,

including policy variables, with the exception of current government expenditure. The results are shown in Figure 1.

What the chart shows is that the NAIRU calculated as the fully-dynamic solution to an entire open economy macro-model has two characteristics. Firstly, for a given level of inflation, the NAIRU fluctuates considerably, varying from just under one million to over three million. Secondly, it reveals a trade-off which persists over the period, in that the NAIRU for ϕ = 5% is everywhere in excess of that for a higher rate of inflation (ϕ = 10%). However, the absolute amount of the difference between the two varies over time. We next discuss the rationale for these two features.

The time-varying NAIRU

For each of the target rates of inflation the calculated NAIRU increased rapidly after a fall in 1980. There are then steady increases in the NAIRU, even for a 10% constant inflation target. A large part of the explanation for this lies in the nature of the dynamic solution used. Essentially, this takes unemployment as a proximate determinant of inflation, and in turn treats government expenditure as the instrument for effecting changes in unemployment. Other deflationary techniques are not allowed in the scenario. These include monetary policy, for example, high interest rates with high exchange rate, and other, more efficient, fiscal methods of reducing inflation (for example, decreases in indirect taxes). Thus the limitation of the present exercise is that it does not seek the optimal policy mix which would stabilise inflation at minimum cost in terms of unemployment (as was done for Model 7 in section (a) above), but uses only one instrument which operates on inflation only via the Phillips Curve effect in the wage equation.

Both solutions - for ϕ = 5% and 10% - show a similar profile over the solution period. The general reasoning behind these profiles is the same for each case. Thus in the first two years of the period, the NAIRU values radically differ from the actual values of unemployment. Initially, with inflation so high following the public sector pay explosion and the 1979 budget VAT increases, unemployment is rapidly increased over the actual value to decrease inflation (which was 13.5 in 1979 and 17.9 in 1980 as measured by the RPI). The large appreciation of the exchange rate introduced a substantial deflationary impulse in 1980, so the NAIRU is calculated to fall towards actual levels, with the previous high levels of unemployment feeding into lower wage increases, after a lag. In 1981 the calculated values of the NAIRU again jump above actual levels (in spite of the fact that these were now rising), as inflation proved slow to decrease even after the large appreciation in the £. For the rest of the period actual and NAIRU values broadly move in line suggesting that, on average, unemployment has been maintained at a level consistent with inflation somewhat below 5%.

The inflation-unemployment trade-off

Finally, we may note what the results of our experiments show for the inflation-unemployment trade-off. As Figure 1 illustrates, there is evidence of such a trade-off, and this is not a short-run (in real time) phenomenon. That is, to achieve a 5% reduction in average inflation, with the same inflationary shocks impinging upon the dynamic model solution, it appears necessary to raise unemployment by between 200,000-400,000, on average. Clearly, this will not always be true. Thus in the early part of the solution, very much larger increases in unemployment are required; in 1979Q4 for example this is of the order of 700,000. Given the variation in the actual level of inflation over the period, and the non-linearity of the model, these differences are to be expected.

(b) The NAIRU with rational expectations

Recomputing the NAIRU using rational forward-looking expectations formation and full consistent solutions also yields an interpretable evidence of a time-varying NAIRU. Thus in Figure 2 we depict a solution for the NAIRU derived from Model 8 with rational expectations, also obtained by employing optimal control. In the case depicted ϕ is equal to 10% per annum. Comparing this result to that shown for ϕ = 10% in Figure 1, the results using rational expectations show a similar, but more volatile, pattern. The increase in unemployment occurs instantly in the present run, in full anticipation of the need to offset future increases in the rate of inflation. This instant increase is successful in the sense that subsequently unemployment is lowered by a noticeable amount compared with the backward-looking solution, and this is done earlier - by the second quarter of 1980, compared to the low achieved in Figure 1 which occurs in 1981Q3. Again, the NAIRU rebounds more rapidly subsequently, indicating the greater volatility we expect from the model

Figure 1.   Comparison of NAIRU and actual unemployment

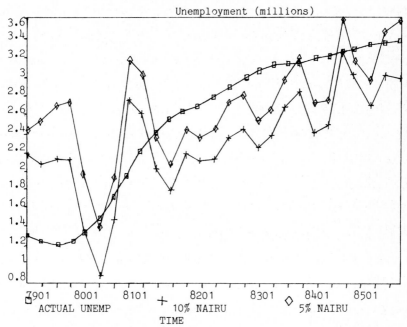

Figure 2.   NAIRU for model 8

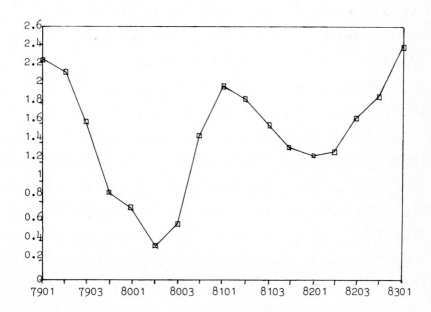

operated in a rational mode.

(c) Allowing for uncertainty in optimal control exercises on non-linear
models
There are two quite different approaches to the modelling and analysis
of uncertainty in contemporary economics; the first of these is what
might be termed 'econometric' uncertainty, that is modelling uncertainty
by allowing for uncertain parameter values, additive error terms and for
the possibility that variables are measured with error. This was
commented on in section 2(ii). The second approach is that of state
uncertainty which derives largely from the work of Arrow and Debreu,
which depicts uncertainty as a number of possible contingent states of
nature.

Earlier we outlined the effects of econometric uncertainty in
formulating optimal control rules using linear models. If on the other
hand we model uncertainty within the framework of state uncertainty a
problem which arises in optimal control analysis, in principle at least,
is the specification of the objective function. Consider the problem
from the point of view of a goverment formulating its welfare function;
it is then appropriate to maximise its expected welfare as long as
certain conditions are satisfied (see von Neumann and Morgenstern
(1947); Luce and Raiffa (1957), chapter 2; Hey (1979), chapter 4).
These conditions are (i) ordering of alternative outcomes, (ii)
applicability of the probability rule, (iii) continuity, (iv)
substitutability, (v) transitivity and (vi) monotonicity. Condition (i)
says that the government should be able to rank any two scenarios

unambiguously. Condition (ii) rules out a government deriving pleasure from the act of gambling on particular views of the world. Conditions (iii) and (iv) combined correspond to independence of irrelevant alternatives. Condition (v) may be violated due to the complexities caused by the multi-dimensional nature of economic welfare, although most decision makers would be prepared to re-appraise their preferences when such inconsistencies are pointed out. Condition (vi) rules out any psychological interaction between the alternative views on the economy and the corresponding probabilities.

Under these conditions we may formalise the government's welfare function as:

$$\text{Max } W = \sum_{s=1}^{S} \pi_s W_s (Y^s) \tag{46}$$

where π_s is the probability of state s occurring.

In the rest of this section we provide an illustration of this form of uncertainty in optimal control analysis. It concentrates solely on uncertainty as to the true model of the economy. To this end the econometric uncertainty reviewed above, which is always inherent in an econometric model, has been ignored, and we concentrate on uncertainty as to which model is the 'correct' characterisation of the economy. Two deterministic models are taken, one characterising broadly Keynesian views and the other being broadly monetarist. Each of these models will represent one possible state of nature, they will then be combined through an objective function of the von Neumann-Morgenstern type to yield a single optimal control problem which will give an economic policy which is optimal under conditions of uncertainty as to the true model.

   To keep this exercise within manageable proportions, we take simplified numerical models, not fully estimated econometric ones. The value of the present exercise then lies partly in the gross behaviour of the two models, and partly in its value as an example of how actual policy formulation could be carried out were enough resources to be made available to repeat the procedure using large scale econometric models. Although the parameters of the models are not estimated, nonetheless they, and lagged values of endogenous variables before t = 1, have been chosen so that the models will roughly approximate the state of the UK economy in 1975.

The Models:

| KEYNESIAN MODEL | MONETARIST MODEL |

$$Y_t = C_t + I_t + G_t \qquad\qquad Y_t = C_t + I_t + G_t \qquad (i)$$

$$C_t = a_{11} + a_{12} Y_{t-1} \qquad\qquad C_t = a_{21} + a_{22} Y_{t-1} + a_{23} \frac{M_t}{P_t} \qquad (ii)$$

$$I_t = b_{11} - b_{12} r_t \qquad\qquad I_t = b_{21} - b_{22} r_t \qquad (iii)$$

$$r_t = c_{11}(\frac{M_t}{P_t})^{-1} + c_{12} Y_t \qquad\qquad r_t = c_{21}(\frac{M_t}{P_t})^{-1} + c_{22} Y_t \qquad (iv)$$

$$\Delta P_t = \Delta P_{t-1} - d_{11} \ln (U_t/d_{12}) \qquad \Delta P_t = d_{21} \Delta P_{t-1} + d_{22} \Delta M_t \qquad (v)$$

$$L_t^D = (Y_t/e_{11})^{e_{12}} \qquad\qquad L_t^D = (Y_t/e_{21})^{e_{22}} \qquad (vi)$$

$$U_t = \frac{L_t^S - L_t^D}{L_t^S} \times 100 \qquad\qquad U_t = \frac{L_t^S - L_t^D}{L_t^S} \times 100 \qquad (vii)$$

$$M_{t+1} = M_t + (\Delta M_t . M_t/100) \qquad M_{t+1} = M_t + (\Delta M_t . M_t/100) \qquad (viii)$$

$$P_{t+1} = P_t + (\Delta P_t . P_t/100) \qquad P_{t+1} = P_t + (\Delta P_t . P_t/100) \qquad (ix)$$

where: Y_t = Expenditure, C_t = Consumption, I_t = Investment, G_t = Government expenditure, M_t = Nominal money stock, P^t = a price index, L_t^D = Labour demand, L_t^S = Labour supply, ΔM_t = the percentage change in M_t, ΔP_t = the percentage change in P_t, and r_t = the rate of interest.

Initial values have to be ascribed to Y_0 and ΔP_0, the values used correspond to actual 1974 figures. Y_0 = 100,000 and ΔP_0 = 17. The only remaining factor which needs to be specified in order to subject these models to an optimal control algorithm is the objective function and which variables are control variables. The control variables are taken to be government expenditure and the percentage change in the money supply. The objective function to be maximised is identical for both models, and is

$$\text{Max } W = \sum_{i=1}^{T} (\Delta P_t^2 + ((U_t - 1.0) . 2.5)^2) \tag{47}$$

This postulates what are taken to be plausible properties: that zero inflation and a one per cent level of unemployment are desired by the policymaker. Also it assumes that high inflation rates (say over 10 per cent) are more acceptable than unemployment rates of a similar magnitude.

The only differences between the two models are in terms of the way money enters the model in equations (ii) and (v). Despite the predominant similarities of the two models there is no reason to expect them to have the same long-run characteristics. These long-run properties may be examined on the assumption of fixed control variables. The Keynesian model yields the following first-order difference equation for national income

$$Y_t = \frac{1}{1+c_{12}b_{12}} \left[a_{12} Y_{t-1} - b_{12} c_{11} \left[\frac{f(Y_{t-1})}{M_t} \right] + a_{11} + b_{11} + G. \right] \tag{48}$$

where $f(Y_{t-1})$ is the relationship between prices and lagged income through the Phillips' Curve. Specifically

$$f(Y_{t-1}) = P_t = P_{t-1} + \left[\Delta P_{t-2} - d_{11} \ln \left[\frac{L^S - (\frac{Y_{t-1}}{e_{11}})^{e_{12}} / L^S}{d_{12}} \right] P_t - 1/100 \right] \quad (49)$$

When unemployment is above d_{12}, the natural rate, $f(Y_{t-1})$ is negative, implying that the rate of inflation is falling. In other words the economy will tend to move towards the natural rate of employment. The only stable equilibrium will be at the unemployment rate d_{12} with zero inflation. This long-run equilibrium point is the point towards which the economy will move, but this may not be attainable if the model exhibits a constraint such as a liquidity trap. If unemployment is above d_{12} then it will be reduced by rising real money supply causing a fall in the rate of interest. But the rate of interest cannot fall below zero so there is a maximum possible level of investment i.e. b_{11}. This may not be sufficient to cure unemployment. So in general when M and G are fixed arbitrarily the economy will move towards a long-run equilibrium point of zero inflation and d_{12} unemployment, but this point may not be attainable for any given level G.

The most important determinant of the long-run equilibrium is, of course, the two control variables M and G. If the optimal control vectors (M* and G*) are substituted into the model, then the long-run equilibrium occurs with zero inflation and unemployment equal to d_{12}. The possibility of a liquidity trap equilibrium with unemployment above d_{12} is removed, as government expenditure can ensure sufficient demand. An interesting point however is that the objective function yields a maximum at 1 per cent unemployment while the model has a long-run equilibrium at d_{12} which is specified as 1.8 per cent. So the optimal control vector will depend, at least in part, on the time horizon taken. If a long time horizon is taken, then the vertical Phillip's Curve is the relevant constraint and the best attainable point will be unemployment equal to d_{12}. If, on the other hand, an extremely short time horizon is taken, then the relevant constraint will be the short run, negatively sloped, Phillips Curve. The resulting optimal solution may then be found by solving the following programming problem

$$W = (\Delta P)^2 + [(U-1)\ 2.5]^2 + \lambda(\Delta P + \ln(\frac{U}{1.8})) \tag{50}$$

which yields the following first order conditions

$$2P + \lambda = 0$$

$$2\ [(U-1)\ 2.5]\ 2.5 + \frac{1}{U}\ \lambda = 0$$

$$\Delta P + \ln(\frac{U}{1.8}) \qquad\qquad = 0$$

with an optimal unemployment inflation mix of U = 1.1%, ΔP = 0.5%.

A parallel analysis for the monetarist model then takes the dynamic equations for output from the monetarist case, i.e.

$$Y_t = \frac{1}{1+c_{22}b_{cc}}\ [a_{22}\ Y_{t-1} + a_{21} + a_{23}\ \frac{M_t}{P_t}$$

$$+ b_{21} - b_{22}\ c_{21}\ (\frac{M_t}{P_t})^{-1} + G_t] \tag{51}$$

In this case with M_t and G_t over time we can define a constant

$$\omega = a_{21} + a_{23} \frac{M_t}{P_t} + b_{21} - b_{22} \, c_{21} \, (\frac{M_t}{P_t})^{-1} + G_t$$

and the long run level of income is

$$Y = A\omega$$

where $A = \{[1 - a_{22}/(1 + c_{22} \, b_{22})] \, [1 + c_{22} \, b_{22}]\}^{-1}$

This long run level of income depends only upon ω, and inflation is zero if M is constant.

Because the model exhibits long-run money neutrality it is possible to determine the long-run inflation rate and unemployment rate separately. It is therefore quite possible to attain the maximum point of the objective function (u = 1%, ΔP = 0). A simple long-run rule for achieving this would be to set ΔM = 0 and adjust G so as to generate full employment over a number of periods. The low real money supply would, in the short term, reduce consumption and investment if the initial position is one with positive inflation. This fall in demand can, however, be offset by high levels of government expenditure. This policy would be similar to Friedman's concept of a monetary rule and it would certainly be optimal in the long run. If the economy starts out of equilibrium however, there is no reason why this policy should be optimal during the adjustment period before the long-run equilibrium is reached. Indeed even within the monetarist model it may be optimal to have a varying rate of growth of the money supply until equilibrium is reached. The zero money supply growth rule would yield the long-run equilibrium eventually but an actual fall in the money supply in the first few years of the policy might yield a faster adjustment process.

Numerical results of the optimal control exercise

The two models are first optimised separately so that the appropriate policies can be found if the true model of the economy was known to be one of the two models. The solution interval is taken to be ten periods. First, the results for the Keynesian model are shown in table 5.

Table 5.   The optimisation of the 'Keynesian' model

Period	Y(£M)	U(%)	ΔP(%)	G(£M)	ΔM(%)
1	100,822	5.0	15.9	15,800	10.7
2	101,071	4.7	15.0	15,770	11.4
3	101,320	4.4	14.1	15,975	11.36
4	101,574	4.13	13.27	16,170	11.44
5	101,833	3.8	12.52	16,350	11.95
6	102,100	3.5	11.85	16,500	11.87
7	102,383	3.17	11.28	16,640	11.79
8	102,689	2.8	10.84	16,800	12.23
9	103,036	2.4	10.55	16,950	12.16
10	103,469	1.88	10.5	17,160	4.4

The optimal policy for the Keynesian model yields steadily falling paths for both unemployment and inflation. The model is clearly converging on its long-run equilibrium but it is doing so fairly slowly. It is seen to be optimal to sustain a fairly high level of unemployment in the early years in order to bring down the rate of inflation more quickly.

The same exercise is conducted for the monetarist model, and the results of this are shown next (table 6).

Table 6.   The optimisation of the 'monetarist' model

Period	Y(£M)	U(%)	ΔP(%)	G(£M)	ΔM(%)
1	104,309	0.89	7.4	19,230	-2.1
2	104,239	0.97	2.6	18,220	-2.1
3	104,210	1.01	0.3	18,785	-2.0
4	104,251	0.96	-0.16	19,100	-0.6
5	104,251	0.96	-0.22	19,150	-0.2
6	104,244	0.97	-0.05	19,150	0.10
7	104,259	0.95	0.02	19,150	0.10
8	104,277	0.93	0.05	19,150	0.09
9	104,289	0.92	0.01	19,150	-0.03
10	104,290	0.92	0.02	19,150	0.03

Contrasting the optimal path of the Keynesian model with this path it is immediately obvious that the monetarist model converges to its long-run equilibrium much more quickly. High government expenditure quickly generates low unemployment levels, while a fall in the money supply quickly brings about a reduction in the inflation rate. The model can be regarded as having reached its long-run equilibrium within the first four years. From the fifth year a monetary rule of the Friedman variety seems to be optimal, but it is not an optimal policy during the approach to equilibrium.

The next question which is posed is what would be the effect of implementing one of these policy sets if the policy makers were incorrect in their choice of the model? This may now be answered by carrying out simulations of each model with the control variables generated by the other model. Table 7 shows the policy derived from the monetarist model, incorrectly applied to the Keynesian model.

Table 7. The Keynesian model with the 'monetarist' control variables

Period	Y(£M)	U(%)	ΔP(%)	G(£M)	ΔM(£)
1	104,335	0.86	17.7	19,230	-2.1
2	104,918	0.50	19.0	18,220	-2.1
3	105,116	0.50	20.2	18,785	-2.0
4	104,692	0.50	21.5	19,100	-0.6
5	103,490	1.8	21.5	19,150	-0.2
6	101,664	4.0	20.7	19,150	0.10
7	99,350	6.7	19.4	19,150	0.10
8	96,613	9.9	17.7	19,150	0.09
9	93,526	13.5	15.6	19,150	-0.03
10	90,178	17.3	13.4	19,150	+0.03

The striking thing about this set of results is that for the first four
or five years the results of this policy might well be considered
preferable to the optimal Keynesian one.   In the first period for
example unemployment is reduced from 5 per cent to 0.86 per cent at the
cost of less than 2 per cent extra inflation.   By the end of the period
however the desirability of the Keynesian policy becomes apparent as
inflation is still over 13 per cent and unemployment is at 17 per cent.
In fact as both G and M are being held constant the model is in effect
performing a huge loop back towards its long-run equilibrium.   As long
as ΔP is positive, unemployment will continue to rise.   Once ΔP becomes
negative unemployment will fall until the long-run equilibrium is
reached.   This illustrates two important points: first that even though
a Keynesian model of this type may have a stable long-run equilibrium it
may take a very long time to reach it, and secondly that Friedman's
constant ΔM rule can be highly sub-optimal in a non-monetarist model.

Now consider the effect on the economy if the Keynesian plan were
implemented when the monetarist model was the true one.   Results for
this are shown in table 8.

Table 8.   The 'monetarist' model with the Keynesian control variables

Period	Y(£M)	U(%)	ΔP(%)	G(£M)	ΔM(%)
1	100,797	5.0	13.9	15,800	10.7
2	100,799	5.0	12.65	15,770	11.4
3	100,879	5.0	12.00	15,975	11.36
4	101,045	4.8	11.72	16,170	11.44
5	101,276	4.5	11.84	16,350	11.95
6	101,557	4.2	11.85	16,500	11.87
7	101,848	3.8	11.82	16,640	11.79
8	102,141	3.5	12.0	16,800	12.23
9	102,469	3.0	12.1	16,950	12.16
10	102,859	2.6	8.2	17,160	4.4

In this solution steadily rising levels of G reduce the level of
unemployment, while decreases to the money supply gradually reduce
inflation.   The Keynesian policy thus works quite well within the
monetarist model.   It is, of course, vastly inferior to the monetarist
control path but a government bringing about this effect might well be
considered successful.   It is apparent that it would not be disastrous
to make planning decisions on the basis of the Keynesian model, even if
this were the inappropriate model.

The problem facing the economic planner is however a profound one;

whichever model he bases his economic policy on, he runs the potential risk of generating a sub-optimal path for the economy. If he plans on the basis of the monetarist model he runs the risk of an immense economic depression if the Keynesian model is the true one. If, on the other hand, the Keynesian model is used for economic planning then the economy may still perform way below potential if the monetarist model is the true one. This problem of model uncertainty is an ideal one for the application of the state uncertainty case outlined earlier. In order to resolve this problem we maximise the following objective function

$$\text{Max } W = - \sum_{i=1}^{T} \left[\Pi_K \{ (\Delta P_t^K)^2 + ((U_t^K - 1.0) \cdot 2.5)^2 \} \right. \tag{52}$$

$$\left. + \Pi_M \{ (\Delta P_t^M)^2 + ((U_t^M - 1.0) \cdot 2.5)^2 \} \right]$$

Subject to the state equations given by both economic models, Π_K and Π_M are the respective probabilities of Keynesian and the 'monetarist' models representing the true state of nature. The superscripts K and M refer to the two models. This problem has been solved on the assumption of equal probability weighting between the two models, that is $\Pi_K = \Pi_M = 0.5$. The following table gives the resulting solution.

Table 9. Solutions with uncertain states:

(a) The 'Keynesian' model with the state uncertain optimal control path

Period	Y(£M)	U(%)	ΔP(%)	G(£M)	ΔM(%)
1	101,901	3.7	16.0	16,850	2.3
2	102,201	3.4	15.6	16,570	2.3
3	102,660	2.8	15.2	17,255	2.3
4	102,579	2.9	14.7	17,350	2.3
5	102,700	2.8	14.2	17,950	2.3
6	102,672	2.8	13.8	18,330	2.3
7	102,684	2.8	13.3	18,870	2.3
8	102,519	3.0	12.8	19,250	-1.3
9	102,798	2.7	12.4	20,400	-0.7
10	103,146	2.3	12.1	21,450	0.0

(b) The 'monetarist' model with the state uncertain optimal control path

Period	Y(£M)	U(%)	ΔP(%)	G(£M)	ΔM(%)
1	101,876	3.7	9.6	16,850	2.3
2	101,643	4.0	5.9	16,370	2.3
3	101,795	3.8	4.1	17,255	2.3
4	101,756	3.9	3.2	17,350	2.3
5	102,243	3.3	2.7	17,950	2.3
6	102,828	2.6	2.5	18,330	2.3
7	103,638	1.6	2.4	18,870	2.3
8	104,410	0.7	0.5	19,250	-1.3
9	105,752	0.5	-0.1	20,400	-0.7
10	107,418	0.5	0.0	21,450	0.0

In the tables, neither result would be as good as the one generated by the optimal control path for each individual model, which is, of course, to be expected. But the possibility of a disastrous result, such as the one yielded by the 'Keynesian' model when the optimal 'monetarist' path was applied to it, is eliminated. No matter which of the two models were in fact truly representative of the real world the outcome of the optimal control trajectory would be acceptable.

In the Keynesian world unemployment is maintained at a reasonably low level while inflation is being gradually reduced. If the monetarist model were true, unemployment would initially rise and then decline over the rest of the period while inflation would be virtually eliminated by the end of the period. It is interesting to note that this 'uncertainty optimal' policy tends to use the constant money growth rule of the monetarists while also adopting the active fiscal policy of the Keynesians!

Conclusion

Uncertainty over which is the most appropriate model for policy formulation poses a serious problem. It has been argued that the solution to this problem may not be found by the use of empirical testing and that, indeed, the appropriate model may even change over time. A technique for formulating policies under the existence of this kind of state of nature uncertainty has been developed and applied to the two simple models so that an economic policy may be formulated which allows for this uncertainty. The technique proposed is an extremely general one being able to deal with problems with many states of nature;

in fact the only practical limits to its range of applications is in terms of the computer hardware available. The weakness of the work presented here lies primarily in the two models themselves. The models presented must be seen as purely an illustration of the proposed approach to policy formulation rather than a definitive set of policy tools.

THE ISSUE OF TIME INCONSISTENCY IN MACRO POLICY

1. Introduction

This chapter will survey some of the important ingredients in the 'time-inconsistency' debate which has attended the publication of the original article by Kydland and Prescott (1977). To its authors, and indeed to many commentators on this issue subsequently, the time-inconsistency proposition was interpreted as a decisive argument against the use of control theory in the design of economic policy. With rational expectations, policies which are optimal at one point of time may cease to be so later when the optimisation is recalculated. It is this property, it is argued, which makes the design of policy in the case of government facing an informed private sector different in kind from the case of policy design with a controller against nature. We will highlight very important qualifications that have been made to this proposition, qualifications which support the existence of optimal time-consistent policies in rational expectations models. These include the extensions of the analysis to reputational equilibria (Barro and Gordon (1983a), (1983b), Currie and Levine (1985), and Backus and Driffell, (1986)) and the re-evaluation of the principle of optimality involved in the derivation of policy rules (Hall (1987), Cohen and Michel (1986) and Hughes-Hallett (1986)). This discussion will occupy sections 2 and 3 below. These applications will all concentrate on linear models, where analytical results are obtainable. In section 4 we provide a further interpretation of time consistency based on Hall (1987), and follow this with a quantitative analysis of the issue of time inconsistency using a version of the National Institute macro econometric model. As the model is non-linear, the analysis in this latter passage is entirely numerical, but is an important addition to the theoretical discussion of the earlier sections, in that it utilises an econometric model.

The material is organised as follows. The next two sections are devoted to an introductory account of concepts used in the time-inconsistency debate. Section 4 then widens the class of models to incorporate a more familiar intertemporal optimal control form of policy design. Section 5 is then largely concerned with the non-linear econometric example.

2. Game theory: some basic concepts

The time inconsistency literature is a particular application of game theory. As such, many of the basic concepts used are best explained in a more general framework, and in this section we will give a brief account of the main ideas behind game theory. A more complete exposition may be found in Intriligator (1971). Two primary sources of particular importance are Luce and Raiffa (1957) and von Neumann and Morgenstern (1947).

In the discussion of control theory and optimisation in chapter 7, the implicit assumption was made that there was one decision maker whose preferences were represented by the objective function, and that the economy generally could be viewed as a purely mechanical set of constraints. This description is, in fact, a rather poor representation of economic behaviour since many decision makers are involved in most economic activities, and the objectives of the decision makers will generally conflict to a greater or lesser extent. Game theory is the extension of conventional optimisation theory to the case of multiple decision makers. The generalisation to two or more decision makers, or players, considerably complicates the problem, as one player's welfare not only depends on his decision and the equations of the system, but also on the decision made by the other player. In its most general form the multiplayer game will not yield a unique stable solution and so much of game theory has involved defining particular types of games which are tractable. Games can be classified by the nature of the payoff function; a zero sum game, a constant difference game or a non-zero sum game. They may be classified by the number of players, a two-player game or an n-player game. They may also be classified by the number of strategies each player may adopt, which may be either finite or infinite. Finally they may be classified by the amount of negotiation before play is initiated, and may be a cooperative game if coalitions between players are allowed, or non-cooperative games.

The most widely explored game is the two-person zero sum game; in this game there are only two players and the set-up of the game is such that each player is competing for a larger share of a total but fixed payout. Even in such a simple game, the possibility arises that no unique solution exists, and locating a solution, assuming one exists, may be analytically very difficult.

The analysis may be extended to allow for uncertainty in the response of one player to the other, to allow for non-zero sum situations and to allow for cooperation between groups of players when there are three or more players. We will not pursue these elaborations here as the essential point which we require is evident, that even in a simple game the assumption made about the other player's behaviour is critical. It is this assumption which is crucial to understanding the time inconsistency debate and so we will now outline a general framework for the types of assumption which are commonly made.

Suppose we consider two individuals who have a respective set of decision variables x^1, x^2 and each individual welfare is a function of his own decision and the decision of the other individual, i.e.

$$U_1(x^1, x^2) \qquad \text{and} \qquad U_2(x^1, x^2).$$

We are dealing with a non-cooperative game so that each individual selfishly maximises his own welfare regardless of the effect on the other individual, subject only to any constraints which we assume have already been substituted into the objective function. The richness of the game arises from the inclusion of terms in the other player's discretionary variables in the first player's utility function. These terms are not, of course, exogenous to the actions of the player, as the other player may alter his behaviour in response to a move by the first player. Because each player's strategy depends on the strategy of the other player, we cannot use standard optimisation techniques to solve such a problem. In fact, the normal solution procedure is an iterative one but we will not pursue that here. We can however characterise

various types of solution. The general solution given when both players

optimise subject to the optimal strategy of the other player is given by

the Nash solution. It may be characterised by a pair of points (x_N^1, x_N^2)

which have the property that

$$U_1(x_N^1, x_N^2) \geq U_1(x_i^1, x_N^2) \quad \text{all } i$$
$$\text{and} \quad U_2(x_N^1, x_N^2) \geq U_2(x_N^1, x_i^2) \quad \text{all } i$$

This states that given that player 2 implements x_N^2, player 1 prefers x_N^1

to any other permissible choice of x^1 open to him, and similarly given

that player 1 implements x_N^1, player 2 prefers x_N^2 to any other

permissible choice of x_2.

To solve a problem for the full Nash solution is difficult, and

often may not be analytically tractable. So two restricted forms of

solution have been evolved which do not have the full optimising

consistency of the Nash solution but which have the advantage of being

much easier to solve. The first of these is the Cournot solution. This

is defined as the solution which occurs when each player forms some

expectation about the behaviour of the other player, and optimises

subject to that expectation. In general this solution will differ from

the Nash solution if the expectation about the other player's action

differs from his finally chosen action. This solution may be

characterised by a pair of points (x_c^1, x_c^2) such that

$$U_1(x_c^1, x_o^2) \geq U_1(x_i^1, x_o^2) \quad \text{all i}$$
$$\text{and} \quad U_2(x_o^1, x_c^2) \geq U_2(x_o^1, x_i^2) \quad \text{all i} \qquad \bullet$$

where x_o^1, x_o^2 is player 2 and player 1's expectation of the other player's action respectively.

The second form of restricted solution is the Stackelberg game. In this game there is a clear leader and follower. The leader announces some action and the follower optimises subject to that announcement. The leader then optimises subject to the optimal behaviour of the follower. This may be characterised as a pair of points (x_s^1, x_s^2) such that

$$U_1(x_s^1, x_s^2) \leq U_1(x_i^1, x_s^2) \quad \text{all i}$$
$$\text{and} \quad U_2(x_o^1, x_s^2) \leq U_2(x_o^1, x_i^2) \quad \text{all i}$$

where player 1 is the leader and x_o^1 is the announced policy. Player 2 plans on the basis of x_o^1 even though it is not an optimal policy for player 1.

In terms of the time inconsistency debate discussed below, the two important cases are the Nash and the Stackelberg game. The Stackelberg game gives rise to time inconsistency and may be thought of as the case where the government announces an economic policy, following which private sector agents then optimise subject to this announcement. However, the policy is not in fact optimal when the time comes to implement it. If the game can be reformulated as a Nash game, the time inconsistency problem disappears.

3. The initial analysis of time inconsistency

The quintessential analysis emphasising the Natural Rate basis to the issue of time inconsistency is that provided in Barro and Gordon (op. cit.). This starts from the suggestion that systematic monetary policy does not affect real variables, but nonetheless there appears to be countercyclical monetary policy directed at influencing real variables such as unemployment (see Barro and Gordon, 1983a). This apparent 'irrationality' in policy formation is then explained in terms of the temporary exploitation of inflation surprises by the government. The basic ingredients of the explanation is a Lucas-type aggregate supply determination of real activity, and an emphasis on long-run equilibrium states. To some extent the first, and more especially the second of these very limiting features are avoided in the models in section 4.

The essentials of the Barro-Gordon (BG) model, it will be recalled, are as follows. Proxy aggregate activity by the Lucas-type unemployment function, i.e.

$$U_t = U_t^n + \alpha(\pi_t - \pi_t^e), \qquad \alpha > 0. \tag{1}$$

where inflation surprises produce movement in unemployment away from the natural rate U^n. The policymaker's objective function is

$$Z_t = a(U_t - kU_t^n)^2 + b(\pi_t)^2, \qquad a, b > 0 \tag{2}$$

Assuming $k < 1$ indicates distortions from the efficiency level of the natural rate due to external effects. The policymaker is assumed to have control of changes in the money supply, which in turn is assumed to determine inflation. Hence π is treated, in effect, as the policy instrument in the exercise. The intertemporal cost function for the policy problem is

$$\underset{U_t}{\text{Min}} \quad \sum_{t=0}^{\infty} \; E(Z(1 + r)^{-t} \mid \Omega_0) \tag{3}$$

where $(1 + r)$ is the discount factor and r is assumed to be constant. Expectations are modelled by requiring that the policymaker minimises (3) in period t, by selecting π_t given the information set Ω_{t-1}. Private sector agents also form their expectations of π_t (π_t^e) using the same information set Ω_{t-1}. Moreover, they are assumed to know that the π_t which the government choose emerges from the minimisation of (3). This feature establishes the nature of rationality in the model. The policy problem may then be simplified by assuming that π_t and future expected inflation π_{t-i}^e, are independent (thus eliminating questions of reputation and credibility, though these are a major topic of subsequent sections to this chapter), so that (3) may be taken to be a simple one-period problem, namely the minimisation of $E(Z_t \mid \Omega_{t-1})$. Simple dynamics can be introduced by allowing for persistence in the supply function, thus (1) becomes

$$U_t^n = \lambda U_{t-1}^n + (1 - \lambda)K + \varepsilon_t, \qquad 0 < \lambda < 1 \tag{4}$$

where K is the constant value the natural rate of unemployment tends to, and ε_t an independently distributed error with zero mean.

The solution to this elementary problem can be thought of as postulating a reaction function for inflation expectations

$$\pi_t^e = h^e(\Omega_{t-1}) \tag{5}$$

and establishing a fixed point. Thus $\pi_t = h^e(\Omega_{t-1})$ is a solution to the policymaker's cost minimisation exercise, given that $\pi_t^e = h^e(\Omega_{t-1})$ in turn determines expected inflation. To locate the solution, the single-period cost function after substituting for (4) and (5) is minimised, i.e.

$$\underset{\pi_t}{\text{Min}} \quad Z_t = a \left[(1 - k)[\lambda U_{t-1}^n + (1 - \lambda)K + \varepsilon_t] \right.$$

$$\left. - \alpha(\pi_t - h^e(\Omega_{t-1})\right]^2 + b(\pi_t)^2$$

The first-order condition is

$$\pi_t = \frac{a\alpha}{b}\left[(- \alpha \ (\pi_t - h^e(\Omega_{t-1})) + (1 - k)[\lambda U_{t-1}^n + (1 - \lambda)K]\right]$$

allowing for $E(\varepsilon \mid \Omega_{t-1}) = 0$. As the private sector knows π_t is selected in this way, $\pi_t - h^e(.) = 0$. Hence they must form their expected inflation as

$$\pi_t^e = \frac{a\alpha}{b} (1 - k) [\lambda U_{t-1}^n + (1 - \lambda)K]$$

or $\pi_t^e = \pi_t = \dfrac{a\alpha}{b} (1 - k) \ \underset{t-1}{E} \ U_t^n = \pi \tag{6}$

as the fixed point equilibrium is given as the selection of π_t which coincides with π_t^e. Equation (6) is then a <u>Nash</u>-type equilibrium to this simple game between the policymaker and rational private sector agents.

To establish some terminology which we use subsequently, we will describe the solution given by (6) as a <u>discretionary</u> equilibrium. Although these terms are not particularly meaningful in this one-period case, this policy is defined as sub-optimal but time-consistent. These terms are fully explained in the more relevant multi-period cases in section 4 below, but the flavour of their usage can be gleaned from the present very limited exercise. To illustrate this, note that the equilibrium in (6) will imply that $\pi_t^e = 0$ is inconsistent, and therefore will not occur. (Since $\pi_t > 0$ will generally be adopted by the government, the expectation of zero inflation will be inconsistent with this choice.) The equilibrium value of π_t from (6) can then be contrasted with a fixed rule for inflation of the form

$$\pi_t^* = h(\Omega_{t-1}) = 0, \tag{7}$$

which can arise where the policy problem is that of our previous analysis, which required the selection of a rate of inflation equal to expected inflation. Equation (7) however produces the same unemployment level (U^n, the natural rate) but a lower inflation rate than the equilibrium solution. Hence (6) is sub-optimal. But in (7) the policymaker has potential for deviating from the rule -

expanding the money supply, raising inflation, producing an inflation surprise and a temporary decrease in unemployment. The rule is thus optimal but time-inconsistent.

Before proceeding with more elaborate formulations of policy games, the general idea of reputational equilibria can be given by a simple extension of this model. There is, in the example already reviewed, an incentive for the policymaker to renege on the policy rule. It is suggested that the rule may nevertheless be made credible when the potential loss of the policymaker's reputation balances his temptation to cheat. This extension explicitly introduces multi-period considerations into the simplified scheme described so far. The essential mechanism is that the cost of cheating today is the effect this higher current rate of inflation has upon expected future inflation rates. Assume there are two possibilities (see Barro and Gordon, 1983b). If $\pi_{t-1}^e = \pi_{t-1}$ then private agents expect the government to conform to the policy rule, but if $\pi_{t-1} \neq \pi_{t-1}^e$, they expect the government to adopt the discretionary policy. Hence, in the first case the government follows the rule, and validates expectations, so maintaining its reputation. In the second case, the government cheats in period t, so next period's expected inflation is the discretionary value (call this $\hat{\pi}_{t+1}$). But, as shown earlier, actual and expected π will coincide. Hence in period t+2 the private sector expects the value for π as given by the rule (call this π_{t+2}^*). Credibility is restored by period 2, and the loss produced by renegeing on the policy rule in period 2, is the expected present value of the relative cost $(\hat{Z}_{t+1} - Z^*_{t+1})$, equal to the cost function evaluated under discretion less that evaluated under the rule (which will be positive).

Whether the policymaker is induced to renege depends on the balance between the current period gain in cheating, $E(Z^*_t - \tilde{Z}_t)$ where $\tilde{Z}_t$ is the cost function evaluated under the cheating policy, versus the expected discounted loss produced by the revision in expected inflation for the t+1 period. In full the relevant criterion is

$$V = E(Z^*_t - \tilde{Z}_t) - qE(\hat{Z}_{t+1} - Z^*_{t+1})$$

where q is the real discount rate. For $V \leq 0$ the policymaker opts for the rule, otherwise he cheats. But if $V > 0$, then the private sector will know that it is in the government's interest to renege on the policy rule.

4. The linear structurally dynamic case

The conclusion of the previous section was that consistent optimal policies may be induced, provided the policymaker values reputation sufficiently. The analysis was couched in terms of a familiar Natural Rate model, and the model was not structurally dynamic, so lagged adjustment was not explicitly incorporated in behavioural equations for example. This section outlines results from linear models which remedy this limitation in the earlier analysis and, what is an added advantage from our point of view, it describes the implications of time-inconsistency in an explicit optimal control analysis of policy choice.

The basic ideas can be established fairly readily using the optimal time consistent feedback rule derived for the general linear model with rational expectations from chapter 7. Recall that for the <u>deterministic</u> form of the model

$$
\begin{bmatrix} z_{t+1} \\ {}_t x^e_{t+1} \end{bmatrix} = A \begin{bmatrix} z_t \\ x_t \end{bmatrix} + B\, W_t + V_t \tag{8}
$$

where ${}_t x^e_{t+1} = x_{t+1}$, and $V_t = 0$, and we optimise the welfare function

$$
H_t = \tfrac{1}{2} \Sigma\, R^t\, (Y'\, Q\, Y + 2\, Y'\, U\, W + W'\, G\, W) \tag{9}
$$

where $Y_{t+1} = (z_{t+1},\ {}_t x^e_{t+1})'$.

The optimal control rule may be written in closed form as (see equation (32) Chapter 7)

$$
W_t = D \begin{bmatrix} Z \\ P_2 \end{bmatrix} \tag{10}
$$

By certainty equivalence this rule also satisfies the stochastic case, when additive error is included in (8) above (see Levine (1984)).

What this example illustrates is the time dependency of the optimal time consistent solution. That is, the optimal rule (10) recomputed at a later date (say $t = n$ instead of $t = 0$) implies that the sum of backward terms be evaluated over a new interval, namely (n, t) instead of (0, t). It is this feature which suggests that the rule may lead to time inconsistency. This arises because the optimal rule sets the co-state variable $p_2(t) = 0$ for $t = 0$, when the program is evaluated over the interval (0, t), but $p_2(t) \neq 0$ for $t > 0$. However, re-optimisation at $t = n$, leads to the co-state being set at zero for the initial period of this new program, i.e. $p(n) = 0$, $n \neq 0$, thereby showing that the policymaker has reneged on the original policy setting (see Currie and Levine (1985)).

In the remainder of this section we note some further analysis of time inconsistency in the structurally dynamic case, before proceeding to our own derivation and implementation of an optimal policy for a dynamic non-linear macro model.

A. The closed loop Stackelberg

The optimal rule (10) may be interpreted as a closed loop Stackelberg solution in the sense that it incorporates the private sector's responses to policy changes when it (the government) formulates its policy. Currie and Levine (op. cit.), for example, illustrate this interpretation by taking an alternative optimal policy rule

$$W_t = (\tilde{D}_1, \tilde{D}_2) \begin{bmatrix} Z \\ \tilde{p}_2 \end{bmatrix}_t$$

where $\tilde{P}_{2t+1} = (P_1, P_2) \begin{bmatrix} Z \\ \tilde{p}_2 \end{bmatrix}_t$

The solution for the non-predetermined variables given this rule may then be interpreted as the private sector's reaction function. In turn, the policy optimisation problem may be recast as optimising the function

W in (9) above, but now incorporating the private sector's reaction
function linking the X vector to the co-state variables (p_1 and p_2), the
predetermined variables (Z), and the government's policy rule.   The
optimal policy rule which now follows is identical to that previously
obtained.

B. Nash solutions

An alternative to the closed-loop Stackelberg, which may be time
inconsistent, is the set of Nash policies (closed and open loop), among
which time consistent policies are obtainable.   Nash policies may be
derived in the framework we use here, by assuming the private sector no
longer believes the government's policy announcements.   The private
sector reaction function then depends upon their assessment of the true
rule (replacing actual values in the previous case with the private
sector's expectations of these).   As neither player in this game, the
government nor the private sector, have knowledge of the other's
reaction function, the equilibrium which is obtained is of the Nash
type.   But since by assumption the government optimises, knowing that
the private sector's decision about X feeds back into the dynamic
behaviour of the system, the resulting policy is a closed loop one.
Time consistent policies are established within the set of closed loop
Nash solutions by, e.g., Cohen and Michel (1986).   Time consistent
policies in the open-loop Nash solution, which takes the X values as
given and defines optimal policies subject to these, may also be
obtained (Buiter (1983)).   A result related to the discussion in section
3 is the perfect cheating solution (Miller and Salmon (1982)).   In this

solution the policy which is announced is of the form implied by the
optimal rule given in chapter 7

$$W(t) = D \begin{bmatrix} Z(t) \\ p_2(t) \end{bmatrix} \tag{11}$$

but assumes the government re-optimises in each time period, which again
entails that $p_2(t) = 0$ for each t.   If (11) above is believed, it is
optimal and time consistent (since the government plans not to follow
announced policy throughout).   But if the announcement is not believed,
then, without credibility, the government ceases to be a Stackelberg
leader. A time-consistent Nash solution then becomes the only available
alternative, and this may be considerably inferior to the Stackelberg
solution.   If the Nash solution is considerably inferior, the
policymaker must weigh the gains from renegeing with the potential
losses due to loss of credibility and the establishment of a Nash
solution.   Intuitively the evaluation of the alternatives are similar to
the discussion of reputations in the static Natural Rate model in
section 3.   The welfare gains from the successful renegeing of policy
can be obtained by evaluating W(t) before and after renegeing. This is
compared to the potential welfare loss sustained if the attempt at
renegeing is unsuccessful, which is given by welfare under the
Stackelberg solutions minus welfare under the Nash.

Our own approach elaborates on the time-consistency of closed loop
Nash solutions, and takes the sub-game perfect Nash solution where the
private sector disbelieves the government's policy announcements, so
their expectations do not depend on these announcements. We show how

this can provide time-consistent policies also.

5. Time inconsistency in a large scale non-linear model

We provide an alternate argument that the Kydland-Prescott conclusion is misleading, which will be intimately concerned with the form of optimisation for rational expectations models. This section, unlike the previous ones, will consider the non-linear case. It is also suggested that the concept of time consistency is identical to the formal principle of optimality which underlies Bellman's equation and therefore, that a properly formulated optimal policy must be time consistent. This echoes in part the analysis for the single non-predetermined case advanced by Cohen and Michel (1986).

Before giving the full model analysis, the gist of the argument is presented in a simple theoretical framework similar to that used by Kydland and Prescott. The National Institute's macro Model 7 will then be used to provide an illustration and numerical confirmation of the theoretical propositions. This necessitates the adaptation of the model to take account of rational expectations, specifically to allow expectations of real disposable income to enter the consumption function. The model amended in this way is then used in control exercises which illustrate the nature and importance of time inconsistency in a large macro non-linear econometric model.

A. Time consistency and the principle of optimality

So far we have operated with fairly general definitions of time consistency. For the next argument however, it is easier if we use

precisely the same formulation as Kydland and Prescott. Time
consistency was defined by Kydland and Prescott within the following
framework. (The notation conforms with their original paper.)

Let $\pi = (\pi_1 \ldots \pi_T)$ be a sequence of policies for period 1 to T
and let $x = (x_1 \ldots x_T)$ be a corresponding sequence for economic agents'
decisions. A general social welfare, or objective, function is
specified as

$$S(x_1 \ldots x_T, \pi_1 \ldots \pi_T) \tag{12}$$

Further agents' decisions in t depend upon all policy decisions and
their past decisions.

$$x_t = x_t(x_1 \ldots x_{t-1}, \pi_1 \ldots \pi_T) \qquad\qquad t = 1 \ldots T \tag{13}$$

A time consistent policy is defined in the following way:

  'A policy π is consistent if, for each time period t, π_t maximises
  (12), taking as given previous decisions, $x_1, \ldots x_{t-1}$ and that
  future policy decisions (π_S for S>t) are similarly selected.'

This definition is quite clear, but just to paraphrase it, if π^0 is the
vector of planned policies at time 0 then if the problem is resolved at
a later date (t) given that $\pi_0^0 \ldots \pi_{t-1}^0$ have occurred, the new optimal
policy $\pi_t^* \ldots \pi_T^*$ will be the same as $\pi_t^0 \ldots \pi_T^0$ if the policies are time
consistent.

Contrast this with the definition of the principle of optimality stated in Bellman (1957) (repeated in Intriligator (1971)):

'An Optimal Policy has the property that, whatever the initial state and decision [ie. controls] are, the remaining decisions must constitute an optimal policy with regard to the state resulting from the first decision.'

This definition of the principle of optimality is clearly identical to the time consistent definition. It would seem therefore that an optimal policy which satisfies the principle of optimality must be time consistent, when the principle of optimality applies.

B. A reconciliation

The conclusion that the principle of optimality implies time consistency is clearly at variance with Kydland and Prescott's demonstration of an optimal but time inconsistent policy. In order to disclose the source of the inconsistency a generalisation of their two period model is made. The results obtained are easily generalised to the n period case.

The welfare function is still

$$S(x_1, x_2, \pi_1, \pi_2) \tag{14}$$

where

$$x_1 = X_1(\pi_1, {}_1\pi_2^A) \tag{15}$$
$$x_2 = X_2(x_1, \pi_1, \pi_2, {}_1\pi_2^A) \tag{16}$$

where ${}_1\pi_2^A$ is the announced policy in period 1 to be implemented in period 2. In this model in period 1 agents have no knowledge of the true policy plans for period 2, but only know the policy makers' announced plans, where in this general framework there is no restriction on policy makers to announce their true plans.

In order to derive the Kydland and Prescott result we impose the constraint:

$$\pi_2 = {}_1\pi_2^A \tag{17}$$

and maximising S in period 1 with respect to π_2

$$\frac{\delta S}{\delta x_2}\frac{\delta X_2}{\delta \pi_2} + \frac{\delta S}{\delta \pi_2} + \frac{\delta S}{\delta x_1}\frac{\delta X_1}{\delta \pi_2} = 0 \tag{18}$$

Now if the constraint $\pi_2 = {}_1\pi_2^A$ is relaxed and we again maximise S with respect to π_2, we get

$$\frac{\delta S}{\delta x_2}\frac{\delta X_2}{\delta \pi_2} + \frac{\delta S}{\delta \pi_2} = 0 \tag{19}$$

The two equations are different assuming the third term in (17) is non-zero, so the optimal policy is shown to be time inconsistent. In this form the result clearly depends upon imposing the constraint (16) in the first case but not in the second. In effect all that is being said is that the relaxation of a binding constraint has produced a better optimal solution in the second period. In general it is always true that the removal of a binding constraint will have this effect.

In order to derive a time consistent policy, all that needs to be done is to treat the constraint (16) in a consistent fashion. Either it must be on in both periods, or it must be off in both periods. The case where the constraint is imposed in both periods is trivial, but where it is off in both periods an interesting third first-order condition emerges.

Maximisation of (13), (14), (15) without constraint (16) with respect to π_1, $_1\pi_2^A$, π_2 gives

$$\frac{\delta S}{\delta \pi_1} + \frac{\delta x_1}{\delta \pi_1}\frac{\delta S}{\delta x_1} + \frac{\delta x_2}{\delta \pi_1}\frac{\delta S}{\delta x_2} = 0 \qquad (20)$$

$$\frac{\delta S}{\delta \pi_2} + \frac{\delta x_2}{\delta \pi_2}\frac{\delta S}{\delta x_2} = 0 \qquad (21)$$

$$\frac{\delta S}{\delta x_1}\frac{\delta x_1}{\delta_1\pi_2^A} + \frac{\delta S}{\delta x_2}\frac{\delta x_2}{\delta_1\pi_2^A} + \frac{\delta S}{\delta x_2}\frac{\delta x_2}{\delta x_1}\frac{\delta x_1}{\delta_1\pi_2^A} = 0 \qquad (22)$$

The first two equations now reveal a time consistent optimal path for π_1 and π_2. The third equation measures the effect the government may have through pure announcement effects. In a multiperiod model the partial derivatives $\delta x_1/\delta_J\pi_K^A$ would be expected to be a function of the government's credibility. So if in earlier periods $_J\pi_K^A$ had not turned out to be equal to π_K (J<K), the effect would be to reduce the value of $\delta x_M/\delta_N\pi_L^A$ (where N>K, N<L≤M). In the limit, if all $\delta x_i/\delta_J\pi_K^A = 0$, the government would have no credibility and therefore its announced policies would have no effect on actual behaviour.

This framework not only yields time consistent policies, but it also yields a set of policies which optimally exploit the ability of the policy maker to influence events by announcing future policies which it does not intend to carry out. By definition these policies are optimal and must therefore be as good as, if not better than, any fixed rule.

An alternative way of thinking of the solution to the time
inconsistency problem lies in considering the conditions under which it
is known that the principle of optimality fails. Typically, now
considering only a linear system, if we write the model as
$$Y' = MX' + Z.$$
Y is a vector of N endogenous variables for all time periods T,
$$Y = (Y_{11} \cdots Y_{1N}, Y_{21} \cdots Y_{2N} \cdots Y_{T1} \cdots Y_{TN}),$$
X is a matrix of M control variables for T periods, M is a matrix of
parameters, and Z is a vector of exogenous factors.

If M is a lower block triangular matrix then the model will be
strictly causal in nature which simply means that there are
contemparaneous effects and lagged effects but the future does not
affect the past.

When a model is solved assuming fully model-consistent
expectations, this introduces terms in M which mean that it is no longer
block triangular. Under this condition the principle of optimality is
known not to hold. But the rational expectations hypothesis has never
been interpreted literally as being complete and perfect foresight (ie.
that agents actually <u>know</u> the future). What is hypothesised is that
agents use the available information in the best way, to predict the
future, including the use of the relevant economic model. This does not
mean that future events actually influence the past, but only that the
expectation of future events conditional on the best use of current
information influence events. In terms of equations (19)-(22), π_2 is
not in the information set of individuals in period 1; all that they
have available is $_1\pi_2^A$ - the announced policy. So it is easily seen

that making the simplifying assumption that $\pi_2 = {_1}\pi_2^A$, and substituting actual future policy, destroys the block triangular nature of the model, and it is this feature of the solution procedure which induces time inconsistency.

This is an unreasonable assumption to make however. If such information were available, there would have been no need for the rational expectations hypothesis.

The next section will outline an optimisation procedure which maintains the block triangularity of the model, allowing for expectations to be formed rationally. This may be viewed as something of a compromise between the solution outlined in equations (19) to (22), which is impracticable, and the solution which arises when setting expectations equal to the actual outcome and carrying out a simple optimisation procedure.

C. Rational and consistent expectations

So far it has been tacitly assumed that consistent expectations are rational, but we need to be more precise in our use of these terms, so in our subsequent discussion we will use the following definitions. An expectation is said to be <u>consistent</u> if the expected outcome is equal to the actual outcome in any given situation. More specifically, in a model context, an expectation is consistent if it is equal to the solution of the model, regardless of the setting of the control variables. An expectation will be defined as <u>rational</u> if it is equal to the actual outcome of the model when control variables are set in an optimal fashion.   Clearly, therefore, a rational expectation must be consistent, but a consistent expectation may not always be rational.   An example makes this easier to understand.   If we state a government objective function and a set of control variables, then the result of optimising the model subject to an announced objective function will yield a set of rational expectations.   A model can, however, be solved for an arbitrary non-optimal set of control variables on the basis of consistent expectations.   But these expectations will not be rational, as they are not based on the optimal set of control variables.

The relevance of this distinction to the time inconsistency debate is that if expectations are truly rational, then the individuals who form the expectations will do so by optimising the government's objective function subject to the model in each of the future time periods.   So when the government comes to formulate its own plans, those plans will not affect expectations.   If the government announces a future policy which will actually be abandoned, then individuals will be able to calculate this and, on the rational expectations assumption, expect only what will actually happen.   This rational model can be described in the following way.   Maximise

$$S(x_1, x_2, \pi_1, \pi_2) \tag{23}$$

where

$$x_1 = x_1(\pi_1, E(\pi_2)) \tag{24}$$

$$x_2 = x_2(x_1, \pi_1, \pi_2) \tag{25}$$

Now $E(\pi_2)$ is derived by individuals optimising S in period 2 themselves; it follows, therefore, that in period 1, $\delta E(\pi_2)/\delta \pi_2 = 0$.

That is, whatever the government says in period 1 that it will do in period 2 has no effect on expectations because individuals know what it will really do.

The first order conditions for this problem are:

$$\frac{\delta S}{\delta \pi_1} + \frac{\delta x_1}{\delta \pi_1} \frac{\delta S}{\delta x_1} + \frac{\delta x_2}{\delta \pi_1} \frac{\delta S}{\delta x_2} = 0 \qquad (26)$$

$$\frac{\delta S}{\delta \pi_2} + \frac{\delta x_2}{\delta \pi_2} \frac{\delta S}{\delta x_2} = 0 \qquad (27)$$

This is again a time-consistent optimal solution; indeed, the solution is the same as (19) and (20). This demonstrates that the time inconsistency result is not the product of the rational expectations hypothesis, but rather it is the result of the assumption that individuals naively believe that the government will actually implement its announced policies even when they do not plan to do so. The optimal solution characterised by (25) and (26) is, of course, a special case of (19), (20) and (21) where both $\delta x_1/\delta_1 \pi_2^A = 0$ and $\delta x_2/\delta_1 \pi_2^A = 0$. In this case we have an example where people's expectations are correct, yet time inconsistency does not arise.

This type of solution may be interpreted in game theoretic terms with non-co-operative behaviour as a Nash equilibrium and is formally identical to that proposed by Buiter (1984), and described in Currie and Levine (1985). This is the 'subgame perfect' solution to the problem of time inconsistency. It essentially solves the problem of time inconsistency by assigning such a high degree of rationality to individuals that they give no weight to the government's announced policies in their decision making.

The solution outlined in equations (19) to (21) is formally a Stackelberg (leader-follower) game solution where time consistency is produced by allowing the leader to choose a perfect cheating solution (see Hughes-Hallett and Rees (1983) and Miller and Salmon (op.cit.)).

As argued above, the Stackelberg model is almost certainly a more accurate representation of the real world. But to properly implement the Stackelberg solution we must provide a complete model of expectations so that the perfect cheating solution becomes a time consistent option. Given the impracticality of this task, the next section will suggest a way of finding the Nash subgame perfect solution for a large non-linear model. This solution may be viewed as a special case of the Stackelberg perfect cheating model where no weight is given to the government's announced policies by private decision-makers.

D. An empirical example using an estimated model
In this section the National Institute's Model 7 is amended to introduce forward expections into its consumption sector. Consumption expenditure is dependent, among other things, upon expected income over the next three quarters. The solution techniques outlined earlier are then used in an optimal control framework to derive the optimal level of government expenditure over eight quarters, given an objective function involving unemployment and inflation. The process is then repeated,

each time dropping the first quarter of the run. This should produce a set of time inconsistent optimal solutions on the basis of consistent expectations. Expected output will then be derived rationally as the solution to a separate optimisation procedure and a time consistent optimal solution will be found.

The National Institute's Model 7 has been augmented by using two equations for durable and non-durable consumption which have terms in expected real disposable income. These equations have been estimated by using an explicit expectations series which was constructed using the National Institute's own ex ante forecasts of real output growth (see Hall, Henry and Wren-Lewis (1984) for further details).

The results for durable consumption were: (in logs)

$$CD_t = -3.78 + 0.63\ CD_{t-1} + 1.4\ Y^e_t - 4.3\ Y^e_{t+2}$$
$$\quad\ (2.8)\quad (6.5)\qquad\quad (1.9)\qquad (1.9)$$

$$+\ 3.5\ Y^e_{t+3} \tag{28}$$
$$\ (2.0)$$

$DW = 1.5 \quad R^2 = 0.95 \quad SE = 0.058$

Estimation period 1966 Q1 - 1983 Q2 (figures in parenthesis are t-statistics)

CD = Real durable consumption; Y^e = Expected real disposable income.

In turn, the results for non-durable consumption were, (in logs)

$$CND_t = 0.24 + 0.69 \; CND_{t-1} + 0.13 \; CND_{t-2} - 0.13 \; IL_t$$
$$(1.4) \quad (5.6) \qquad\qquad (1.3) \qquad\qquad (4.7)$$

$$+ 0.06 \; Y_t^e - 0.36 \; Y_{t+1}^e + 0.46 \; Y_{t+2}^e \qquad\qquad (29)$$
$$(0.5) \qquad (1.4) \qquad\qquad (2.2)$$

DW = 1.9 R^2 = 0.99   SE = 0.008

Estimation period 1966 Q1 - 1983 Q2

CND = Real non-durable consumption;   IL = $\Delta_4 LOG(CPI)W/Y$, i.e. the inflation loss on real wealth relative to income, where W is real wealth.

The baseline optimisation run was carried out over the period 1981 Q3 - 1983 Q2 using a POST MORT optimisation mode.

The results of this optimisation are shown in the tables below. Table 1 shows the actual level of government expenditure in the first row and the second row shows the solution value of the optimisation problem over all eight quarters. Each of the next rows shows changes in the control path when the problem is resolved using subsequent quarters as the initial starting values. The optimal paths from the earlier runs are incorporated in the quarters before the starts of the later runs as initial conditions. The importance of time inconsistency is illustrated in this table most dramatically by the optimal level of government expenditure in the eighth quarter in row 2 and row 9. When the optimisation is carried out for the whole period the solution for the final quarter is 14800.1. But when the optimisation is for the last quarter only, with the time-inconsistent optimal path implemented before

Table 1.   An example of a time-inconsistent optimal path based on
             consistent expectations

NIESR Model 7

£m 1980 prices

Quarter	1	2	3	4	5	6	7	8
Actual base government expenditure	12245.0	12046.0	12171.0	12175.0	12183.0	12413.0	12662.0	12493.0
Optimal values for full time period	13025.7	12885.1	12865.1	13495.0	14250.2	14705.3	15000.3	14800.1
Starting 2nd quarter	–	12883.8	12863.9	13493.7	14248.7	14706.8	15001.8	14801.6
Starting 3rd quarter	–	–	12863.9	13493.7	14248.7	14706.8	15001.8	14801.6
Starting 4th quarter	–	–	–	13493.7	14248.7	14706.8	15366.4	15161.3
Starting 5th quarter	–	–	–	–	14084.5	14873.1	15366.4	15161.3
Starting 6th quarter	–	–	–	–	–	14693.6	16173.0	15957.1
Starting 7th quarter	–	–	–	–	–	–	16387.9	16606.7
Starting 8th quarter	–	–	–	–	–	–	–	16605.1

this, the solution changes to 16605.1. The time-inconsistent optimal path is defined by the diagonal elements of table 1; this is the best the government can do if it is willing to renege on its announced policies and if people, nonetheless, continue to believe in these announced policies.

If we now turn to the fully rational case defined earlier it is evident that the solution technique is not so simple. To the government's control exercise, individuals' expectations are now given as an exogenous input. These expectations are, however, formed by individuals carrying out the government's optimisation exercise and these expectations must be consistent with the plans finally reached by the government. So the problem is to choose an exogenous set of expectations which will yield an optimal government path which will actually fulfil these expectations.

In terms of the equations for our simple example the relevant optimisation problem is presented as equations (22) to (24), and the first order condition of this problem ((25) and (26)) will yield the general solution

$$\pi_1^* = f_1(E(\pi_2)) \tag{30}$$
$$\pi_2^* = f_2(E(\pi_2)) \tag{31}$$

i.e. the optimal government policy is a function of what people expect it to do in period 2. The solution to the first order condition represented as (21) and (22) will produce a mapping from individuals' expectations into the optimal government policy. On the assumption that this mapping has a fixed point, the rational expectation which people should hold will be $\overline{\pi}_2$ such that $\overline{\pi}_2^* = \overline{\pi}_2 = f_2(\overline{\pi}_2)$, ie. the fixed point of the mapping.

The problem of locating this fixed point for a large econometric model is far from trivial. The algorithm we employ for finding this solution involves the following steps:

(1) Set an arbitrary set of expectations Y_1^e.

(2) Optimise the model with respect to the objective function subject to the set of exogenous expectations, giving values $\tilde{Y}$.

(3) If the values of $\tilde{Y}$ produced by the optimal control variables are sufficiently close to Y^e then stop. If not, then set $Y_2^e = \tilde{Y}$ and go back to (2).

Stages (2) and (3) are repeated until convergence is achieved and a fixed point for (31) and (32) is found.

Applying this algorithm to the entire econometric model using the objective function specified in (30), gave the fully rational solution for government expenditure shown in table 2.

This optimal solution is now time consistent as there are no gains to be made by governments announcing incorrect policies for the future, as these will not be believed.

One interpretation which may be placed on the two sets of results presented in tables 1 and 2 is that they represent two extremes.   In

table 1 expectations are set equal to announced government policy.   In

table 2 expectations are arrived at in a way which takes absolutely no

account of announced policy, but instead uses information about the

Table 2. An example of a time-consistent optimal path based on rational
          expectations

   NIESR Model 7

£m 1980 prices

Quarter	1	2	3	4	5	6	7	8
Optimal government expenditure	215001.1	11971.9	12001.0	13532.7	14730.3	13144.0	16108.4	16466.9

model and its objective function only.   It would seem reasonable that a

rational individual (using the term rational in a more general sense

now) would use all the information in the best possible way and so both

sets of information should be used.   It is possible to consider a

further alternative using an expectation formation mechanism based on a

weighted average of the announced policy and the separately derived

'rational' policy.   The weights might even vary over time so that when

governments have been seen to stick to their announced policies for a

reasonably long period, individuals would assign a high weight to the

announced policy.   When a government has recently reneged an announced

policy, a high weight may be assigned to the rationally formed

expectation.   Such a scheme is particularly appealing as the costs

involved in forming a truly rational expectation (as defined above) are

clearly much higher than the costs of simply believing the government's announced policy.

6. Conclusions

We have reviewed some of the time-inconsistency literature in this chapter, and have suggested a number of conclusions. In summary it has been shown that time inconsistency is not the inevitable consequence of using rational expectations in a model. Rather it is the consequence of the assumption that people believe the announced government policy will be carried out. Time consistent optimal policies can be derived formally by splitting the government's actions into an announced policy and a true (non-announced) policy. Time consistent optimal policies can also be derived in the special case where expectations are formed rationally by individuals optimising the model and the known objective function (the sub-game perfect Nash solution) and therefore giving zero weight to the announced policy plan in their expectations formation procedure. This chapter has then demonstrated a technique for locating the second of these solutions for the case of a large non-linear model.

Blanchard, O. and Kahn, C. (1980), 'The Solution of Linear Difference
    models under Rational Expectations', Econometrica, 48, July.

Buiter, W. (1982), 'Saddlepoint Problems in Continuous time Rational
    Expectations Models: A general method and some macroeconomic
    examples', Centre for Labour Economics, Discussion Paper No.
    114. London School of Economics.

Dornbusch, R. (1976), 'Expectations and Exchange Rate Dynamics', Journal
    of Political Economy', 84.

Haache, G. and Townend, J. (1981), 'Exchange rates and monetary policy:
    modelling sterling's effective exchange rate', Oxford Economic
    Papers, 33..

Hall, S.G. (1987), 'A forward looking model of the exchange rate',
    Journal of Applied Econometrics, 2.

Hall, S.G. (1984), 'On the solution of high order symmetric difference
    equations', Oxford Bulletin of Economics and Statistics.

Hall, S.G., Henry, S.G.B., Payne, J. and Wren-Lewis, S. (1985),
    'Employment and average hours worked in manufacturing' British
    Review of Economic Issues, 7, 16.

Hall, S.G., Henry, S.G.B, and Wren-Lewis, S. (1986), 'Manufacturing
    stocks and forward looking expectations in the UK' Economica
    Hansen, L.P. and Sargent, T. (1980), 'Linear rational
    expectations models for dynamically interrelated variables'
    Journal of Economic Dynamics and Control.

Hansen, L.P. and Sargent, T. (1982), 'Instrumental variables procedure
    for estimating linear rational expectations models' Journal of
    Monetary Economics No. 9, pp. 263-296.

Hayashi, F. and Sims, C.A. (1983), 'Nearly efficient estimation of the time series models with predetermined but not exogenous instruments' Econometrica.

Henry, S.G.B. (1979), 'Forecasting employment and unemployment', in The Economics of the Labour Market eds Hornstein, Z., Guce, J., and Webb, A., HMSO, London.

Henry, S.G.B., and Wren-Lewis, S. (1984), 'The aggregate labour market in the UK: some experiments with rational expectations models' in Contemporary Macroeconomic Modelling, Ed. Malgrange, P. and Muet, P., Blackwells.

Kennan, J. (1979), 'The estimation of partial adjustment models with rational expectations' Econometrica, 47, No. 6, pp.1441-1445.

Layard, R. and Nickell, S. (1985), 'The causes of British unemployment' National Institute Economic Review, No. 111, pp.62-85.

Layard, R. and Nickell, S. (1986), 'Unemployment in Britain' Economica Supplement.

Nickell, S. (1984), 'An investigation of the determinants of manufacturing employment in the United Kingdom' Review of Economic Studies LI pp. 529-557.

Pagan, S. (1984), 'Econometric issues in the analysis of regressions with generated regressors', International Economic Review, 25.

Sargan, J.D. (1964), 'Wages and prices in the United Kingdom, a study in economic methodology' in Hart, P.E., Mills, G. and Whittaker, J.N. (eds) Econometric Analysis for National Economic Planning, Butterworth, London.

Tinsley, P. (1971), 'A variable adjustment model of Labour Demand' International Economic Review, October

HM Treasury (1985), 'An expectational model of manufacturing employment in the UK' mimeo, HM Treasury, London

Wickens, M. (1982), 'The efficient estimation of econometric models with rational expectations' Review of Economic Studies XLIX pp. 55-67

Wickens, M. (1986), 'The estimation of linear models with future rational expectations by efficient and instrumental variable methods' Discussion Paper No. 8601, University of Southampton, Department of Economics

Banerjee, A., Dolado, J.J., Hendry, D.F., Smyth, G.W. (1986), 'Exploring equilibrium relationships in econometrics through state models: some Monte Carlo evidence' Oxford Bulletin of Economics and Statistics, Vol. 48, No. 3, pp. 253-78.

Box, G.E.P. and Jenkins, G.M. (1970), 'Time series analysis: forecasting and control', Holden-Day, San Francisco.

Brown, T.M. (1952), 'Habit persistence and lags in consumer behaviour', Econometrica, 20, pp.355-71.

Currie, D. (1981), 'Some long-run features of dynamic time series models', Economic Journal, 363.

Davidson, J.E.H., Hendry, D.F., Srba, F. and Yeo, S. (1978), 'Econometric modelling of the aggregate time-series relationship between consumers' expenditure and income in the United Kingdom' Economic Journal No. 88, pp. 661-92.

Davis, T.E. (1952), 'The consumption function as a tool for prediction' Review of Economics and Statistics, 34, pp.270-77.

Dickey, D.A. and Fuller, W.A. (1979), 'Distribution of the estimation for autoregressive time series with a unit root', Journal of American Statistical Association, vol.74, pp.427-31.

Dickey, D.A. and Fuller, W.A. (1981), 'Likelihood ratio statistics for autoregressive time series with a unit root', Econometrica, vol.49, pp.1057-72.

Evans, M.K. (1969), Macroeconomic Activity, Harper and Row, New York.

Evans, G.B.A. and Savin, N.E. (1981), 'Testing for unit roots; 1', Econometrica, Vol. 49, pp.753-77.

Fuller, W.A. (1976), Introduction to statistical time series, Wiley, New York.

Granger, C.W.J. and Newbold, P. (1974), 'Spurious regressions in econometrics', Journal of Econometrics, 2, pp.111-20.

Granger, C.W.J. (1980), 'Long memory relationships and the aggregation of dynamic models', Journal of Econometrics, Vol. 14, pp.227-38.

Granger, C.W.J. (1981), 'Some properties of time-series data and their use in econometric model specifications', Journal of Econometrics, Vol. 16, pp.121-30.

Granger, C.W.J. (1983), 'Co-integrated variables and error-correcting models', UCSD Discussion Paper.

Granger, C.W.J. and Engle, R.F. (1985), 'Cointegration and error correction; representation, estimation and testing'.

Granger, C.W.J. and Weiss, A.A. (1983), 'Time series analysis of error-correcting models' in Karlin, S., Ameniya, T. and Goodman, L.A. (eds.) Studies in Econometrics, Time Series and Multivariate Statistics, New York Academic Press.

Haavelmo, T. (1947), 'Methods of measuring the marginal propensity to consume', Journal of American Statistical Association, 42, pp.105-22.

Hall. S.G. (1986), 'An application of the Granger and Engle two-step estimation procedure to United Kingdom aggregate wage data', Oxford Bulletin of Economics and Statistics, Vol. 48, No. 3, pp.229-41.

Hall, S.G. and Brooks, S.J. (1985), 'The use of prior regression in the estimation of error-correction models', Economic Letters, 20, pp.33-7.

Hall, S.G. and Drobny, A. (1986), 'A suggested procedure for testing equilibrium specifications in the Granger and Engle two-step estimation framework', NIESR, mimeo.

Hall, S.G. and Drobny, A. (1987), 'Some long run features of dynamic time series models: the implications of cointegration' Presented at the European meeting of the econometric society, Copenhagen.

Hall, S.G., Henry, S.G.B. and Trinder, C. (1983), 'Wages and prices' in Britton, A.J.C. (ed.) Employment, output and inflation, Heinemann, London.

Hendry, D.F. (1973), 'Stochastic specification in an aggregate demand model of the United Kingdom', Econometrica.

Hendry, D.F. (1986), 'Econometric modelling with cointegrated variables: an overview', Oxford Bulletin of Economics and Statistics, 48, 3, pp.201-12.

Hendry, D.F. and Mizon, G.E. (1978), 'Serial correlation as a convenient simplification, not a nuisance: a comment on a study of the demand for money by the Bank of England', Economic Journal, 88, pp.549-63.

Hendry, D.F. and Morgan, M. (1986), 'Classics in the statistical foundation of econometrics', Cambridge University Press.

Hendry, D.F. and von Ungern-Sternberg, T. (1981), 'Liquidity and inflation effects on consumers' expenditure' in Denton, A.S. (ed.), Essays in Theory and Measurement of Consumer Behaviour, Cambridge University Press.

Hooker, R. (1901), 'Correlation of the Marriage rate with Trade', Journal of the Royal Statistical Society, 64.

Jazwinski, A.H. (1970), Stockastic Processes and Filtering Theory, Academic Press, New York, London.

Jevons, S. (1884), Investigations in Currency and Finance, London, Macmillan.

Johansen, S. (1987), 'Statistical Investigation of Cointegration Vectors', Institute of Mathematical Statistics, University of Copenhagen, mimeo.

Kuznets, S. (1942), 'Uses of national income in peace and war', National Bureau of Economic Research Occasional Paper no. 6.

McCallum, B.T. (1976) 'Rational Expectations and the Natural Rate Hypothesis: some consistent estimates.' Econometrica, 44

Nelson, C.R. and Kang, H. (1981), 'Spurious periodicity in inappropriately detrended time series', Econometrica, Vol. 49, No. 3.

Nelson, C.R. and Plosser, C. (1982), 'Trends and random walks in macroeconomic time series: some evidence and implications', Journal of Monetary Economics, vol.10, pp.139-62.

Phillips, A.W. (1957), 'Stabilization policy and the time forms of lagged response', Economic Journal, 67, pp.265-77.

Phillips, P.C.B., Durlauf, S.N. (1986), 'Multiple time-series regression with integrated processes' Review of Economic Studies, Vol. 53, pp. 473-95

Sargan, J.D. (1964), 'Wages and prices in the United Kingdom: a study in economic methodology' in Hart, P.E., Mills, G. and Whittaker, J.N. (eds.), Econometric Analysis for National Economic Planning, Butterworth, London.

Sargan, J.D. and Bhargava, A. (1983), 'Testing residuals from least
    squares regression for being generated by the Gaussian random
    walk', Econometrica, Vol. 51, pp.153-74.

Stock, J.H. (1985), 'Asymptotic properties of lest squares estimates of
    cointegrating vectors', mimeo, Harvard University.

Yule, G.U. (1926), 'Why do we sometimes get nonsense-correlations
    between time series? A study in sampling and the nature of time
    series', Journal of the Royal Statistical Society, vol. 89, pp.1-
    64.

Andrews, M. (1983), 'The aggregate labour market - an empirical investigation into market clearing', Discussion Paper No. 154, Centre for Labour Economics, LSE.

Andrews, M. and Nickell, S. (1986), 'A disaggregated disequilibrium model of the labout market', Centre for Labour Economics, London School of Economics, Discussion Paper No. 251.

Artus, P. and Muet, P.A. (1983), 'Investment, output and labour constraints, and financial constraints: the estimation of a model with several regimes', Paper presented to the European Econometric Society meeting, Pisa.

Barro, R. (1984), 'Macro Economics', John Wiley & Sons.

Beenstock, M. and Warburton, P. (1984), 'An economic model of the UK labour market' Working Paper No. 64, City University Business School.

Clower, R.W. (1965), 'The Keynsian counter-revolution: a theoretical appraisal' in The Theory of Interest Rates, by Hahn, F.M. and Brechline, F.P.R., (Eds), London, Macmillan.

Fair, R.C. and Jaffee, D.M. (1972), 'Methods of estimation for markets in disequilibrium", Econometrica, 40, pp. 497-514.

Goldfeld, S. and Quandt, R.E. (1980), 'Econometric Modelling with non-normal disturbances', Econometric Research Program, memo No. 265, Princeton University.

Gourieroux, C., Laffont, J. and Monfort, A. (1980), 'Disequilibrium econometrics in simultaneous equation systems', Econometrica, 48.

Hall, S.G., Henry, S.G.B., Payne, J. and Wren-Lewis, S. (1985), 'Employment and average hours worked in manufacturing', British Review of Economic Issues, 7, 16.

Laffont, J. and Monfort, A. (1979), (1979), 'Disequilibrium Econometrics in Dynamic Models', Journal of Econometrics, 11.

Layard, R. and Nickell, S. (1985), 'The causes of British unemployment', National Institute Economic Review, No. 111, pp. 62-85.

Leijonhufvud, A. (1968), On Keynesian Economics and the Economics of Keynes, London, Oxford University Press.

Maddala, G.S. and Nelson, F.D., (1974), 'Maximum likelihood methods for models of markets in disequilibrium' Econometrica, 42, pp. 1013-1030.

Maddala, G.S. and Chandra, A. (1983), 'Estimation of disequilibrium models UK Inventories under rational expectations', paper presented to the European Economic Society, Pisa, August.

Monfort, A. (1983), 'Comment on Quandt's paper' in Econometric Reviews, vol. 1, no. 1.

Muellbauer, J. and Portes, R. (1978), 'Macroeconomic models with quantity rationing', Economic Journal, pp. 788-821.

Quandt, R.E. (1982), 'Econometric disequilibrium model', Econometric Reviews, vol. 1, no. 1.

Rosen, H.S. and Quandt, R.E. (1978), 'Estimation of a disequilibrium aggregate labor market', Review of Economics and Statistics, LX, pp. 371-9.

Smyth, D. (1983), 'The British labour market in disequilibrium: did the dole reduce employment in interwar Britain?', Journal of Macroeconomics, vol. 5, no. 1, pp. 41-51.

Stenius, M. and Viren, M. (1984), 'Some further results on Rosen and Quandt's labour market model', European Economic Review, 26, pp. 369-77.

Whitley, J. (1983), 'Endogenising Incomes Policy', Discussion Paper no. 23, Institute for Employment Research, University of Warwick, Coventry.

Anderton, R. and Dunnett, A. (1987), 'Modelling the behaviour of export volumes of manufactures', National Institute of Economic and Social Research, mimeo.

Caruth, A. and Oswald, A. (1987), 'Wage Inflexibility in Britain; theory, facts and estimation.', Centre for Labour Economics, London School of Economics, mimeo.

Cuthbertson, K. (1985) "Bank Lending to UK Industrial and Commercial Companies" Oxford Bulletin of Economics and Statistics, May Vol 147, No. 2.

Hall, S.G., Henry, S.G.B, and Wren-Lewis, S. (1986), 'Manufacturing stocks and forward looking expectations in the UK' Economica Hansen, L.P. and Sargent, T. (1980), 'Linear rational expectations models for dynamically interrelated variables' Journal of Economic Dynamics and Control.

Hall, S.G. and Henry, S.G.B. (1987a), 'Wage Models' National Institute Economic Review, February.

Hall, S.G. and Henry, S.G.B. (1987b), 'Wage Models : Some further results', National Institute of Economic and Social Research, mimeo

Layard, R. and Nickell, S. (1986), 'Unemployment in Britain' Economica Supplement.

Minford, A.P.L. (1983), 'Labour Market Equilibrium in an open economy', Oxford Economic Papers, 35, supplement.

National Institute (1985), Model 8 Listing, National Institute of Economic and Social Research, London, mimeo.

National Institute (1986), 'National Institute Model 9'

Wickens, M. (1982), 'The efficient estimation of econometric models with rational expectations' Review of Economic Studies XLIX pp. 55-67.

Anderson, P.A. (1979), 'Rational expectation forecasts from non-rational models' Journal of Monetary Economics, 5, pp. 67-80.

Fadeev, D.K. and Fadeeva, V.N. (1963), 'Computational methods of linear algebra'. Freeman and Co., New York.

Fair, R.C. (1979), 'An analysis of a macro-econometric model with rational expectations in the bond and stock market', American Economic Review, Vol. 69.

Fair, R.C. (1984), 'Specification Estimation and Analysis of Macro-econometric models', Harvard University Press.

Hall, S.G., (1984), 'On the solution of high order symmetric difference equations', Oxford Bulletin of Economics and Statistics, 46, 1 pp. 85-88.

Hall, S.G., (1985), 'On the solution of large economic models with consistent expectations' Bulletin of Economic Research.

Holly, S. and Beenstock, M. (1980), 'The implication of rational expectations for the forecasting and the simulation of econometric models', London Business School, Discussion Paper.

Holly, S. and Zarrop, M.B. (1983), 'On optimality and time consistency when expectations are rational', European Economic Review, February.

Hughes-Hallett, A.J. (1981), 'Some extensions and comparisons in the theory of Gauss-Seidel iterative techniques for solving large equation systems', in proceedings of the 1979 Econometric Society Meeting, Essays in honour of Stefan Valavani, S, E.G. Charatsis (Ed.), Amsterdam.

Klein, L. (1983), 'Lectures in Econometrics', North Holland.

Lipton, D., Potterba, S., Sachs, J. and Summers, L. (1982), 'Multiple
    shooting in Rational Expectations Models'.

Lucas, R.E. Sr. (1976), 'Economic policy evaluation: a critique' Journal
    of Monetary Economics, Supplement, pp. 19-46

McNees, S. (1975), 'An evaluation of economic forecasts', New England
    Economic Review, November/December.

Minford, A.P.L. and Matthews, S.K. (1978), 'A note of terminal
    conditions and the analytical solution of rational expectations
    models', Liverpool International Transmission Project Working paper
    no. 7805

Minford, A.P.L. et al (1984), 'Unemployment, cause and cure', Martin
    Robertson, Oxford

NI Model, Britton (ed.) (1983)

Norman, M. (1967), 'Solving a non-linear econometric model by the Gauss-
    Seidel iterative method', Paper presented at the Econometric
    Society meeting

Wallis, K.F. (1984), 'Comparing time series and non-linear model based
    forecasts', Oxford Bulletin of Economics and Statistics, vol. 46,
    no. 4, pp. 383-389

Wallis, K.F. (1985), (ed.) 'Models of the UK Economy (A second review by
    the ESRC Macroeconomic Modelling Bureau). Oxford University Press.

Young, D.N. (1971), 'Iterative solution of large linear systems', New
    York Academic Press

Bianchi, C. and Calzolari, G. (1980), 'The one period forecast error in
    non-linear econometric models', International Economic Review, 21,
    pp. 201-8.

Bianchi, C. and Calzolari, G. (1982), 'Evaluating forecast uncertainty
    due to errors in estimated coefficients: empirical comparison of
    alternative methods', ed. G.C. Chow and P. Corsi, John Wiley and
    Sons Ltd.

Calzolari, G. (1980), 'Antithetic variates to estimate the simulation
    bias in non-linear models', Economic Letters, 4.

Cooper, J.P. and Fischer, S. (1972), 'Stochastic simulation of monetary
    rules in two macro-econometric models', Journal of the American
    Statistical Association, 67.

Cooper, J.P. and Fisher, S. (1974), 'Monetary and fiscal policy in the
    fully stochastic St. Louis econometric model', Journal of Money,
    Credit and Banking, No. 6, pp. 1-22.

Corker, R., Ellis, R. and Holly, S. (1983), 'Uncertainty and forecasting
    precision', London Business School, Discussion paper No. 98.

Dunham Jackson (1921), Bulletin of the American Mathematic Society No.
    27, p.160.

Evans, M.K., Klein, L.R. and Saito, M. (1972), 'Short run prediction and
    long simulation of the Whorton Model' in Hickman (1972).

Fair, R.C. (1980), 'Estimating the expected predictive accuracy of
    econometric models', International Economic Review, 21, pp. 355-78.

Fair, R.C. (1984), 'Specification Estimation and Analysis of Macro-
    econometric models', Harvard University Press.

Fisher, P.G. and Salmon, M. (1983), 'On evaluating the importance of non-linearities in large macro-econometric models', ESRC Macromodelling Bureau, Discussion Paper No. 2.

Fitzgerald, V.W. (1973), 'Dynamic properties of a non-linear econometric model', in Pencavel and Williams (1973).

Fromm, M.G., Klein, L.R., Schink, G.R. (1972), 'Short and long term simulation with the OBE Econometric Model', in Hickman (1972).

Green, G.R., Liebenberg, M. and Hirsch, A.A. (1972), 'Short and long term simulation with the OBE Econometric Model', in Hickman (1972).

Haitovskiy, Y. and Wallace, N. (1972), 'A study of discretionary and non-discretionary monetary and fiscal policies in the context of stochastic macro-econometric models', in Zarnowitz (1972).

Haldane, J.B.S. (1948), 'Note on the median of a multivariate distribution' Biometrica, No. 35, p.414.

Hall, S.G., (1984), 'On the solution of high order symmetric difference equations', Oxford Bulletin of Economics and Statistics, 46, 1 pp. 85-88.

Hall, S.G., (1985), 'On the solution of large economic models with consistent expectations' Bulletin of Economic Research.

Hendry, D.F (1984), 'Econometric evaluation of linear macroeconomic models', mimeo, Nuffield College, Oxford.

Henry, S.G.B and Johns, C.B. (1985), 'Simulations on NIESR Model 7' NIESR mimeo March.

Hoel, P.G. (1962), 'Introduction to mathematical statistics' John Wiley Inc., New York, London.

Kendall, M.G. and Stuart, A. (1969), 'The advanced theory of statistics', Charles Griffin & Co. Ltd. London.

Mariano, R.S. and Brown, B.W. (1981), 'Bib parametric stochastic prediction in a non-linear simultaneous system', Presented at the North American Econometric Society.

McCarthy, M.D. (1972), 'Some notes on the generation of pseudo structural errors for use in stochastic simulation studies', in Hickman (1972).

Muench, T., Rolnick, A., Wallace, N. and Weiler, W. (1974), 'Tests for structural change and prediction intervals for the reduced forms of two structural models of the U.S.: The FRB-MIT and Michigan quarterly models', Annals of Economic and Social Measurement 3.

Nagar, A.L., (1969), 'Stochastic simulation of the Brooking Econometric Model', in Duessenbery et al (1969).

Schink, G.R. (1971), 'Small sample estimates of the variance-covariance matrix of forecast errors for large econometric models: The stochastic simulation technique', University of Pennsylvania PhD dissertation.

Sowey, E.R. (1973), 'Stochastic simulation of macro-econometric models: Methodology and interpretation', in Pencavel and Williams (1973).

Wallis, K.F. (1984), 'Comparing time series and non-linear model based forecasts', Oxford Bulletin of Economics and Statistics, Vol. 46 No. 4, pp. 383-389.

(for section (ii) Uncertainty in the linear case.

Bray, J. (1975), 'Optimal control of a noisy economy with the UK as an
example', Journal of the Statistical Society, 138A, 339-66.

Corden, W. (1981), 'Taxation, real wage rigidity and employment',
Economic Journal, 91.

Currie, D. and Levine, P. (1985), 'Time inconsistency and optimal
policies in deterministic and stochastic worlds' Programme of
research into small macromodels, Paper No. 30.

Economica (1986), Special Issue.

Goldfeld, S., Quandt, R. and Trotter, H. (1966), 'Maximisation by
quadratic hill climbing', Econometrica, 34, pp. 541-51.

Henry, S.G.B, Karakitsos, E and Savage, D. (1982), 'On the derivation of
the efficient Phillips Curve', Manchester School, June.

Hey, J.D. (1979), 'Uncertainty in microeconomics', Martin Robertson,
Oxford.

Himmelblau, D.M. (1972), 'Applied non-linear programming', New York
McGraw Hall.

Kendrick, D. (1981), Stockastic Control for Economic Models, McGraw-
Hill, New York.

Luce, R.D. and Raiffa, H. (1957), 'Games and Decisions; Introduction and
Critical Survey' John Wiley and Sons, New York.

National Institute (1986), 'National Institute Model 9'

Polak, (1972) 'A survey of methods of feasible directions for the
solution of optimal central problems' IEEE Transactions on
Automatic Control AC-17, (1972), 59, pp. 591-596.

Powell, M.J.D (1964), 'An efficient method for finding the minimum of a function of several variables without calculating derivatives' Computer Journal, vol. 7, pp.155-162

Spendley, W., Hext, G.R. and Himsworth, F.R. (1962), 'Sequented application of simplex designs in optimisation and evolutionary operation', Technometrics, 4, pp. 441-61.

Backus and Driffill (1986), 'The consistency of optimal policy in stochastic rational expectations models', Centre for Economic Policy Research, Discussion Paper No. 124.

Barro, R. and Gordon, D. (1983a), 'A positive theory of monetary policy in a natural rate model', Journal of Political Economy, 91.

Barro, R. and Gordon, D. (1983b), 'Rules, Discretion and Reputation in a model of Monetary Policy', Journal of Monetary Economics, 12.

Bellman, R. (1957), Dynamic Programming, Princeton N.J. Princeton University Press.

Buiter, W. (1983), 'Optimal and time consistent policies in continuous time rational expectations models', LSE Econometrics programme Discussion Paper No. A39.

Cohen, D. and Michel, P. (1986), 'How should control theory be used by a time consistent government?' Centre for Economic Policy Research, London. Discussion Paper No. 141.

Currie, D. and Levine, P. (1985), 'Time inconsistency and optimal policies in deterministic and stochastic worlds', Programme of research into small macromodels, Paper No. 30.

Hall, S.G. (1985), 'On the solution of large economic models with consistent expectations', Bulletin of Economic Research.

Hall S.G., Henry S.G.B., Wren-Lewis S (1984), 'Manufacturing stocks and forward looking expectations in the UK', NIESR Discussion Paper No. 64.

Hall, S.G., (1987), 'An Investigation of time inconsistency and optimal policy formulation in the presence of rational expectations using the National Institute Model 7', Applied Economics, 19, No. 9.

Hughes-Hallett, A. and Rees, H. (1983), Quantitative Economic Policies and Interactive Planning, Cambridge University Press, Cambridge.

Hughes-Hallett, A. (1986), 'Is time inconsistent behaviour really possible?', Centre for Economic Policy Research, Discussion Paper No. 138.

Intriligator, M.D. (1971), Mathematical Optimization and Economic Theory,, Prentice Hall, New Jersey.

Kydland, F.E. and Prescott, E.C. (1977), 'Rules rather than discretion: The inconsistency of optimal plans', Journal of Political Economy, Vol.85, No.3.

Levine, P. (1984), 'Problems of implementing macroeconomic policy as an optimal feedback rule when expectations are rational', London Business School, Centre for Economic Forecasting, Discussion Paper No. 139.

Miller, M. and Salmon, M. (1984), 'Dynamic games and the time inconsistency of optimal policy in open economies', Economic Journal (Supplement), Vol.95, pp.124-138.

Miller, M. and Salmon, M. (1985), 'Dynamic Games and the Time Inconsistency of Optimal Policy in Open Economics', Economic Journal, 85.

References to section 2. Game theory: some basic concepts.

Intriligator, M.D. (1971), 'Mathematical optimisation and economic theory', Prentice Hall, New Jersey.

Luce, R.D. and Raiffa, H. (1957), Games and Decisions; Introduction and Critical Survey, John Wiley and Sons, New York.

von Neumann, J. and Morgenstern, O. (1947), Theory of Games and Economic Behaviour, 2nd Edition, Princeton University Press, Princeton, New Jersey.

Maximising the log-likelihood function

The analytical derivation of the log likelihood function for a disequilibrium model has been well known for some time. The practical maximisation of such a function is not a straightforward task however and a number of studies have failed at this stage. Even if we make the assumption that the likelihood function is not unbounded (and Quandt, 1982 has shown that this need not be a valid assumption), the function may still exhibit both discontinuities and multiple maxima. Under such conditions no algorithm, as far as we are aware, will guarantee to find the global maximum and in practice the discontinuities can cause many algorithms to fail at a point which is not even a local maxima.

The program for estimating disequilibrium models which we have developed tries to cope with these problems in two ways. First, there are five separate optimisation algorithms available as well as a number of combinations of the five algorithms. Second, when the chosen optimisation procedure has finished the program carries out a series of grid searches around the solution point. Examining one parameter at a time it searches to see the effect of either increasing or decreasing the parameter value on the log likelihood function. A series of graphs are then produced to show the shape of the function around the chosen point.

The five methods of optimisation used are: the Powell (1964) conjugate directions method which does not need to calculate derivatives of the function at all; a Quasi-Newton algorithm which calculates

numerical derivaties; a Quasi-Newton algorithm which requires a set of
analytical first derivatives only; a version of the Zoutendijk method
of feasible direction (see Polak 1972); and a non-linear simplex method
(Nelder and Mead, 1965) which is relatively inefficient but is robust to
function inaccuracies and discontinuities. There are also a number of
options for iterating between these routines, using the solution values
from one routine as the starting value for another. In general we would
expect the Quasi-Newton methods to be the most efficient techniques for
a well behaved function.   But in the face of local maxima or
discontinuities these techniques can go badly wrong as, in essence, they
use the information available at one point of a function plane to infer
something about a wide region of that plane. The less efficient simplex
and method of feasible directions techniques tend to draw less
information from the current point, but instead proceed with a process
of sets of line searches which are more likely to find ways around a
nearby discontinuity or local maxima. A sensible general procedure
would seem to be to use the simplex technique to generate a set of
starting values for one of the Quasi-Newton approaches.   We would
generally expect the derivative based optimisation routines to get
closer to a maximum than non-derivative algorithms, once the starting
point was sufficiently close to the maxima for the derivatives to be
meaningful.

The grid search around the solution point has a number of uses;
first, it is a useful check on the reliability of the solution point,
such an investigation can never confirm that a point is definitely
either a global or local maxima, but it can often show that a point is

not a global maxima by indicating a move which would improve the function value.   Passing a simple grid search test is therefore a necessary, though not sufficient, condition for a maximum.   The second use is where an optimisation algorithm has failed due to a discontinuity; in this case simple graphs may suggest a new starting value for a key variable on the correct side of the discontinuity. If a function is very difficult to maximise it is even possible to carry out a manual iteration procedure based in part on the information provided by the grid search.

In practical estimation, before any of the optimisation algorithms were implemented, a set of OLS regressions were performed on the general model after the data sample had been split according to the direction of movement of the de-trended real wage.   These regressions provided a sensibly scaled set of parameters as starting values for the maximum likelihood estimates.   In practice it is important to have good estimates of all the parameters; if even one parameter is given an unrealistic value the likelihood function may be a very long way from its optimal value.   Bearing this point in mind a +1 -1 dummy was constructed and used as a proxy for excess supply and demand in the wage adjustment equation.   This allowed the full version of the wage adjustment equation to be estimated by OLS with a suitable scaling procedure applied to the parameter on the dummy. These OLS results then constituted the starting values for the optimisation procedure.

The most successful optimisation strategy then proved to be

maximising the function using the simplex method first, and then using the Quasi-Newton method with analytical gradients to finish the procedure. Typically the second step produced only small changes in parameter values although the log likelihood function increased by about 5 or 6.

Finally we might usefully comment on the evaluation of the likelihood function. Relatively little empirical work has been done on disequilibrium models so far and one result of this is that any researcher is unlikely to have more than one program available to carry out the estimation. This means that it is impossible to check the implementation of that program against another performing substantially the same task. Consequently there will always be a significant area of doubt as to the correct evaluation of the disequilibrium likelihood function itself. We found that two checks were especially useful in validating the likelihood function. The first was to derive estimates of the covariance matrix of the parameters in two ways: from a numerically estimated Hessian matrix and from a Hessian matrix constructed from analytical derivatives. If these two are not fairly close it indicates that the numerical derivatives are substantially different from the analytical derivatives at the solution point. This may indicate an error either in the coding of the function evaluation or the derivative evaluation. The second check involves using a set of starting values derived from OLS estimation which therefore produces a set of estimates which actually do fit fairly well. Given that this likelihood function, like any other, is simply minimising a weighted and transformed set of model errors, we would not expect the optimisation

process to move to a substantially worse fitting model. If this happens

in optimisation then this strongly suggests an error in the likelihood

function evaluation.   Our program includes simple analysis of the

model's predictions over its estimation period which allows an easy

check on overall model fit. In the early stages of program testing both

of these procedures proved useful in locating errors in implementation.